Wacky Eire

First published in 2012 by
Liberties Press
7 Rathfarnham Road | Terenure | Dublin 6W
Tel: +353 (1) 405 5701
www.libertiespress.com | info@libertiespress.com

Trade enquiries to Gill & Macmillan Distribution
Hume Avenue | Park West | Dublin 12
T: +353 (1) 500 9534 | F: +353 (1) 500 9595 | E: sales@gillmacmillan.ie

Distributed in the UK by
Turnaround Publisher Services
Unit 3 | Olympia Trading Estate | Coburg Road | London N22 6TZ
T: +44 (0) 20 8829 3000 | E: orders@turnaround-uk.com

Distributed in the United States by
Dufour Editions | PO Box 7 | Chester Springs | Pennsylvania 19425

ISBN: 978-1-907593-48-2
2 4 6 8 10 9 7 5 3 1

A CIP record for this title is available from the British Library.

Cover design by Sin É Design
Internal design by Liberties Press
Printed by Bell & Bain Ltd

Wacky Eire

Geraldine Comiskey

LIB
ERT
IES

To Mam and Dad – and Irish mammies everywhere.

Contents

Preface

As a roving reporter, I often feel like a gypsy crossed with a rally driver – whose navigator has just gone crazy. One minute, I'm ambling along at a leisurely pace, enjoying the view, having the craic with the locals; the next it's total mayhem as scenery, animals and people jump out at me. Ireland's winding roads are no place for the person who likes life to be predictable – there's a surprise around every bend.

I feel privileged to have had a close-up, driving-seat view of this strange little island, to have seen more of my native land than most inhabitants have in their lifetimes – and to have taken part in some of the wackiness. I don't subscribe to the traditional view that a journalist should be a disembodied voice, reporting on other people as if they were animals in a wildlife documentary. When I'm reporting on something amusing, it's far more interesting if the joke is on me too.

Of course I can't get involved in a story when I'm in my other guise, as a serious news reporter – but I have found that my walk on the wacky side has helped me to be a better all-round journalist than I would have been if I had restricted myself to straight reportage. I have learned, for example, that people are far more complex than they appear at first. It's often said, but rarely understood, that you should never judge a book by its cover. Ireland has many wise fools – and many foolish wise-guys who can't see beyond the mask of a jester or the tears of a clown. Having walked many miles in some strange shoes, I know what it feels like to be an outsider and an insider all at once, to be shunned and welcomed. And I feel honoured to have met many fascinating people, who have shown me their wacky side.

And I've come to believe that Ireland is a magical place, where ordinary people enter chrysalis every time the fancy takes them – and sometimes when they don't expect! The Queen and Barack Obama went native in spectacular style. Every night of the week, rugged farmers are transformed into twinkletoed rhinestone cowboys as they head into their local hotels to strut their stuff at country'n'Irish dances. Several times a year, respectable men and women strip off and show off their wobbly bits to the world – usually the *Sunday World*, if I have anything to do with it.

And of course, just like my newspaper, I was born here, bred here and am read here. So when I tell you Ireland is the wackiest place on earth, I'm speaking from experience.

Acknowledgements

Most of the people I'd like to thank for making this book possible would be mortified to find their names in these pages. Some, who unintentionally helped me, would be furious. So I won't expose you this time; you know who you are, and I hope you see the funny side while you're reading it.

Huge thanks to Sean O'Keeffe, Caroline Lambe, Clara Phelan, Alice Dawson and Dan Bolger at Liberties Press.

A big toast to my literary agent, Jonathan Williams, who spotted my potential as an author long before I did and put in countless hours, not just on this book but on others to come, and to the *Sunday World*'s news editor, John Donlon, the Godfather of Irish journalism, who indulged and encouraged my wacky side while continuing to take me seriously when it counted. I am also grateful to the *Sunday World*'s deputy news editor, investigative journalist and author himself, Eamon Dillon, for some of my wackiest assignments ever; fellow author and investigative journalist Jim 'Agent of the Devil' Gallagher for recruiting me as his disciple; showbiz editor and investigative journalist Eugene Masterson, and crime reporters Alan Sherry and Niall Donald for some great ideas (and in Niall's case pretending to be my 'husband' at a swingers' party); novelist and crime writer Niamh O'Connor for encouraging me to give the literary world another go; three successive picture editors, Gavin McClelland, Dave Dunne and Owen Breslin and my many colleagues, past and present.

The *Sunday World* is a breeding ground for authors, and great credit is due to Editor Colm MacGinty, and MD Gerry Lennon, who have always given us the freedom to develop our own styles and identities through its pages. My own profile got a huge international boost as a result of Managing Editor Neil Leslie's decision to send me after Thierry Henry. Special thanks to Assistant Editor J. P. Thompson for sending me off on a few wacky adventures outside Ireland; Sarah Hamilton for dealing with all the correspondence, messages and strange packages that arrive for me in the newsroom; Seán Boyne for publishing my very first *Sunday World* article and giving me a crash course in how to write tabloid-style when he was news editor; Fashion Editor Fay Brophy for her part in my 'wedding'; social network section editor Daragh Keany for taking a gamble on me and being a good sport about it, and to all the staff and contributors who make the *Sunday World* a bestseller every week.

It was a treat to work with so many brilliant photographers down the years, in Ireland and abroad, who combined artistic talent and investigative skills with a sense of mischief – and, on occasion, doubled up as bodyguards. They include legendary *Sunday World* snappers Val Sheehan, Liam O'Connor and Ernie Leslie, who have worked with me on everything from wacky features to hard news, and (in alphabetical order): Gary Ashe; Marti Berenguer of Solarpix; Matt Britton; Bryan Brophy; Mary and Patrick Browne of P. J. Browne's Photography;

Acknowledgements

Kevin Byrne; Arthur Carron (of Collins picture agency); James Connolly (PicSell8); Aidan Crawley; Frank Dolan; Andrew Downes; Mark Doyle; Ann Egan; Christy Farrell; Willie Farrell; the late Austin Finn; Philip Fitzpatrick; Brenda Fitzsimons; Mick 'de fish' Flanagan; Brian Gavin (Press 22 agency), Noel Gavin; Rory Geary; Keith Heneghan; Ciara Hennigan (JMac Photography); Pat Hogan (of Provision agency); Emma Jervis (Press 22 agency); Mark Kelleher; Michael Kelly; Clare Keogh; Eamonn Keogh (of McMonagle Photography); Barbara Lindberg; Peter Lomas; Martin Maher; Hany and Carmel Marzouk; Philip McCaffrey; Mick McCormack; Brian McEvoy; Jason McGarrigle; Eoin McGarvey; Billy macGill; Andy McGlynn; Ciaran McGowan of the *Irish Sun*; Philip McIntyre; Jack McManus; Don McMonagle (McMonagle Photography); Peter McParland; Mike and Daragh McSweeney (Provision agency); Adrian Melia; Gerry Mooney; Pat Moore; Robert Mullan; Paul 'Nico' Nicholls; and Solarpix Agency in Marbella, for giving me a taste of international fame; the late Dave O'Connor, his wife Marie and son Ken; Pat O'Leary; Conor O'Mearain; Valerie O'Sullivan; Willie Smith; Dave Stephenson; Lorraine Teevan; Dylan Vaughan; Jim Walpole; Eamon Ward, and Ciara Wilkinson.

I am indebted to the *Irish Sun*'s crime editor, the legendary Paul Williams, and their picture editor, Padraig O'Reilly, for their timely advice and encouragement while they were working for the *Sunday World*, and to my past bosses, notably my taskmasters at the *Irish Daily Star*, the great Bernard Phelan, *Star Chic* magazine editor Moira Hannon and columnist Terry McGeehan. I would also like to thank Des Gibson, Fiona Hynes and Paul Mallon at the much-missed *Irish Daily Star Sunday*; *Daily Mirror* Editor-in-Chief Jumbo Kierans and his team, including News Editor Niall Moonan, Deputy News Editor James McNamara, Pat 'Buddha' Flanagan, Declan Ferry and Lindsay Fergus, who all put the quirky stories my way when they were at the helm; Christian McCashin, who was my editor at the *Irish Sunday Mirror*; Paul Drury and Ronan O'Reilly at the *Irish Daily Mail*; Paul Clarkson and Fiona Wynne of the *Irish Sun*; Eoghan Corry of *Travel Extra*, who first sent me on my wacky way when he was Features Editor at the old *Irish Press* and Deputy Features Editor Seán Mannion; the late Dermot Walsh and Johnny Roche of the *Wexford People* and Jan Van Embden, who took me on as teenager at the *Bray People*; Ken Finlay, who gave me my first official work placement with *Southside*, later to become the *Southside People*, and his successors Jack Gleeson and Neil Fetherston, as well as honchos Tony McCullagh and Ray O'Neill, and all my ex-colleagues at the *Dublin People*.

Thanks to the late Peter Carvosso of the *Evening Herald*, the late Howard Kinlay of the *Irish Times*; and the late legendary *Irish Times* editor Douglas Gageby, who treated me like an experienced reporter right from the start. I'm also grateful to his successor, Conor Brady, for standing up for me and journalism against commercial interests and showing true integrity while I was a teenage trainee, the then deputy editor of the *Irish Times*, James Downey, for some sound advice, the paper's news editor at the time, Eugene McEldowney, former news editor John Armstrong, Mary Maher, Dick Grogan and many others in the *Irish Times* newsroom for the excellent training they gave me on the newsbeat. Thanks also to Jack Fagan for letting me pimp up the *Irish Times* property supplement on occasion; Kevin Myers for letting me give *An Irishman's Diary* a sex-change; Seán Duignan (then of RTÉ) and the late Noel Conway for initiating me into the Leinster

Acknowledgements

House Press Gallery; thanks also to my first ever tabloid news editor, Martin Brennan of the *Evening Herald*, for giving me a good grounding as a newshound, and features editor at the time, Helen Rogers, for her fantastic advice and encouragement; Mike Burns of RTÉ, who took me on as an unofficial trainee back in 1986, and Denis Madden who recommended me to him; to Paul Byrne of TV3 for his generous help and encouragement and to shock jocks Adrian Kennedy, Jeremy Dixon and Niall Boylan for giving me a taste of 'tabloid radio'. Thanks go to my bosses at the *Tribune*, Vincent Browne, the late Michael Hand, Rory Godson, Colin Kerr and *Dublin Tribune* MD Seamus O'Neill. Thanks also to John Moore for giving me my first taste of British tabloid journalism when he was the *Sunday People*'s man in Ireland; Shay Fitzmaurice of the *North Wicklow Times* and Gerry Fitzmaurice of the *North County Leader*; Gráinne Willis and Valentine Lamb of *The Irish Field*.

Special thanks to my old teachers David Rice and Ciaran Carty of the School of Journalism at the College of Commerce in Rathmines, Dublin, and a very special thanks to the late, legendary Mairéad Doyle, who taught me shorthand; to Danny O'Hare, then of the National Institute of Higher Education, who presented me with the Seamus Kelly Memorial Award, and to the award fund's trustees and panel of judges back in 1987, who gave me a huge boost of confidence; to author Gordon Thomas for making me his apprentice; to crime journalist Jim Cusack of the *Sunday Independent* for encouraging me to give journalism another go; my namesake Ray Comiskey of the *Irish Times* for all his advice and help; and to many more who helped me on my way.

Journalists and public relations people necessarily distrust each other, but I have been lucky to have crossed paths with some of the best promoters, publicists, marketing people and event organisers in the business, who have come up with some brilliant ideas for features, helped me gather information under pressure, and accepted it with good grace when my duties as a journalist clashed with theirs as PRs. A very special thanks to Fiona Bolger; Breffni Burke; James Cafferty (Showtours); Dave Curtin; John Drummey; Kaz and Neil Lynas (Propeller PR, Belfast); Niamh Sullivan (Hopkins Communications); Nigel O'Mahony and Michelle Mangan of OMF Publicity; Peter Philips; Hannah Rose Farrington and Dandelion PR; Pauline Madigan; Carmel Dooley; Marion Fossett and Charles O'Brien of Fossetts' Circus; RTÉ press office, especially Karen Fitzpatrick and Rayna Connery; Maureen Catterson and her team at TV3; Linda NiGriofa at TG4; Caitriona Maguire of Lidl Ireland; Tara Gilleece; Melissa Kelly at O'Leary PR; Chris Kelly at Fleishmann Hilliard; Ailish Toohey; Caroline Moody, Nicola Watkins and the PRs at the Irish Defence Forces Press Office – especially former press officers Cmdt Eoin O'Neachtain and my first contact there, Cmdt Declan Carberry, whose decision to break with protocol and allow a female to take part in FCA manoeuvres led to the Seamus Kelly Memorial Award for me.

Bottoms up to Daragh McCoy and Rachel Solon for their dedication to the pursuit of art and fun. Thanks also to Keane Harley for accompanying me on my wacky way. My thanks to former curate of St Anne's Parish Shankill, Fr Doyle, for giving me a big break on the St Anne's parish magazine. Special thanks to the late author Tony Foster and to Ireland's biggest WAG, Mary Cunningham, for their inspiration and encouragement. And thanks to many others who helped me on my way, of whom more anon in one of my upcoming books.

Acknowledgements

Above all, I thank my mother, Nancy Comiskey, for lighting all those candles to St Anthony (they worked!); my dad, Gerry Comiskey, for being the best and wisest dad ever; my sisters, Lorraine and Sallyanne, brothers-in-law Liam Kenny and Denis Sullivan, nieces Laragh and Molly and nephews Mark and Daniel, for providing a refuge from my wacky world. Hope I didn't embarrass you too much!

August 2012
Dublin

CHAPTER ONE: Rebels

The Irish have always had a soft spot for the person who breaks rules, taboos and even laws. Maybe it's because the Republic was founded by rebels . . .

Pothole Man

When a Cavan man told me the potholes up there were big enough to swim in, I took him literally. We ended up going for a dip in the road . . . I brought my diving mask, snorkel, bikini and thigh-high boots; he brought a giant measuring stick and stripped down to his Y-fronts.

But then lorry driver Martin Hannigan was a man on a mission. The dad of six from Cootehill, County Cavan, had been waging war on the local authority for twenty-two years, and the BBC's Terry Wogan had even flown over to interview him in 1994. Songs had been written about him, including a trad number by Sharon Shannon and a reggae ballad that went out on You Tube and local radio. He had erected illegal road signs, published a calendar featuring pictures of Cavan's worst potholes, gone on twenty-four-hour fasts while chained to the railings of Cavan courthouse, and held demos outside Government Buildings in Dublin. No wonder he was nicknamed the Pothole King, I thought, as Martin showed me his battlezone – the pockmarked back-roads of County Cavan. His one-man vigilante attack involved painting circles around the holes. Armed with a spray-can, he usually worked at night so as not to be disturbed. 'The County Council powerwash the paint off – and I just go back and paint them again,' he explained.

In 2008, the County Council took the defiant Pothole King to court for interfering with public property. 'The judge dismissed the case but he said I'd go to jail the next time I painted around a pothole. Still, I'm not putting my spray cans away,' he said as he vowed to defy the court order. 'I think it's a matter of public safety. I'm doing it to warn drivers about the holes. You wouldn't see them in the dark or when it's wet. They fill up with muck and water.'

Pockmarked by craters, some up to three feet deep and fifteen wide, these roads from hell would have put the fear of God into *Top Gear*'s Jeremy Clarkson. They were driving locals around the bend, and the road rage reached boiling-point in 2009. As the National Roads Authority unveiled its multi-billion speed camera project, Martin got angry – and called in the *Sunday World*.

Followed by local photographer Lorraine Teevan, Martin took me on a tour of the county's worst roads, but it was more of an off-road experience – a bumpy safari ride without the exotic beasts. Even the Celtic Tiger had bypassed the B-roads of Cavan.

'I've destroyed two cars on these roads,' Martin said as I hung on to my breakfast. 'All that bouncing around in the potholes wrecked the suspension. And I can't count how many times the exhaust has come off my car. Once I know there are bad potholes on a road, I avoid them – but there are new potholes appearing all the time and they take you by surprise. They are costing motorists a fortune in repairs. Cars are failing their national car test because of the bad roads. And they're an accident waiting to happen. Some of these roads haven't been tarred for twenty-five years.'

At five miles long, Mayo Lane, in the townland of Aghagashlan is the mother and father of bad roads. It's the link between Ballybay and the main Shercock-Cootehill Road, but local drivers are wary of using it as a shortcut. However, the seven families who live there have no choice.

It was the road to heartbreak for a bereaved family, when the undertaker could not get the hearse down the road. 'Someone suggested taking the coffin out and carrying it, but that would have been riskier – it's so easy to trip in a hole. So, instead of bringing the man's corpse home for his wake, they had to bring him straight from the mortuary to the cemetery,' Martin said.

As we bumped along Mayo Lane, local pensioner Hugh Connolly stopped us to tell us how the potholes had made him a 'prisoner'. The bachelor, who had been living in a caravan on the boreen for fifteen years, said he was often stranded. He had to walk three miles to the shops and pubs in the nearest town, Cootehill.

'I don't even have a car – there'd be no point. It would be wrecked. The taxis won't even come down this road. A few have tried but they had to reverse. It's too narrow to turn.'

Less than half a mile up the road, Martin's sturdy Volkwagen Passat got one of its 12-inch wheels stuck in a huge crater. I could feel the car sliding back into the hole as Martin drove in first gear out the other side. Yards on, we hit another pothole – on a dangerous hairpin bend. Then we came across a twenty-yard stretch of water and could go no farther. Martin said some holes were fourteen inches deep. And one was twenty-one foot long, seven foot wide at each end and ten foot wide in the middle.

He had warned me to bring my wellies because we might need to get out of the car. Being the cautious type, I went a bit farther, and wore the nearest thing I had to fishermen's waders: thigh-high PVC stilettos. But, while my kinky boots may have been all the rage in Dublin night-clubs that winter, they were no match for the Cavan puddles. The muddy water was up to two feet deep in some places – and slippery.

As soon as I realised my rain mac wouldn't keep me dry, I stripped off to more suitable attire. A bikini, diving mask and snorkel are not what you'd normally wear on a road trip – but then it's not every day you find roads like swimming pools. And the Pothole King was just as keen to make a hole-y show of himself. 'I don't care if I get pneumonia,' he said as he stripped down to his jocks. The dapper granddad had worn his best suit, complete with collar and tie for our interview, but now it was time for action. 'I've tried everything to get the Council and the National Roads Authority to take notice of this public safety hazard. This is my best shot.'

A month after the exposé in the *Sunday World*, Martin was being hailed as a hero around the world. The wacky photos, showing Martin and yours truly giving it welly, made an impression as far away as Detroit, USA, where envious anti-pothole campaigners had to admit that our holes were bigger than theirs. Martin was hailed as a hero by bikers, truckers and motorists around the world.

But the flip side was a deluge of hate-mail. 'I got anonymous letters saying insulting things about myself and my family. Someone sent me a blank Christmas card with a note: 'This will be your last Christmas'. One weirdo posted Martin a copy of the *Sunday World* article – with 'RIP' scrawled on it. Martin believes he knows who sent the hate mail. 'This fella has a grudge against me. When he saw me in the *Sunday World*, it really got under his skin.' But he vowed to continue his war:

'I've hundreds of spray cans in my shed, and I'm going to start painting circles around the potholes again when the snow is all gone.'

Martin's wife, Sylvana, even dubbed yours truly 'the Pothole Angel'. 'People are saying the *Sunday World* was right to do it. It was a bit of fun, but it drew attention to a serious issue. And Martin is getting a lot of slagging about the pictures! You don't get many men who are prepared to strip down to their underpants and get into a pothole in the road. We can't walk down the street without people stopping us.'

But Martin's stunt had yet to prick Cavan County Council's conscience or make a dent in what he described as their 'stubborn refusal to do anything about the most dangerous potholes in the country'. A Council spokesperson told the *Sunday World*: 'In relation to potholes, there is a maintenance programme in place for each area,' but declined to expand.

However, nearly a year later, the Hole-y War that had motorists' knickers in a twist ended and the Pothole King was finally able to pull up his Y-fronts – because Ireland's biggest pothole was no more! Martin felt like King of the Road as he told me that the council had thrown tar into it. 'The road is as smooth as a golf course now,' he said.

For the Pothole King, it was a hole in one.

Cockerels and Chainmail

He had many nicknames: The Birdman, Pirate Paddy, The Man in the Iron Suit and even Hugh Hefner. And every one of them suited him. When he wasn't spinning old vinyl LPs in his sitting room where he ran a pirate radio station, or making love to his 'bit of fluff', as he charmingly called his latest lover, he could be found in the stands at a local GAA match – with a chicken on his head. Or down by the river, astride an ancient moped with no wheels – wearing a medieval-style chainmail suit and brandishing a sword as he defended the honour of his province, Leinster, against neighbouring Connacht.

And while it was not exactly the Playboy mansion, or Dublin Zoo, Paddy Farrell's council house, in the town of Lanesboro, County Longford, had more wildlife.

His Russian fiancée, Lana, was happy to share the two-bedroom Council house with a golden labrador called Lucky and a cat, Paddy Garfield. They were all that remained of his menagerie, after Council officials ordered him to get rid of his flock of chickens.

Neighbours in the terrace, which is part of a housing scheme for senior citizens, complained that chicken Gloria and her mate Gaynor were keeping them awake with their amorous crowing and clucking at 5 AM.

Paddy, who was also running a pirate radio station, Big L, from his parlour, said he was especially fond of the hen because she shared his love of country 'n' Irish music. 'Gloria is a fan of Big Tom and the Mainliners [a showband from County Monaghan] like me. She hatched her chicks on a Big Tom LP – it was like she was hatching them on the great man himself!'

While Gloria was the love of his life, Paddy, who admitted to being 'over sixty', said his forty-two-year-old fiancée was just a 'bit of fluff' on the side. 'She's just my part-time girlfriend. She's a wild woman and she goes off on me sometimes when we have rows. But I don't mind because I was a wild boy when I was younger.'

The couple's volatile relationship was played out on the pages of the *Sunday World* – it was livelier than anything you'd see on a TV soap. When Lana disappeared for a few weeks after a tiff, Paddy called me to say he had replaced her – with two ginger cats. He revealed he had named the kittens Podge and Rodge – not after RTÉ television's risqué puppets but 'because that's what I used to call Lana's breasts when we were making love!'

The couple's on-off relationship had begun when Paddy found her homeless and broke on the streets of Longford, having being lured to Ireland with the prospect of work picking mushrooms.

It was thanks to Lana that Paddy's pirate radio station occasionally blasted out Russian pop. Paddy said his radio station was so popular, even the local cops turned a blind eye to it. 'I broadcast from my spare bedroom – right behind the Garda station.' But the 'young-at-heart' pensioner said Lana was just one of the women in his life.

Paddy's own grown-up kids had all flown the coop, and he had been sharing his Council house with his pets since his wife died four years previously.

Next time I saw him, he was decked out in his medieval-style chain-mail suit. His neighbour, Gezza Shurger, had taken six months to make the hooded tunic the old-fashioned way, using pliers to link the individual iron rings. He was hoping to flog it for a grand to a theatre, film company, museum or battle re-enactment group.

Paddy said he and Gezza were like old-fashioned knights – loyal to each other and always ready to rescue damsels in distress. It was strange to find medieval values such as chivalry mixed in with the hedonistic culture of Hugh Hefner, in a small country town. But a few years later, Paddy and Lana got married. They moved to a new house – and the animals came too.

The Ming and I

He earned the nickname 'Ming the Merciless' because he looked and dressed like the comic-book character. And, long before he turned up in Dáil Éireann wearing a bespoke hemp suit, the bearded, pony-tailed leftie was notorious for posting spliffs to journalists.

One thing was certain: Luke 'Ming' Flanagan was not your bog-standard politician. Just one week after he had helped turf out the government in February 2011, the freshly elected TD got in some practice for the cut-throat world of national politics by sharpening his blade! He led sixteen of his neighbours on to the bog to break the soil – and the law. 'I'm willing to go to jail for the right to cut turf,' he said as he dug his own patch on the bog near Castlerea, County Roscommon – one of thirty-two bogs around the country that are off-limits to turf-cutters under EU rules.

The Mighty Ming was defending the rights of turf-cutters all over the country to cut their own briquettes. 'We have the support of bog-cutters in Offaly, Kerry, the Dublin Mountains – everywhere there's a bog. We even have Loyalist members across the border. In 2012 another twenty-three bog complexes will be covered by the ban and in

2014 a further seventy-five. They're trying to get rid of turf-cutting altogether,' he explained.

Ming's message to the Eurocrats and the National Parks and Wildlife Service was: 'Bog off'. While the rest of the nation knew him for his campaign to legalise the auld weed, in counties Roscommon and Leitrim it was all about the auld sod. And, as he declared war on his home turf, it was clear Ming was King. Since his election, he had achieved rock-star status among his constituents.

But he didn't mind getting his shoes and trouser-hems wet as he jumped ditches and trudged through the mud like a trooper. 'It's only muck. And there's plenty of that still in Leinster House,' he said as he gave me some turf-cutting tips.

Ming laughed at my efforts to wield the *slean* – an ancient bog-cutting tool. No matter how hard I tried, I barely made a dent in the turf. Still, with him doing all the hard work, 'The Ming and I' made a good team – until I called the plants that grow on the bog 'grass'. Ming, who knows his grass from his weed, laughed: 'You wouldn't call that grass! It's sphagnum.' He revealed that he knew the name of every creature living on the bog. But, luckily for this city slicker, the creepy crawlies were taking a day off. 'On a very hot day you'd get eaten alive with midges,' Ming said, 'but I love being out here in the fresh air. You get a great tan from it.'

He has been cutting turf since he was a little boy helping his parents. 'We used to have a picnic. I remember once my mother brought a sponge cake. It was covered in flies but we still ate it. Everything tastes nice here. You work up a great appetite.'

His own Ming Dynasty was made up of 'bog men', he added. 'My grand-uncle Harry Fleming cut turf here for sixty-seven years. Between him, my father and myself, we cut €150,000 worth of turf out of it. But the National Parks and Wildlife Service think it's OK to throw us three-grand compensation for turfing us off the bog. If they offered me a million, I wouldn't take it. We cut it for domestic use – to light our fires and heat our homes. It saves a family €500 a year.

'All our national resources are being taken out of the hands of the people – our oil and gas off the west coast, our fisheries, and now our bogs. If we give up our right to grow our own fuel supply, I suggest we cut the two colours off the Irish flag and just go with the white flag.

'The last time Irish people were evicted from the bogs was in 1915 – and a relation of mine, Father Michael O'Flanagan, stood up to the State. He led a group of turf-cutters onto a bog near Cliffony, County Sligo. When the authorities saw there was a priest leading them, they backed down because they didn't want to go up against a person in authority. Now I have the mandate of the people – so maybe they'll listen to me.' Ming said everyone should be allowed cut in their own local bog. 'We'd have to do a twenty-mile round journey to get to the nearest bog where we're allowed to cut – so much for protecting the environment! The legislation was brought in without consulting us. The documents were all in Latin. And when we eventually got to look at the maps they used, they were out of date – there were drains marked in that were there forty years ago.

'We know the bog but we're being forced to obey laws made by people who have no understanding about it. They're not even environ-mentalists. We arranged a meeting with a group from the National Parks and Wildlife Service and five of them came down in one car each. You'd think they'd come in a bus run on vegetable oil if they cared about the environment. We place the top of the bog in mounds so the flora will grow again. You'd imagine they would be pleased we're looking after the bogs for them. We also watch out for illegal dumping. If any bog-cutter was caught dumping, we'd kick him out of the association.'

But it was clear that the nearest these people would get to breaking the law was cutting a few briquettes for the fire. Local man Joe Connally was weaving his tractor carefully among the mounds of stacked turf so as not to disturb them. Michael Fitzmaurice, chairman of the Turf Cutters' and Contractors' Association, said he hoped Ming would be able to get the ban reversed. 'He's our best hope.'

Ming has continued to champion the illegal turf-cutters and others who broke 'bad laws'. One thing is for certain: instead of merely preserving our heritage, Ming is keeping it alive – along with the twin Irish traditions of rebellion and a sense of community.

I went back onto the bog with Ming in 2012, to join him in lifting a sod of turf which had been cut by a local farmer. 'I could go to prison for this,' he said. He introduced me to ten locals who said they were being 'terrorised' by the police and Irish Air Corps – who were flying over the bog to take aerial snaps of the illegal turf-cutting.

HeLL Plates

He had been branded Ireland's worst driver – after failing his driving test ten times. So when Ray Heffernan invited me for a spin in his car, I was all set for a Top Scare. The sixty-one-year-old separated dad of two had just taken the Department of Transport to court for the seventh time, to challenge the results of his most recent driving test. But he lost his case after the judge heard he drove over a roundabout and clocked up five 'potentially dangerous faults', nineteen serious faults and two minor faults during the test in his native city of Cork in 2011.

Driving tester Kevin Condren said Mr Heffernan asked: 'So where is this mini roundabout?' – after driving right over it. The tester said he 'felt in danger' at least five times, because Mr Heffernan drove through stop signs, failed to signal or respond to instructions, 'over-revved' the engine and 'his observation was particularly poor'.

So I made sure to wear my hard hat when Ray offered to let me test him on his driving skills in Cork city and suburbs. After half an hour in the passenger seat, I was in a tailspin. I could see why Ray and the driving testers were bumper-to-bumper. Because, while he was as skilful as a stunt-driver when it came to difficult manoeuvres, he was awful when it came to the mundane things such as stopping at traffic lights, keeping to the correct side of the road – and driving over things in the middle of the road!

Ray denied he had ever driven over a roundabout on his driving test. 'There was no roundabout. That driving tester perjured himself in court. And I never failed my test,' he insisted as I got into his Nissan Almera. 'The test was wrong. It was a lady tester the last time and she told me she feared for her life in my car. I hope you're not nervous – because I'm a safe driver. You won't need the hard hat,' he added as I put on the builder's helmet I had bought especially for the trip.

Ray also denied that he had assaulted a driving tester after failing his test four years previously. Still, I kept my wheel brace handy just in case we got into a scrap. As we set off from his home in Mayfield, I was comforted by the fact that Ray was driving on familiar streets – until I noticed he was driving a bit far from the kerb. He slowed down to look at a cardboard box right in the centre of the road – then drove right over it! 'There was nowhere else to go – and I didn't even touch it,' he said – after I heard the box snagging on the axle and crunching under the back wheels. 'There could have been something in it,' I pointed out.

Teetotaller Ray had no excuse for driving down the middle of the road, but he had a go anyway: 'If I went over on the right I'd hit a car on the other side of the road.'

The next big beeper was on Brian Boru Bridge as we crossed the River Lee. Ray drove slowly towards the red light, seemed to be looking at it – and then went right through it! When I pointed it out, he blamed me for distracting him. 'I was talking to you,' he explained. In fairness, there was nothing in front of him, and the car behind – driven by photographer Billy macGill, with a camera attached to his dashboard – was a bit too close. And I felt it was safer to jump the light than jam on the brakes – but I didn't tell Ray that.

After that, it was all smooth cruising as I gave him the test-drive from hell. Cork's steep hills are a driver's nightmare, unless you're Jeremy Clarkson. So I was impressed by Ray's handling of the gears and throttle-control. Patrick's Hill had been too tough even for Lance Armstrong on his bicycle as he participated in the Irish leg of the Tour de France the previous year, but Ray took it smoothly in second gear. And he ran rings around the parked cars and trolley bays in a packed Dunnes Stores car park in Ballyvolane – without the aid of a parking sensor. He had to stop for a smoke after that. 'They didn't let me smoke on my driving test. You're not allowed,' he said.

But I really took my (hard) hat off to Ray when he tackled the notoriously tight car-park at the back of the Maldron Hotel, which had received road-rage reviews on tell-tale tourists' website Trip Advisor. The entrance, which was just wide enough for an average family car, was even tighter than usual, because there was a car parked on one side and a delivery truck with the ramp down on the other. Ray drove in slowly, then looked around in horror since there was barely space to move. I suggested reversing back down the ramp, but brave Ray offered to do a five-point turn. 'In a four-wheel drive car, you can turn on a sixpence,' he explained. It was only then that I realised why he was going so slow. 'I always have it in four-wheel-drive. That's the only setting it has,' he said.

Ray admitted that he often left it in four-by-four at speeds of up to sixty-five mph. 'The fastest I'd ever drive it would be sixty, sixty-five miles per hour on the motorway. I'm not a boy-racer. If I'm a dangerous driver, why am I not in a coffin now? I've been driving for forty-four years and I had just one accident, in 2008 – and that was the other fella's fault. He had to pay me through his insurance. I was stopped on the road turning right, and he went into me.'

The retired plasterer said he clocked up twenty thousand miles a year. 'I'd do about a hundred miles a week, just to the shops – Lidl, Aldi and Dunnes. But I drove a lot in England. I've driven in fog and on ice. My first car was a Ford Prefect – I've driven all kinds of cars. I didn't drive in the snow and ice last winter because it was too dangerous.'

Ray first took the test in 2004 – and was shocked when he failed. He vented his road rage on the then Transport Minister, Martin Cullen, sending him three hundred letters and bombarding him with calls. He still claims that there is a 'conspiracy' against him. 'I'm black-listed by all the driving testers. Even if I did my test in another part of Ireland, they'd fail me.'

After his seventh failure, in 2008, he booked a test in England. 'I had it all arranged to do it in Leeds, but there was flooding in England. The cars were floating down the road like matchboxes. So I came back and tried it again here.' But Ray was already infamous in the UK: Hockley Driving School has put his story on their website as an example of what NOT to do on your driving test.

Still, as the *Sunday World*'s roving reporter, with plenty of mileage under my belt, I thought Ray was cool behind the wheel. And so did photographer Billy McGill, a former rally driver. I was impressed at the fact Ray ignored his mobile phone ringing and made a big show of turning his head to look left and right. It was just a shame he didn't see that red light. My verdict at the time: I'd pass him – because he drives too bloody slowly.

A few months after I met him, Ray failed his test for the eleventh time and lost his eighth court case against the Department of Transport. He has since applied to sit the test a twelfth time.

Achill Henge

It had clearly been built as some kind of statement. But a wall of silence surrounded 'Achill Henge', a gigantic replica of Stonehenge on Achill Island, when I visited the place with a photographer.

Several people, including an elected representative in County Mayo, said they were 'afraid' to talk. One man even made serious allegations – but declined to speak on the record. Two women collecting signatures for a petition to 'Keep Achill Henge' refused to give their names or be photographed. 'We've filled up a few pages with signatures. It will bring tourists – we've got a lot of people asking for it. It will be good for tourism. But that's all we're saying.' Another woman said: 'You won't find anyone to talk about it. People are afraid – They're afraid of things they can't talk about. We want it to stay, that's all we're saying'. Others who had previously spoken to the press decided to keep schtum this time. They were hoping Mayo County Council would stop asking questions and simply give it the thumbs up if its creator, Joe McNamara, lodged a second appeal against the decision to knock it. Less than a month after it was erected, the local authority voted to knock it.

To many, the brazen builder had the dangerous appeal of an outlaw in a Wild West movie – someone to be wary of, but nonetheless to be admired for his stand against the authorities. And he achieved national cult-hero status when he was jailed for a weekend before Christmas 2011, after he was found in contempt of court – because he had he ignored two County Council injunctions ordering him to stop work on the building. It had been erected without planning permission between 25 and 27 November 2011.

The concrete structure was just the latest attention-grabbing stunt by McNamara, originally from Achill but living at Dun na Carraige in Blackrock, County Galway. He had first hit the national headlines when he rammed a cement-mixer into the gates of Leinster House in September 2010. The truck had the words 'Toxic Bank' and 'Anglo' painted on its sides. McNamara climbed onto the roof of the truck through the sun roof as the truck cruised towards the gates, causing just €35 worth of damage.

He was arrested just before it hit the gates, but the policemen on duty were unable to stop the lorry. McNamara later told the Gardaí he was unable to stop it himself because the brakes had been cut, which was confirmed in court by a mechanic. His own defence team said McNamara himself had cut the brakes. The judge dismissed charges of dangerous driving and criminal damage and dismissed all other charges. The forty-one-year-old, who owed Anglo Irish Bank €7.5 million, said he was doing it because he was 'pissed off'.

Two months later, he parked a cherry-picker emblazoned with the words 'Anglo Toxic Bank' outside Leinster House, sat in the crow's nest and played loud music until he was arrested and charged with dangerous driving. But the charges were again struck out. On that occasion,

McNamara told reporters there would be no more protests. His solicitor told the court he regretted any inconvenience and waste of court and state resources.

But one year on, the Anglo Avenger resurfaced as the Achill Avenger. Standing four-and-a-half metres high and thirty metres in diameter, 'Achill Henge' was said to have been built in one night on common land next to land owned by McNamara's relations, the Stokes family.

Local Fine Gael councillor Michael McLaughlin was so impressed he declared it a potential tourist attraction, a 'work of art' and 'genius'. He told a meeting of Westport Town Council: 'People will travel from all over to see it and I think it could be one of the major tourist attractions in the west of Ireland. If left, it will still be standing strong in five thousand years, and will continue to pose questions and generate debate; that's what good art does. It is public art in my opinion. There's a fine line sometimes between genius and madness, but I certainly think this is genius. I know there are planning breaches and, by the letter of the law, it should come down. But I think an exception should be made. First of all, from an engineering point of view, it is a fantastic piece of work. He did it all himself and I wouldn't say it is even one quarter inch out of place – and he got it built in one weekend.'

But archaeologists based on the island condemned it on the grounds that it was built over a historic old railway line – and may even have destroyed a genuine Bronze Age site less than half a kilometre away. Theresa McDonald, who runs the Achill Archaeological Field School, told the local paper, the *Mayo News*: 'We don't know how extensive the site is, it could stretch to the site of the Henge.' She said the developer would have been made aware of it had he applied for planning permission.

The members of Achill Historical and Archaeological Society also wrote to the local paper to condemn the unauthorised structure. Secretary Gerard Mangan said the fake tomb would have 'grave implications for the future preservation of other archaeological sites in the area'.

The massive structure impressed some ESB workers from Castlebar, who turned up when the *Sunday World* sent me to check it out in January 2012. As I stood there with photographer Keith Heneghan, the two men suddenly emerged out of the fog. They declined to be named or photographed. One declared it a 'great bit of engineering', given that the boggy land had to be levelled out and 'it was built in one night, so I heard'. Keith and I had driven and trekked up a long mud track, which had been freshly gouged into the marsh by heavy machinery. As we turned a corner, it loomed out of the gloom, looking like the ruins of a lost city. Its classical lines and modern components reminded me of the artist Giorgio Di Chirico's paintings of a post-apocalyptic world, and I could finally understand why the local councillor had described it as art. The structure was clearly intended to be at least twice as huge; steel brackets protruded from the tops of the vertical slabs. Inside was an unfinished circular concrete path and a square of concrete in the centre. Graffiti artists had already made their mark, using the local slate stone to scrawl their names, OXO games and single words ranging from the rude ('balls') to the bizarre ('ears').

Meanwhile, the mysterious McNamara once again broke his silence when he announced at a public meeting in Galway that he planned to run in the next general election. The crowd parted as the dark, brooding Mayo man appeared in the room and interrupted the meeting, which had been held to protest against the closure of local airline Aer

Arann. Once again, McNamara had bulldozed his own agenda to the fore.

Friends and foes alike could only tremble at the prospect of seeing him unHenged.

CHAPTER TWO: Animal Passions

As an agricultural nation, the Irish have always been close to animals – sometimes too close. They are our workmates, friends, food. . . . And sometimes they show us who's boss.

Woodstock for Farmers

It's not often a townie gets to hobnob with eighty thousand culchies. So when the *Sunday World* sent me to the Ploughing Championships, I was 'on the pig's back' (as they say in rural Ireland when they're feeling smug). This was the ultimate muckfest – it was Woodstock for farmers. And my editor thought it would be fun to put a city slicker in the middle of it. Until then, my knowledge of the countryside had been largely gleaned from watching *Killinascully* – a sitcom on Irish channel RTÉ about a bunch of country bumpkins.

My experience with tractors had been limited to cursing them from behind on winding country roads. And, while I was very fond of livestock, it usually came in the form of milk on my cornflakes.

Some years previously, I had made the pilgrimage to Ireland's biggest annual agricultural show with my boyfriend – another townie – and we had entered a raffle for a Hereford bullock. The hard-working farmers were unable to hide their shock when we told them we wanted to keep the beast in a suburban garden – as a pet! He reminded me of a little bullock I had befriended as a child while staying with my country cousins –and, as a veggie, I was determined to save this one from the abattoir. It was a major gaffe, we soon realised, and the cynic in me was convinced that our raffle tickets had gone missing before the draw.

Anyway, I got my revenge when the *Sunday World* sent me along with another city-slicker, Dublin snapper Val Sheehan – who specialised in glamour photography and fashion. Together, we were the perfect tabloid team – and, we thought, the antithesis of the green welly brigade. The news editor, John Donlon, thought it would be a good idea for me to wear pink wellies – just to give those country folk fair warning that a Dubliner was among them. I went one better and dug out my psychedelic festival boots (I had worn them on a mucky day in Marley Park), along with a denim mini-dress. Val hadn't brought his wellies, and the hems of his smart trousers were soon covered in mud. Within minutes of our arrival in the grounds of Farmley Castle in Cuffesgrange, County Kilkenny, we were asked to enter the Most Appropriately Dressed Couple contest. We had to tell the lady we couldn't, because we were working for a newspaper – she didn't seem to believe us, and we couldn't blame her. Neither did the PR official, who seemed to think we were taking the Michael.

However, as we wandered around, it soon became clear that we fitted right in. This was the most diverse bunch of people I had ever seen. GAA jerseys representing every county clashed with cowboy hats, hot pants, biker jackets, tweeds, moth-eaten jerseys and rubber boots ranging from Dunnes Stores' finest to posh Hunter wellies. Yuppies in brand new Barbour riding macs mingled with sons of the soil in well-worn overalls and flat caps, while pin-striped politicians tucked their smart trousers into wellies. There were comedians and live bands, including Crystal Swing, and salesmen were flogging just about every-thing on earth – even earth itself, in every form imaginable, from tracts of land to bags of topsoil. For most of the people there, it was less about land – and more about landing a bargain. You could buy anything from a herd of heifers to a remote-controlled toy helicopter, a combine-harvester or a bra. You could pick up an old cow – or an old farmer. Cowboy hats, goth T-shirts and outfits suitable for Ladies' Day at the Races vied for place alongside horses' tack and handymen's tools. The sideshows included a pony-gymkhana, sheep-shearing contest, fashion shows, cookery demos and the odd spontaneous sing-song.

I fell in love with a Charolais calf from Thurles. Just eight months old, the little fellow had no name – and was unlikely to be given one, since he was destined to end up a burger. 'Or a piece of prime steak,' his minder said. I gave the poor creature a hug and went for a bite myself – a veggie burger, much to the amusement of some teenage boys. 'Eat a real burger, it won't make you fat,' one said. At the Ploughing, vegetarians were still a novelty.

Still, I did get into a beef with the liveliest bull in the field – a bucking bronco! He might have been just a machine, but then I was a fake farmerette, so we were perfectly matched. Or so I thought until he bucked me off. As I flew through the air, I thought of a few words that rhymed with 'buck'. But I got back up for another ride. The lads from young Irish farmers' organisation Macra na Feirme ('Sons of the Farms'), who had supplied the mechanical bronco, told me to hang onto the rope – but I just couldn't resist grabbing the horns. At my best attempt, I lasted all of sixteen seconds. The record so far during the event was thirty-four seconds, according to Denis Drennan and Thomas Quirke of Macra na Feirme. In hindsight, I should have worn jeans – my bare knees got shredded on the hog's-hair hide. But I had the last laugh when a macho cowboy, complete with Stetson and handlebar moustache, came out bow-legged, moaning, 'It's not good for men!' Forget *Brokeback Mountain* – he looked a bit broke-back!

It was time to find myself a real country man, I thought as I was lured into a tent to the strains of *Aon Focail Eile* – a naughty play on words in the Irish language. Its composer and singer, the country-woman's crumpet, Richie Kavanagh, was surrounded by sexy farming lasses and their blokes as he belted out his hit. But I still managed to get a squeeze out of him. Val had persuaded me to get up on the stage. 'Who are you?' Richie asked. I retorted: 'Who the focail are you?' After a few seconds talking bullocks with him in front of a lively crowd, I was ready for the funny farm myself. So he let me go with a message to his farming friends: 'This girl wants a ride on your tractors.'

The real star of the Ploughing Championships every year is Godfrey Worrell from Kildare, who has been raking in the awards since 1996, with the help of his plough-horses, Jenny and Jim. These black beauties are always immaculately groomed and decked out in antique harnesses.

Pensioner Martin Bellew from County Tipperary was delighted to see an old threshing machine in action. 'I used to work one of those when I was a young lad. You never see them now – you might see an old thresher in a pub but there's usually a part missing. Now young people can see how they work.' He said life in the countryside had changed a lot since his youth. 'It's all big machines now. The old way was hard work – but I miss it.'

Some of the farmers were just there to pick up a new tractor – but others found a new religion. In a true sign of the times, the Church was making a comeback – but this time round spiritual types were spoilt for choice. Punters grabbed free copies of the *Irish Catholic* – before heading into tents to sign their souls over to the Free Presbyterians, Baptists, Church of Ireland and a host of other religions. Others simply wrote on the Ecumenical Prayer Wall – asking God for health, happiness and money to pay the mortgage.

At least health was free. Huge queues formed outside the Irish Heart Foundation tent, where medically trained volunteers offered free check-ups. Something that would cost €50 at the GP's was not to be sneezed at – and well worth the short walk from the burger-van. I steered well clear of this – whatever about the healthy outdoor life, I have always had a phobia of doctors. Still, I gave the chipper a miss and went for a fruit-and-yoghurt smoothie – and was surprised to see quite a lot of old-school farmers doing the same.

Then I got into a potentially life-threatening situation when a big bull took a keen interest in my red top. I tried covering up with a shirt –but the beast seemed to think I was acting the matador. Luckily his owner had him on a tight tether.

The Ploughing Championship moved to Athy in 2009, and the venue was so popular that the organisers held the event there for two more years. Rain failed to dampen the visitors' enthusiasm in 2010. The tractors came in handy – for pulling jeeps out of the muck! But snapper Ciaran McGowan and I struck a blow for city slickers when we drove across the corn stubble instead. Country folk who had laughed at my little Mazda Mx-5 sports car followed us.

The following year, there was no disguising the fact that I was a faux farm gal, when I met my match – a plastic cow! Despite the make-believe mammaries, Daisy had to be milked the old-fashioned way. Photographer Conor O'Mearain got me to sit down on a three-legged stool and imagine I was an old-fashioned milkmaid – albeit one in

Penneys' shorts and Dunnes Stores' wellies. But it was an udder story getting to grips with her slippery teats. Luckily, I got a few tips from her owner, Jim Dockrey, and Aoife Kinsella of the Farm Relief Service, which runs courses in all aspects of agriculture. 'Young farmers love to have a go at traditional milking – it makes them appreciate the modern machinery all the more,' Jim explained.

Some lazy cows just stood around looking glamorous. And Jim's prize heifer was more fake than the plastic cow, I realised when he let me peek into her grooming kit – a four-by-two foot box of toiletries and cosmetics especially for cows! Not even my hairdresser sister had such an array of brushes and combs. The bovine beauty kit included 'Showbiz' shampoo (especially for cows), setting lotion, styling mousse, volumising mousse and hairspray. Jim had even varnished her hooves before putting her on show. The All Ireland Angus-Cross Champion was the daughter of a white shorthorn cow and a handsome black Angus, but her plush black hide owed more to Jim's skills as a 'moo-tician'. And as she fluttered her long eyelashes, a bullock strained at his tether and lowed longingly.

Meanwhile frisky farmers confessed they were really only there to look for wives – unlike the adulterous couple from RTÉ soap *Fair City*, 'Jo and Tommy', who were supposed to be having a roll in the hay somewhere on the seven hundred acres.

But it didn't take much to create a scandal at 'The Ploughing', as I discovered when I obligingly posed with a man and his vintage tractor, which he was raffling for charity. He later rang to ask me to keep the photos out of the paper. 'It's my eighty-seven-year-old mother,' he said. Apparently some corners of rural Ireland were not quite ready for denim shorts and a little bit of cleavage.

A week later, pop princess Rihanna came up against the same prudish attitude in County Down, when an elderly farmer booted her out of his field for cavorting topless as she filmed her new video. Clearly there is no place in the Irish countryside for nature of the bodily kind.

Boozy Bull

The last time he went on the lash, he was barred from the pub. And television companies were soon bidding for the footage of him head-butting his fellow drinkers and destroying the furniture. But the raging bull finally got to enjoy a booze-up – thanks to the *Sunday World*. We were moved by the story of the thirsty beast that escaped from a cattle mart and went in search of the perfect pint.

Like anyone who has been shown the door before closing time, Arthur the bull got into a fierce temper. Terrified locals scattered as the big beast ran amok for thirty minutes, charging at the barman, goring another man and making a hole in a wall. The frustrated creature then appeared to be trying to play snooker – with his horns!

But all was forgiven when the owner of the Porterhouse Pub in Kingscourt, County Cavan poured a pint especially for his famous four-legged customer. Cyril Rafferty said he had no beef with the bull. 'He's one of my quieter customers if the truth be told.' But instead of letting him back into the boozer, Cyril brought Arthur's pint to him. And he got the *Sunday World* to serve it up on the farm.

It was not quite what I expected when the newspaper's resident booze expert, Pub Spy, sent me off in search of a 'horny beast' on a Friday night. And I was even warier when the other punters told me about their scary experience. Martin O'Leary had been standing at the bar when the creature burst in the side-door. 'It all happened in a flash,' he said. His mate Seán Martin added: 'I've never seen anything move as quick. He ran out the front door and the bull started attacking the rest of us. We legged it out the door but this Englishman, Malcolm Nevin, got in the way of the bull and was lucky to escape. The bull gouged one fella's arm. Little Sharon Carroll, the barmaid, warned us. She said, "Don't open the back door – there's a bull outside!" But this guy went out for a smoke – and left the door open.'

Seán, a Dub like myself, added: 'You know you're in the country when a bull drops into the pub for a pint. I moved up here sixteen years ago but I've never seen the like of this.' The former Dublin City Ramblers bassist even planned to write a song about the incident, 'The Ballad of the Bull'. Meanwhile Cyril was even thinking of changing the name of the pub. But first he had a bidding war on his hands as television companies fought for the exclusive thirty-minute CCTV footage.

Days after the bull's rampage, Cyril was still repairing the damage to his pub furniture. They may have been shorn down to stumps, but the bull's horns had still taken the side off the snooker table – and gored an enormous hole in the wall! 'Then he collapsed on the floor and the lads from the mart came in to take him away. He went quietly enough – he was herded out the back door just like any other troublesome customer. He must have had one hell of a hangover,' Cyril said.

I hoped the creature wasn't in a bullish mood as we headed up to the farm outside Inniskeen, County Monaghan where he was recuperating from his night on the tiles. It was well after closing time when we got him a nice creamy pint in the nearby Dan McNello's pub. It's best known as poet Patrick Kavanagh's favourite haunt, but from now on McNello's and the Porterhouse will be known as the Bull Boozers. Cyril pulled a perfect pint of Guinness for the bull, who may need the strength for his new career –as a stud! Then the farmer Stephen Farrell, who had got his Uncle Tommy to buy the fifteen-month-old Limousin on his behalf, let yours truly serve the bull his first ever pint.

And, judging by the bull's satisfied slurping noises, it was worth waiting for.

A Baaaad Haircut

As an animal-lover, I'm all in favour of pampering our four-legged friends. But I was ready for the funny farm when I was told to give the animals . . . a haircut. Beauty and the Beast is best left to fairytales, I thought as I tried my hand at sheep-shearing.

In my fake hillbilly outfit (a denim mini-dress with wellies), I might have looked like the lost member of the Beverly Hillbillies, but I couldn't fool the sheep, I realised as I did my best to make them bald – and ended up giving them Mohicans.

It hadn't looked like such a bad idea when All Ireland Champion sheep-shearer George Graham offered to give me a crash course on a farm near Borris, County Carlow. Farmer Michael O'Gorman and his son Michael Junior were happy to let me loose on their flock with an electric shears. I even got some tips on hair-cutting from my sister Sal, a hairdresser. But I noticed the sheepdogs kept well out of the way; with yours truly wielding the shears, there was a chance they'd end up looking like that poor mutt in the Specsavers ad.

This was not what George and his mate Alex Reid from New Zealand had in mind as they let me help them practise for the All

Ireland Sheep Shearing Championships. George, who had hung onto the Irish record for twenty years, could shear 483 sheep in nine hours – or one sheep every twenty seconds. The third-generation sheep-shearer from Ballyoughter, County Wexford, hoped to shave one second off his time during the contest in Portlaoise, but I took a lot longer. I wondered just what I had let myself in for as I watched the muscular six-footer drag a huge sheep out of the pen. At sixty kilo-grammes, she was a real handful and her hooves looked as if they could do some damage. Worse, we had to start off by de-fluffing her lady bits! Giving a big animal the equivalent of the Hollywood bikini wax was a job for Rambo, I decided as I let George do this delicate job. This was the first time the ewe had ever been sheared. So I was surprised when she lay back like a *Playboy* centrefold. In seconds, George had turned her into the sheep equivalent of Pamela Anderson.

But I had to finish her makeover. First I had to put on a pair of special sheep-shearing moccasins so I wouldn't slip on the wooden board, which was greasy with oil from the sheep's wool. I was nervous as George handed me what looked like a giant electric barber's trimmer and told me to give the sheep a short back and sides. I was afraid of hurting her, so I skimmed the fluff off the edge of her coat, but George told me to go in closer. 'The wool is more valuable when it's all in one big coat,' he explained. George taught me to stretch the skin with one hand and hold the blade close with the other. It took me ages to shear the poor sheep and, every so often, she would look up at me with big confused eyes. Soon she got bored and began answering the other sheep in the pen with mournful bleats. I was sure she was grumbling about me. Every so often, she would lie back and put all her weight on me – but whenever I let her slip, she kicked. 'Handling the sheep is the hardest part,' George explained. 'The shearing is easy.' I wasn't so sure about that. But I was so impressed by my sheep at the end of her make-over that I named her Dolly Ewing.

George said not all sheep are so docile. One of Dolly's friends had bitten him the day before – on the nipple. 'It's still very painful,' he grimaced. Given my choice of dress, I got a bit worried. But luckily the sheep did nothing more than nuzzle me.

In thirty-five years as a globe-trotting sheep-shearer, George has had some serious run-ins with the creatures. 'I've been bitten, kicked and even head-butted by sheep. The sheep in New Zealand are twice the size of the ones here. Imagine being attacked by a 120-kilogramme sheep.' Rams can weigh up to two hundred kilos but are sometimes easier to handle, he added. 'You can get a big ram and he's very placid. The hardest things for me to shear are lambs. They're so small, there's nothing to grab onto. And they're slippery.'

I wasn't about to shear a lamb. But I was chuffed when the only lamb in the flock let me hold him for a few moments – though he wasn't too keen to pose for *Sunday World* photographer Ciaran McGowan (who is now with the *Irish Sun*). The minute Ciaran pointed the lens at him, he wriggled free and ran into the next field. Like a naughty toddler, he stopped and looked around the hedge to see if we were chasing him. Then he disappeared into the flock of baldy ewes. They fussed over him like aunties, licking him and nudging him towards his mother.

In two days, the lads had sheared 660 sheep. But there was still a pen full of fluffy creatures waiting for their haircut. Just counting them was sending me to sleep – and giving me nightmares. So I took a break – on a giant bale of wool. It was so soft and springy, I imagined

I was sitting on a cloud. Just as I was relaxing, the heavens opened and we had to get the sheep inside. 'Wet wool is hard to cut – and it's dangerous to use the electric shears in the rain,' George explained. Sheep dogs Jack and Jill, Ted, Kim and the boss dog, Glenn, expertly rounded up the flock and put them in a shed until the rain had stopped. George revealed he had worked in worse weather. 'I've sheared sheep in minus-fourteen degrees in Canada – it's so cold, you have to do it indoors.'

He said the only thing he didn't like about sheep was mutton stew. 'I'll do anything with a sheep except eat it.' In between shearing, he teaches sheep-shearers on farms and agricultural colleges. His twenty-one-year-old son, Brendan, had just won the Junior sheep-shearing contest at Balmoral, near Belfast. Brendan's mum is a hairdresser – though her clients will not be asking for this particular cut.

At €2 a sheep in 2010, George was a lot cheaper than a barber. And he was certainly not fleecing the farmers; the price of wool jumped by 50 percent that year. Farmer Michael and his son, Michael junior, said they would never attempt to shear sheep themselves. 'It's a job for the professionals,' they laughed as they watched my efforts. I was not ready to take on the likes of George in the contest, but even he had to admit my sheep looked magnificent.

Where the Buffalo Roam – in Cork

It's not often we find big, hairy, horny beasts willing to pose for photos, but there was nearly a stampede as a herd of buffalo jostled to get into a picture for the *Sunday World*. Never mind the fact that the nearest a bovine creature usually gets to 'Cheese' is in a burger – this bunch, born and bred in Italy, had come to Ireland especially to make the finest cheese in the world – mozzarella. And clearly they thought I was just as tasty as their own milk – because they tried to ciao down on me! As they chewed my hair and the hem of my dress, licked my hands with their sandpaper tongues, head-butted and even rugby-tackled me, I wondered if I was in the middle of a bovine bunga-bunga party. I steered clear of their curled horns and massive cloven hooves, but soon realised that they were just treating me like one of the herd.

And I was chuffed when Betty the Buffalo gave me a ride. But it was a hairy experience in more ways than one, as she tried to take me on a tour of her pasture near Toon's Bridge, Gouganebarra, west Cork. 'She might bolt but she'll stop at the river,' her owner, farmer Johnny Lynch promised as I tried to persuade the huge creature to stand still for photographer Daragh McSweeney. Despite being a water buffalo, Betty was a bit wary of the River Lee! But before she could give me the rodeo of my life, her mates butted in – literally.

'They get jealous of her,' ten-year-old Kieran explained as he gave me a few tips on how to handle Betty. The plucky lad had tamed the whole herd of sixty buffalo, but Betty was his special pet. At the tender age of two, she weighed four hundred kilos – and was expected to reach nearly double that size within two years. Kieran was hoping to train Betty or one of her mates to jump like a horse. And the idea was not as far-fetched as it seemed – about the same time, German teenager Regina Mayer was making headlines around the world with her jumping cow Luna.

Meanwhile the sight of a herd of buffalo in Ireland was surreal enough. They had come a long way from the hills of Cremona in northern Italy, but the herd of sixty buffalo had settled in well in the twelve months since Johnny and his business partner, local cheesemaker Toby Simmonds, shipped them over in 2010.

Johnny's fields used to be full of the familiar black-and-white Friesan cows. And neighbours still weren't used to seeing the herd of buffalo galloping over the hills. 'Some of them thought I was mad at first. Some of them still do! And people drive down from Cork City just to see the buffalo,' he said.

He milks the buffalo on his farm with the help of wife Geraldine, young Kieran and his other son Peter (eighteen). 'We use the same milking machinery that's used for the Friesian cows. The buffalo are no different – except they produce creamier milk and more of it.' The animals thrive on Irish grass and grow faster than their Italian cousins,

Johnny added. 'They've really made themselves at home in West Cork and they love to wallow in pools when the weather is hot.'

The Mozzarella Mob, as they were dubbed, were soon showing the local cattle who was boss. 'On hot days, they stand in a circle around the pools and keep the Friesians out. They keep the water for themselves – and they guard it with their horns!' Johnny had to reinforce all the metal furniture in the milking parlour because the boisterous buffalo would wreck it otherwise. 'They are very docile but they are playful,' Johnny said as the animals tried to herd *him*.

The milk is turned into cheese at the old creamery in nearby Toon's Bridge village. It was a cheesy moment for sure when head cheese-maker, Seán Ferry used the vintage cheesemaking equipment, which had lain idle for thirty years, to make the first ever batch of Real Irish Mozzarella. Johnny's business partner, Toby Simmonds, had been using the building for his Real Olive Company, producing such delicacies as rock-hard Parmesan cheese, which he sold at farmers' markets. He used a 50 percent grant from the west Cork Development Partnership to convert the machinery to make mozzarella – though, until Johnny got the buffalo, Toby still had to import the delicate buffalo cheese directly from Italy. 'You can make a kind of mozzarella from ordinary cows' milk, but it's not as good. The real stuff has to come from buffalo milk – and it has to be very fresh,' Toby explained. He pointed out that mozzarella takes just seven hours to mature, and Italians say it should be eaten on the same day it's made. It's used in salads, panini and stuffed aubergines. It can last a week if it's stored in brine – but then it's only suitable as a pizza topping.

Italians have been guarding their precious secret for nearly a thousand years, since medieval crusaders brought a herd of water buffalo from Asia to Naples.

A Moo-ving Story

It was the latest twist in a moo-ving story, when a herd of cows had a lucky escape from the abattoir – because they were too fat to travel by cable-car! The ten cows were stranded on remote Dursey Island, off the Beara Peninsula in west Cork, in the winter of 2011, because the Cork County Council had imposed a new weight restriction on passengers. Their owner and eight other local farmers were threatening to block tourists' access to a scenic walking trail if they were not allowed bring their cows on the cable-car – the only link with the mainland. Travelling 250 metres above sea-level, the 219-metre trip takes about ten minutes.

Months later, the sheep got a reprieve too – when the ban was extended to all livestock. Cork County Engineer Noel O'Keeffe said: 'The risk to humans is too great and there are no European codes that permit carriage of animals on cable cars.' But he admitted that there might be a moo-turn – if the cable-car could be modified to carry animals as well as people.

The nine farmers, who, between them, kept about sixty cows and five hundred ewes on the island, were supported by the Irish Farming

Association's regional chairman, Richard Connell, and local TD (member of the Irish parliament) Noel Harrington, as well as tourists and hundreds of neighbours, including the cable-car operators – who went on strike in solidarity with the farmers.

Farmer Ger Murphy, who lives on the mainland but has grazed his cattle on the island every summer for as long as he can remember, was adamant: 'If there's no cows on the cable-car, there'll be no walking trail. The Council want us to let tourists walk across our land, but they won't let us keep our livelihood. They want Dursey for tourists and only tourists, but we're not in the tourism business – we're farmers.'

Mr Murphy was frustrated when I interviewed him for the *Sunday World*. 'I have cows near calving. The grass is getting thin over there on the island. In the winter, it's just bare rock. There's nothing for them to eat. They'll starve to death.' He said he couldn't keep bringing them hay as he had just come out of hospital. Even with the help of his son and some neighbours, it would mean stuffing the cable car with hay and making several trips a day throughout the winter, as the little cabin was barely big enough to carry one cow or six people.

Cork County Council's health and safety officers had reduced the weight limit following an engineers' report, and finally banned all animals in February 2012. And Mr Murphy predicted the outright ban two months before it came into force. He told me: 'They're messing us around. First they told us we could transport cattle up to 544 kg, then it was 450, now it's 400 kg. Next they'll go the whole hog and ban livestock altogether. The weight restriction is bad enough. An adult cow normally weighs 450-500 kilogrammes – if a big animal was any lighter it would be suffering from malnutrition and you wouldn't get anything for it at the mart. And a man would have to travel with the animal so that would add to the weight. There's no other way to get them across from the island. Dursey Sound is one of the most treacherous stretches of water in the world. You'd have to tie the cow to a boat with ropes, and you'd run the risk of losing an animal. And they'd get seasick and it would be very frightening to them. It would be dangerous managing a big animal in rough seas. We've been moving cows to and from the island by cable-car for forty-two years and we've never had an accident.'

The cows were not the only ones to be stranded; three of the temporary cable-car operators went on strike to support the nine farmers and eleven human inhabitants. Six of the islanders, aged from early-forties to mid-sixties, were cut off from the land for a weekend.

Full-time cable-car operator Paddy Sheehan sympathised with the farmers – though he did not join in the strike because he was off duty that weekend, for the first time in years. 'I usually work seven days a week and I wouldn't like to see people stranded,' he said. 'But it's crazy to ban cows from the cable car. We've been bringing them over for forty-two years and we never had one accident. The cows are quiet enough because they can't do anything when they're being lifted through the air. Anyway, it's not every day you'd be bringing fully grown cows over. It's only when you have an old cow and she's finished breeding, you have to get rid of her so you bring her across to the mart. But it's mostly young cattle and sheep that would be coming across. There's no other way to move them; the sea is too wild.'

Mr Sheehan said a group of twenty Polish tourists had been disappointed to find out that there were no cows on the cable car. 'They came here especially to go on the cable-car. I think they enjoyed the ride in the cable-car as much as the island. The only dampener for them was that there were no cows going over for them to see. Tourists love it. They take pictures of the cows in the cable-car. You'd never see anything like it anywhere else in the world.'

In the nearby town of Castletownbere, locals were fuming at the proposed ban. In Murphy's restaurant, owner John Murphy, who also happened to be the chairman of Beara Tourism, said he was one hundred percent behind the farmers. 'This health and safety thing has gone crazy!' He said farmers had been using that cable car to transport cows since it was launched by the late, legendary Taoiseach [Irish Prime Minister] Jack Lynch. 'Jack Lynch and his wife Maureen were the first to travel in it.' Waitress Kerrie O'Neill said: 'It's good that it's there for the cows – but I wouldn't go in it myself in this weather! It would be awful if it wasn't there.'

Noel Harrington said: 'It's been there since 1969 and there's never been an accident. It has a blemish-free record – what other mode of transport can claim that? It's unique in the world. There isn't a cable car anywhere that is used for animals.' He said locals had been milking its value as a tourism attraction. 'And in a time of recession, we want to keep the tourists coming.' But Councillor Jerry Sullivan pointed out: 'If the engineers say it's a health and safety issue, they must know what they're talking about.' Though he added that he had sympathy for the farmers.

Rosarii O'Neill, who grew up on the island, where she still owns a cottage, as well as a B&B on the mainland, could see both sides of the argument. 'It will make life hard for the farmers, but you have to move with the times.'

It made life difficult for the *Sunday World* too. We wanted a picture of a cow on the cable car – which would explain why I was wearing a milkmaid costume at dawn as I waited with photographer Billy macGill for the cable car operator to arrive.

It was a dark, stormy morning in the middle of winter 2011, and we had each driven more than two hours through terrible weather in the dark to reach to remote tip of the peninsula. But it was worth it to get the perfect picture. At just fifty-four kilogrammes (last time I checked), I was sure I well within the freshly imposed weight limit of 400 kg – and I had an inflatable cow handy, just in case my breakfast put me over the latest limit.

The first trip was scheduled for 9 AM, but there was no one manning the car. A man drove up in a green van just after nine, looked at us sheltering in the doorway of a public toilet beside the cable-car, then drove off. There was no phone number to call – and anyway there was no mobile-phone coverage or public phone. We later found out that that was the weekend the cable-car men went on strike.

Still, I had a moo-ving experience just sitting in the cable-car. Rocking in the Force Ten winds, the tiny cabin felt like a carnival ride. The wind sang on the wires, and I felt that at any moment the cable-car could break free and go flying across the sea. A bottle of holy water was tethered to the bolt inside the sliding door. I blessed myself and got the hell out!

Sow Scary!

As a typical townie, I regard the countryside as the perfect place to chill out. So when I heard about a farm where pigs roam free and cows listen to rock 'n' roll, I thought I was in for a relaxing day. But I was ready for the funny farm after I got into a tug of war – with an angry pig! There's nothing like a hundred-kilogramme monster to put manners on a city slicker, and I'd be telling porkies if I didn't say I was afraid of the giant Landrace sow who was nearly twice my weight and could have gobbled me up in seconds. Frothing at the mouth and glaring at me with her mean piggy eyes, she bared her saw-like teeth and growled at me like a dangerous dog! With her enormous, upturned snout and a ridge of stubble on her humped back, this was no Babe.

It was like a scene from the horror movie *Hannibal Rising*. I half expected Anthony Hopkins to turn up in his gimp mask, as the big pig grabbed a bucket I was holding. I've done more rash things than feed a pig, but this creature was in no mood to wait for her dinner. With the bucket clenched in her massive jaws, she shook it to loosen my grip. Our undignified tussle ended when she pushed her snout against my hand and tossed the bucket into the air. For one awful moment, I wondered if Spud the Sow was about to give up her veggie lifestyle and make a ham sandwich out of me. And I wondered why I had ever given up meat in sympathy for creatures like this.

Luckily, Spud was behind bars in her pen. But, moments later, she had escaped and was wandering around the farmyard – just inches away from *Sunday World* photographer Mick Flanagan and myself. Farmer Joe Brady saved our bacon as he calmly herded Spud back into her enclosure, where her five little piglets were dozing. 'Higgledy-piggledy,' he coaxed. That seemed to be the magic word. But, as soon as he had filled her trough, Spud butted him out of the way with her snout and tucked into her meal of barley, peas and soya.

'She's a divil – I keep the children away from her,' Joe said. Seven-year-old Ellen and ten-year-old Finn had named her Spud because she was partial to potatoes, but, as Joe explained, Spud was nothing like Peppa Pig. 'When the pigs get to that size, the hunger and aggression take over and they're unpredictable.'

She may have been territorial, but she barely noticed when Joe grabbed one of her piglets. The little fellow squealed in terror and tried to wriggle free. It was hard to believe this four-month-old baby would grow into a monster like his mammy in just eight months. As I held the little piggy, I felt his heart beating frantically. But he calmed down and soon he was making happy grunting noises. I just hoped he wasn't mistaking me for his mammy.

As soon as they're weaned, piglets roam free on Joe's farm near Mullingar, along with a herd of saddleback pigs and some Angus cattle. All fed on organic food, they are raised in the traditional way – the best way, Joe says.

And the proof is in the (blood) pudding. Foodies from all over the country flock to Joe's farm shop on Saturdays, to pick up freshly pre-pared pork, bacon, ham and beef. With prices ranging from €6.50 for a leg shank of pork to €22 for striploin beef, it's not cheap, but Joe points out: 'It costs €200 to fatten a pig for eight months. I only feed them with the best organic food and they eat no meat products at all.' He also supplies local restaurants with the beef, which is hung for four weeks. The animals are slaughtered locally and sent back to the farm in the form of sausages, rashers, rib steaks and burgers. And I have to say, even as a veggie, I much prefer them that way.

'It's not a pet farm – it's a working farm,' Joe reminded me as he introduced me to some scary saddleback sows. They fought viciously to stick their snouts into the trough, and I nearly felt sorry for one poor pig who was getting nipped by all the others – until Joe pointed to her bum. 'Look at the fat on that!'

They had seemed docile at first as Joe stepped over the electric fence into their field. 'This one has been to visit her boyfriend, so she should be pregnant,' he said as he ran a hand along her back. But she showed she was up for some action as she raised her curly tail. Joe said that was a sign that she was sexually aroused! 'It's like when a woman puts on a sexy negligee.'

While she was keen to hog a bit of male attention of any kind, Miss Piggy was a bit boar-ish when I tried to make friends. She grunted and tried to nip my wellies. 'Who's the muppet now?' she seemed to be saying as I tried to escape over the electric fence without getting barbecued. She may not have been adept at giving karate chops like the puppet, but I sincerely hoped she'd end up as pork chops! Her pregnant mate was friendlier and just sniffed my leg.

I was glad their boyfriend, a big boar named after the macho rapper

Will.I.Am, was not around. But clearly he had been busy. Another saddleback sow had recently given birth to thirteen piglets. At five weeks old, they already weighed five kilos each and were as big as Rottweilers. 'When they're born, they're the size of a small Jack Russell,' Joe revealed. One little piglet squealed angrily as he lifted it up to show me its jagged teeth and leathery black snout. 'Touch his snout,' Joe urged me. 'Doesn't it feel lovely? Isn't that the finest leather?'

Meanwhile, Joe's herd of Angus cattle were in the mood for some fun as they played hide-and-seek with us. It turned out they were also fond of the odd tune! 'If I play music in the tractor, the cows follow me,' Joe revealed. 'They love hard rock and I've discovered that they like the Manic Street Preachers. They know once the music is playing, they're going to get fed.'

Joe sometimes looks like a hip, Irish version of the Pied Piper as he drives his vintage 1960s' tractor across the fields with the music blaring out of it and a procession of cows marching behind. The tractor, which he has restored to its full glory, was a present from his next-door neighbour, author J. P. Donleavy – who often pops in for some bacon. J. P.'s notorious fictional character Sebastian Dangerfield would have a lot in common with Joe's randy bull and boar.

CHAPTER THREE: Ireland's Soul – Spirituality and the Supernatural

Ireland was once known as the Island of Saints and Scholars. And it still is, for those who believe. But, nowadays, religious practice takes many forms.

The Holy Stump of Rathkeale

To most people it looked like any old tree-stump. But to the devotees who prayed at its gnarled roots and blessed themselves after they had touched the fresh wounds in its trunk, it was the Holy Grail. And to two rival bookies it was the subject of an unholy bidding war.

The residents of the village of Rathkeale, County Limerick, mounted a twenty-four-hour vigil at the stump in the grounds of Holy Mary's church – after the woodcutter who had chopped down the tree saw the Virgin Mary in it. Locals were afraid the parish priest would have it removed – despite his protestations to the contrary.

Irish bookie Paddy Power bid €6,200 for the stump– beating a Canadian casino's $5,000 (€3,200) offer – but it wasn't enough to tempt the parish priest to sell the stump. Power said he wanted to stop the stump moving to Sin City! But online casino GoldenPalace.com hoped to add it to its collection of odd religious items – along with a slice of toast apparently showing the Virgin Mary's face and Pope Benedict's old VW Golf. Power said: 'We don't want to see our holy tree stump paraded around the world in some kind of carnival of the bizarre, alongside a mouldy slice of toast. If we are successful with our bid, we will endeavour to preserve the tree stump and make it accessible to all those who choose to visit it. You can bet on it!'

The parish priest, Canon Joe Dempsey, held firm: 'I'm not having it removed. I can't see what all the fuss is about,' he said – adding that he could not see the vision of the Virgin Mary in the stump. 'As far as I can see, it's just an auld tree stump. But if people want to pray around it, sure why not? They can pray at all the other auld tree stumps in the grounds if they want.'

Canon Dempsey said he had been 'a bit surprised', on returning from his holidays, to find that the churchyard had been turned into a pilgrimage site. For a few crazy weeks in 2009, thousands of believers from all over Ireland and the UK flocked to the rural village to see what appeared to be an image of the Mother of God in the grain of the sawn-off stump. The vague shape, which apparently showed her holding Baby Jesus on her lap, was first spotted by woodcutter Eddie Tierney and his colleague Anthony Reddan, while they were felling trees in the church grounds. Spookily, Mr Tierney's chainsaw suddenly stopped after he had cut the stump of the seventy-year-old willow, exposing the image. 'The tree wouldn't let him cut it any more. It gave him a message and that was that,' a local lady told me when I visited the place to write an article for the *Sunday World*. The shy woodcutter would not talk to me, but neighbours said he spent hours at the site, simply praying, for several weeks after his 'miraculous' discovery in 2009. His supervisor, Community Council boss Noel White, wanted to put a glass casing over the tree-stump to protect it from pilgrims who were taking pieces of bark as relics. Within a week of the 'apparition', more than two thousand had people visited the site to kiss the stump, rub it and pray. They even held an all-night vigil one night, saying decades of the Rosary over and over until dawn.

The churchyard was packed when I arrived with photographer Ciaran McGowan. A crowd four-deep surrounded the stump, kneeling and praying, some silently, others aloud. More queued up – people of all ages, from all parts of Ireland and the UK, mostly members of the travelling community.

The pilgrims said they had been upset when the curate, Fr William Russell, told a large crowd to go away. 'He put them away from the stump because he said there was no evidence that the Virgin Mary was there. The priest is all confused about it. He can't see what we see. He thinks it's just a tree,' pensioner Paddy Shannon said. It was a Holy Headache for Fr Russell, who had had the misfortune to be left in charge while the Canon was on holidays. Fr Russell just 'didn't get it', some of the local people said after he rubbished their belief on local radio, pointing out 'You can't worship a tree'.

But many of his parishioners insisted the image in the trunk was clear. Mr Shannon said even his grandchildren had spotted it straight away. 'The only one who can't see it is the priest as far as I know,' he said. 'It's beautiful. You get a lovely feeling when you're near it. There's something special there all right,' he added.

Cancer patient Gerry Heffernan (sixty-one) from London was among the many who believed that the stump had miraculous powers. Mr Heffernan, who was visiting family in the area, stood in front of the stump, head bowed, praying for a cure. 'You get a happy kind of feeling when you touch it,' he said, adding that he hoped to bring his wife and kids from England over to see it. A lady in a wheelchair also arrived with her carer, who brought her close so she could kiss the stump. In her eagerness, she nearly fell out of the wheelchair.

Throughout the week, people with various illnesses paid a visit, some with their nurses. Some even hailed it as a miracle for business in the town, which until then was best known for its large Traveller population – 30 percent of the householders described themselves as Travellers in the national census. The lavish mansions on its outskirts lie empty most of the year, their owners off travelling around Ireland or the UK. It is a world apart from the thatched cottage toy town appearance of Adare, just two miles down the road. Thanks to my *Sunday World* colleague Eamon Dillon, Rathkeale has also gained international notoriety as the venue for bare-knuckle fist-fights among Travellers, who converge on the town several times a year for organised bouts.

But for a few weeks in 2009, it was more like My Big Fat Gipsy Shrine, as worshippers poured into the little village, parking caravans on every backroad. For the likes of local Eurospar shopkeeper Derek Downes, who was clearly under pressure as he tried to serve the huge crowds, the stump was a mixed blessing. But he didn't want to talk about it. 'I prefer not to get involved in any of this. I run my own show down here and I keep to myself.'

The McCarthy family had come from Tralee especially to see the stump. Granny Kathleen McCarthy pointed out that she could be regarded as an expert, as she was a regular pilgrim to other sites where Our Lady had appeared. 'I go to Knock and Lourdes a few times a year, I've been to the Holy Land, I was in Millstreet three years ago when Our Lady appeared in a well, and I was in Ballinspittle when the statues were moving. It's the same thing again – it's Our Lady appearing on earth,' Mrs McCarthy said. Her daughter Geraldine McCarthy added:

'I'm not as religious as my mother, but I can see it too.'

Geraldine's children Britney (eight), Candice (five) and William (one) were all fascinated by the 'miracle'. Britney wanted her experience recorded in the *Sunday World*: 'I can really see it! It's Holy Mary.' Declan Hogan brought his two-year-old daughter Jasmine to touch the tree. The child pressed her tiny hand against it, giggling.

Locals Sinead Picard (twenty-eight) and her friend Bridget Daly (twenty-five) were sceptical at first – but got a shock when they saw it. 'I can see it better in photos. You can make out the figure of a woman holding a baby,' Sinead said. Both young women described themselves as Catholic but not particularly devout – until then. 'I'd go to Mass but just once a week. I'd believe in God,' Sinead said.

Twelve-year-old Michelle Lowe and her friend Aisling Donovan (fourteen) saw a bit more than most people. 'We saw a girl kneeling down beside her,' said Michelle. 'And she's holding Baby Jesus.'

Retired milkman Frank Markham, who pointed out that he had never missed Mass in seventy years, said the vision had strengthened his faith because it was 'bringing people of all ages back to the Church'.

Two local woman said they had got 'a very peaceful feeling' when they touched the stump. The image is 'very clear – you can see her veil and the shape of her head,' they added but declined to be named because they are public representatives.

James Hogan said the image brought him closer to God too. Sitting in his white Merc as he guarded the site, with Tiger Woods tattooed on his arm, he looked more like a Hell's Angel than a worshipper at a shrine to Our Lady. And he admitted: 'I wouldn't go to Mass every Sunday – but I'll go to every Mass on this weekend to see what the priest says about the tree stump!'

Together with his brother Declan and some other local men, James was mounting a twenty-four-seven vigil over the shrine. They took it in turns to park in front of the church every day. 'We're doing this in case the priest has it taken away. He can give us all the reassurances he wants – we don't trust the clergy,' James said.

But he wasn't a Holy Joe, as I realised when he showed me a mobile phone picture of the stump clearly bearing an image of Michael Jackson! 'If he was here, he'd get up off that stump and start dancing! Then we'd have a show!' he guffawed, adding: 'Our Lady won't mind me having a laugh. I'll say a few Hail Marys.' He added: 'Rathkeale is known for lots of things like the bare-knuckle fights. But now it'll be known for something else. Even if the priest doesn't believe it, he shouldn't be stopping the people from praying.'

Canon Dempsey said that the outbreak of religious fervour had not boosted the numbers attending Mass. 'Sure there's always a big crowd at Mass here every Sunday anyway. It's no different.' But he said he would not turn the people away from the stump, which was by then festooned with Rosary beads, flowers and prayer cards. 'They're doing no harm. If they want to say a few prayers I won't stop them.' He added: 'It seems to be dying out a bit. I only saw three people there last night – this time last week there were hundreds.'

The religious fervour seemed to dissipate as quickly as it had begun. But the occasional pilgrim can be found praying at the stump.

Holy Joe

With his strong Dublin accident and penchant for wearing anoraks, Holy Joe Coleman was nothing like the conventional image of a mystic – in fact, his down-to-earth demeanour served only to convince his devotees that he was to be trusted. And an estimated fifteen thousand people turned up to 'see the Virgin Mary' with Joe at Knock Shrine, County Mayo, on Halloween 2009.

Coleman first came to my attention when the *Sunday World* received a press release announcing that the Virgin Mary was to appear at Knock Shrine on Halloween. This was followed by a few reports from people who claimed she had actually popped up in front of them, whilst they were praying with Joe. Soon the word spread – largely through an intensive PR campaign involving press releases, a website, tapes, videos and pamphlets. Joe was also holding regular 'seeing' sessions at other shrines, including a rock face in the wilds of Donegal.

Meanwhile, Coleman's friends were spreading the rumour that a 'boy from the Travelling community' had been cured of blindness – a claim which was later rubbished by the Travellers' organisation, Pavee Point, who said, after extensive research, that they could find no such boy.

It was just one of many controversies which erupted over a six-month period. But even Doubting Thomases had to admit that Holy Joe Coleman and his sidekick, chef Keith Henderson, certainly put on a holy show wherever they went. Whether they were drawing crowds to Knock basilica, or busloads of pilgrims to remote Kerrytown Shrine near Loughanure, County Donegal, Joe and Keith had the kind of pulling power about which politicians and rock stars could only dream.

Joe said he had been having 'visions' of Our Lady since 1986, but it was only in 2009 that he came to public attention, when he claimed to have seen the Virgin three times in as many months – once in Donegal and twice in the old chapel at Knock, where he insisted that he had seen her statue moving. 'The statue comes alive, she opens her arms, a lovely pink cloak comes around her, there are stars above her head, she turns into Jesus, then into Padre Pio, and then back to herself. While the vision is happening, I can see nothing else in the chapel,' he told the *Mayo News*.

On Halloween 2009, it was a real horror story for the health and safety authorities at Knock Shrine when Joe packed the basilica with his followers. But instead of the fire-and-brimstone 'messages' from the Mother of God, which had been his hallmark in the weeks up to then, what they got this time was Hell itself. It was like an Apocalyptic scene as twelve thousand screaming pilgrims tried to run out of the full-to-capacity church all at once, stepping on terrified children, pushing wheelchairs out of the way and knocking over tables.

Meanwhile Joe sat motionless in the front pew, surrounded by friends, including Keith Henderson, whose face was frozen in a manic smile.

Terrified mum Lizzie Connors from New Ross, County Wexford, picked up a lady whose wheelchair had been turned over. Mrs. Connors later told me she had feared for the safety of small children after the crowd nearly trampled her five young daughters. 'There were ladies in wheelchairs being shoved across the floor by the crowd. The children wanted to go out and see what the fuss was about but I kept them with me. I come to Knock four times a year and I do believe in Our Lady – but I think she's always here. We don't need someone to bring her here to us. I don't think Our Lady would want little children to be hurt or people in wheelchairs to be knocked over.' But little Mag piped up: 'I saw Our Lady on the Altar!'

Geraldine Bourke from Charlestown, County Mayo, said she was afraid her daughters Aoife (eleven) and Saoirse (eight) and niece Louise (thirteen) would get hurt or lost in the crush. 'It was terrifying. You'd nearly get killed in the crowd. All I could hear was shouting.' Clinging to her aunt, Louise told me she had been 'frightened'.

During the commotion, the self-styled mystic slipped out, surrounded by friends – but was mobbed on the way to his car. Meanwhile, his friends passed on his mobile number to believers. One girl told me: 'I'm calling him to get healed.' Her face was pale and gaunt, her eyes listless; it was clear that Joe was her last hope.

Earlier, the crowd had crammed into the basilica to pray along with Joe for ninety minutes. Outside, stewards employed by the shrine management kept the crowds out, since the basilica was packed to capacity. They blessed themselves, muttered decades of the Rosary as they strafed their beads, and some even knelt on the ground. It was surreal to see such unity in diversity. Well-heeled elderly couples rubbed shoulders with Travellers. The young female Travellers cut a dash as they joined in the Rosary sessions, showed lots of cleavage in black leather bra-tops, and bum-cheek in their matching leather mini-skirts. These ensembles were teamed with suspenders, ripped stockings and over-the-knee boots. Joe later went on radio to say that Our Lady expected young ladies to dress modestly.

He refused to let his followers earwig on his chat with the Mother of God. But, while one might have expected him to have a guardian angel, he surrounded himself with human minders. Refusing my offer, on behalf of the *Sunday World*, to sit beside him as he had his supernatural experience, Coleman told me before the event: 'I'm going to have protection around me. I don't think it would be possible to be with me while the apparition is happening because, when I'm talking to the Blessed Mother, I need some privacy.' But with twelve thousand watching him closely in the packed basilica, it was anything but private. There was near-hysteria when his face appeared to go neon-red – but it turned out it was the light from a camera phone.

Then his friend, Galway-born Brenda Walsh, led the crowd in decades of the Rosary. In her pink funfur jacket, Brenda drew the crowd's attention straight away as she started the event by shouting at the murmuring crowd to 'Stop talking in Our Lady's House! Shss! Everybody say shsss!' Some obediently joined her in a loud 'shss' that echoed around the vast basilica. Others sniggered or continued talking.

Brenda later told me: 'I asked Joe if he could see Our Lady and he said yes. He said she was here. He was in ecstasy.' She said she did not see an apparition but 'heard the rumble, then the rumble seemed to be coming from my stomach – and now it's in my soul. I felt Our Lady calling me to get up and calm the crowd. There was a loud murmur and it needed to be silenced for us to hear Our Lady.'

Outside, Mary Fox from Ballina said she had seen 'the sun dancing and turning different colours. I saw Our Lord's face in it, then it turned into Our Lady.' She added that she had seen the Blessed Virgin at Knock earlier that month – the Mother of God had appeared at 3 PM, exactly as Joe Coleman had predicted, she said. 'The last time I collapsed when I saw her. I came here the last time because I had just lost a baby and I wanted to pray to Our Lady for my lost baby. My partner came with me and he's with me today again – but he doesn't believe.'

Teresa Curley from Ballaghadereen, County Roscommon, who was there with her twelve-year-old son Kalvin, said she had found the atmosphere different to the previous time. 'There was a great feeling of peace at three o'clock the last time but this time there was nothing but panic.'

And spirits ran high when Joe unleashed an unholy fury on Knock Shrine manager Pat Lavelle, after Mr Lavelle rubbished Joe's claims. Coleman grabbed Mr Lavelle by the coat and shook him – an attack he later admitted on radio. Local photographer Mick McCormack snapped Coleman's loyal friend and promoter, top PR lady Mary McGovern-Egan, laughing as she watched the bizarre altercation, but for Mr. Lavelle it was further proof that 'Holy Joe' was not so pious.

Meanwhile, Joe's followers were hell-bent on having 'visions' – or getting 'healed' by Joe.

Mum-of-two Breege Queenan, from Boyle, County Roscommon, was convinced she and others had had a brush with the supernatural on an earlier occasion as she stood with Coleman and a crowd of eight thousand in front of Knock's old church. She had been staring at the gable wall where the Virgin is believed to have appeared in 1879, along with St Joseph and St John, waiting for a sign. Just eleven people were there to see the first Knock apparition – a far cry from the masses who joined Coleman on his spiritual journey.

'People saw different things,' Mrs. Queenan said of her own experience. 'One man's hands turned orange and everyone was trying to touch him – he was getting very frustrated. Some said they saw the Host in the sky. Others like myself saw the sun changing colour and dancing in the sky.' Some of the crowd said the sun 'danced and shimmered' for ten minutes before vanishing into the clouds.

Most of the crowd ignored parish priest Monsignor Joseph Quinn's plea over the tannoy to come into the nearby basilica, where Mass was taking place as part of the annual pilgrimage organised by the Dominican fathers. 'Everyone was on a high,' Mrs. Queenan said. 'There was an amazing atmosphere. You couldn't move in the crowd but everyone was very gentle.' She added that she 'wasn't very excited' by that because she had seen it before in Medjugorje. 'But my video of it happening in Medjugorje was ruined – the sun glared on the camera lens. So this time I turned the camera on the glass wall in front of the gable, to film the sun's reflection. While I was looking at it through the lens, it looked like the sun was turning blue, red and green – and dancing in the sky. I showed the camera to the girl who was with me and she thought it was amazing. But it was nothing to what I saw when I played the video at home.

'It was Our Lady, I am sure of it. The camera does not lie. You can see that it is the figure of a woman in the clouds. At first when I looked at the video I saw a woman's face, then when I looked at it a bit longer I could see her sitting in the sky, just above the sun and to the right of it.'

She showed it to her two daughters, Annamarie (twenty) and Katy-Jane (seventeen), who 'saw it straight away. And my father, who's ninety-two, saw it very clearly. I brought the video into the old folks' home where I work and everyone there saw exactly the same image. These are people who wouldn't all have the best eyesight but still they saw it.

'The only one who couldn't see it was my husband – but he's sceptical about that sort of thing.'

At the same time, one Mr O'Shea from Sligo captured an image of a veiled lady from the waist up, standing and pointing to the crowd below. He captured the image on digital camera as he stood in the crowd outside the shrine with his wife, Anne and fourteen-year-old son, Seamus. Mr O'Shea said he was 'surprised' to see the image and had been dubious until then. 'It was curiosity that brought us there. I'm not a deeply religious person. My wife and I haven't been practising our religion. We'd been going to Mass occasionally but not regularly. To be honest, I would never have believed it if I hadn't seen it with my own eyes. I wouldn't believe it if someone told me about it. I didn't show the picture to anyone except my immediate family – and the *Sunday World*. We were afraid people would laugh at us. I'm not a Holy Joe, and I'm a bit embarrassed that I did see it – but I have it on camera.' He added that his wife did not see Our Lady at the time, and could only see her in the photo later. 'She believes I saw what I saw and the photo is proof. She was standing beside me in the crowd when I saw it'. Their son Seamus had seen 'exactly the same image at the same time.' Mr O'Shea described the experience as 'deeply spiritual. I can't explain it but I did feel a deep happiness and there was a warm, golden glow everywhere. I think everyone in the crowd felt that.'

However, like all charismatic people, Joe also attracted the attention of fervent non-believers. Mr Coleman admitted on Joe Duffy's *Liveline* radio programme that he was accepting 'donations' from anyone who came to him for healing. And he was forced to admit that he had charged a girl €40 – after she rang up to tackle him over his claims that he 'never took a penny'. He also admitted that his plane fares and accommodation were paid by supporters. Like royalty, Holy Joe never had to put his hand in his pocket as he went about his 'spiritual' business.

Joe's neighbours in the gritty west Dublin suburb of Ballyfermot, and pilgrims who had met him and Keith on a trip to Medjugorje, were not so charitable when they spoke to me about the pair. And when I went with photographer Val Sheehan to Joe's modest council house to confront him about the allegations that were later made on RTÉ's Joe Duffy show, he used some most un-holy language as he yelled down the stairs at us, and refused to come out to talk. A young man who confirmed he was Joe's son said: 'My father is doing good work, healing people'.

Coleman himself claimed to be 'disabled' following an accident while he was working as a roofer, and was living on Social Welfare Disability Benefit – as well as his cash 'donations'. But when I asked him if he had called on the Blessed Virgin to heal him, his response was less than holy.

Meanwhile Galway ophthalmologist Eamonn O'Donoghue, a consultant ophthalmologist surgeon in University Hospital Galway, blamed the events at Knock when five patients presented at his surgery, suffering from sun-damaged retinae; all had been at the Holy Joe show. Mr O'Donoghue warned that it could lead to blindness and told newspapers it was 'profoundly irresponsible' for anyone to encourage people to stare at the sun.

And holy war broke out at a remote shrine in County Donegal, in late 2009, when Joe's followers began to turn up in their droves – because Joe claimed he had seen the Mother of God there too.

Kerrytown Shrine, in the marshy Rosses area, had been attracting the odd pilgrim since 1939, when two girls claimed they had seen the Blessed Virgin appearing on a rock face. It was almost a secret – and locals preferred to keep it that way. The site, including a whitewashed cottage, holy well and rock face, was being cared for by a trust, having been bought in 1999 by a woman from County Derry, while the land itself was owned by a Donegal couple. Local people – including the landowners – were shocked when I revealed it was full of collection boxes and signs asking for donations. People who had been going there for years to say the Mysteries of the Rosary were now saying the real mystery was: who was collecting the money? By August 2010, the brick box had disappeared but the smaller collection boxes remained.

When I first visited the spot, having read about it on Joe's website, I found it hard to believe anyone would want to set up shop in such a desolate spot. The nearest villages are Loughanure and Crolly – home of trad band Clannad, whose haunting music comes to mind as you drive across the labyrinth of narrow tracks across the open bogland to the shrine. These ancient roads, which are not even on the maps and can be reached only by following hand-painted signs, would put the fear of God into even Jeremy Clarkson. With rain and mist blurring the boundaries between land and lake, the place is more like Atlantis than the mainland. There are some houses dotted around the boreens, but no one answers the door, there are no animals to be seen and few cars.

So, on a rainy winter's day in 2009, I expected to be alone. But within fifteen minutes of my arrival, at least six more cars pulled up, mostly people from other parts of Donegal and Northern Ireland.

They told me they were there to pray, having first heard about the place two weeks previously, when the famous Mr Coleman claimed he was among fifteen people who saw 'crosses flashing in the sky' for about an hour.

There was even a brand new website devoted to the remote shrine, kerrytown-apparitions.com, in which he claimed to have seen not only the Virgin but also Jesus and Padre Pio.

But local people said that whoever had planted the collection boxes in the cottage beside the rock face was seeing euro signs. The first thing I saw on arrival was a vision of sorts – a surreal-looking brick wall, barely a metre in length, with a slot like a postbox and a sign, 'Donations'. Inside the little cottage, there were more collection boxes – I counted at least eight in the two rooms, ranging from a hole in the wall to what looked like a ballot box which had the word 'Petitions' pasted over it. There were also three empty trays labelled 'Rosaries', 'Scapulars' and 'Miraculous Medals' with a note on each: 'Please take one. A gift for you, but should you wish to make a donation, please put it in the donations box in the wall of the main room.' A noticeboard was covered with newspaper cuttings referring to Joe Coleman's 'visions', along with a picture of a crowd at the shrine marked 11 October 2009 (one of the days he had claimed to have seen visions in Knock). Displayed prominently was a printed poster advertising Sunday, 6 December, at 3 PM, as the 'next day of prayer at Kerrytown Rock in the house of the Immaculate Conception.' Given that Jesus was supposed to have been born in Palestine, this would have been a miracle, I thought. But locals were sure the date referred to yet another apparition – of Joe Coleman. And it was clear that Mr Coleman or his followers had done a bit of interior decorating in preparation for his coming. Hanging on the wall were pictures of the Virgin captioned 'Medjugorje' and the Child of Prague and a giant picture of Pope John Paul II with a St Brigid's Cross above it.

Most eye-catching was a huge string of Rosary beads made of what looked like Rune stones – but, instead of Celtic Pagan symbols, each bead bore a picture of the Child of Prague, Our Lady and other figures.

There was also a visitors' book (signatures began on 27 October 2009) and a note stating that a 'committee' looked after the shrine. But no members' names were listed. However Joe's website gave a brief history of the shrine – along with a lot of information about Joe Coleman. His mobile number was given as the contact number for people looking for information about the shrine. The website also bore the same image of the Virgin as a picture hanging inside the Kerrytown cottage, captioned 'Medjugorje'. Followers of Joe Coleman would have been familiar with his pilgrimages to the Eastern European town – where he also claimed to have seen spirits. Kerrytown shrine looked like another Medjugorje or Knock in the making.

It was so bizarre, I knew no one would believe me if I described the place. And I was afraid someone would remove the objects once they realised a reporter was on the prowl; some locals, who had suddenly turned up, seemed wary of me. Before their arrival, I had snapped a few discreet pictures of the cottage and its contents for my own record. The moment I got back to my hotel, I called local photographer Matt Britton, who immediately dashed down to the site. Matt had been present when Joe had one of his 'visions' at the shrine, and was intrigued by the mysterious 'visionary' – as were most of the locals.

The people of the Rosses area of Donegal didn't know what to make of Joe Coleman himself. They were also baffled by the fact that one small room in the cottage was locked. They were even more curious about an extension that was being built on the side of the old cottage –and the foundations for another building in front of it.

A local man said he and his neighbours would prefer the site to remain 'a peaceful place where people come to pray and meditate. 'But a lot of very different people have been coming here for the past two years since Joe Coleman claimed he saw the visions. They are all caught up with these apparitions. They want to see visions. They are all mad if you ask me. You can't make sense of them.' He added that in the weeks since autumn 2009, when Joe's P.R. machine had begun generating a mass of publicity regarding his Knock 'visions', the little shrine had become especially busy. 'There are coachloads of people coming from Dublin and across the border. And that boy Joe Coleman has been here a good bit too. Last time he was there was about two weeks before he appeared in Knock. 'People around here do not want huge crowds like that arriving at our little shrine.' A local girl said: 'We didn't realise anything was happening down at the shrine because we don't go there very often. The last time I was there I was a child on a trip with the Legion of Mary. But we'll be keeping an eye on it from now on'.

Locals were also furious to find a copyright symbol beside the name of Kerrytown on the website kerrytown-apparitions.com. 'What right have they to lay claim to the name of our holy shrine?' a Loughanure man fumed.

After I wrote a series of articles about Holy Joe in the *Sunday World*, I got some hate mail from his supporters, but lots of people thanked me. Within months his 'healing clinic' in the Ballyfermot office of Sinn Féin had been closed down. Holy Joe soon disappeared off the radar, resurfacing in April 2010, with a few appearances – or apparitions if you believe him – at Mount Melleray, County Waterford.

Then in April 2010, he issued a press release claiming that the ash cloud which had stopped air traffic across Europe would 'intensify and get darker' as a sign of the imminent Second Coming of Christ. 'Our Lady told me that God is extremely angry with the evil action of priests, bishops and cardinals in the Catholic Church and that, unless we convert back to our Faith in Ireland, we will not be able to redeem ourselves in the eyes of God at this very important time.' A note at the end of the press release described Joe as 'a simple, uneducated man' and listed his contact details including his website, knockapparitions.com.

He appeared in Knock again in May 2010, having predicted that he would see Our Lady yet again, along with 'crosses in the sky' and 'new moons that have never been seen before with the naked eye'. But on this occasion, he was joined by just twelve followers – or 'apostles', as locals joked.

His next appearance – or apparition – at Knock was in May 2011. This time, church officials told him he would have to wait his turn with the other pilgrims to get into the basilica. He stood outside, eyes bleary as he gazed up at the sun, and soon a crowd of about three hundred joined him – but this time most wore sunglasses. After about two hours, he suddenly crouched, clutched his side and limped away, saying he felt unwell and had just received a 'message' from Our Lady. He didn't hang about to say what that message was, but later issued a statement claiming the end was nigh.

His sidekick, Keith Henderson, was later to die in a freak accident when lightning struck his car as he was driving to Roscommon town, where he lived and worked as a chef.

Penance on Lough Derg

Holidays from Hell bring out the bad girl in me, but I had to behave myself on a trip that was supposed to bring me closer to Heaven. I donned sackcloth and ashes – or, rather, waterproof clothes that kept me wet – to do penance for my sins on the rainswept island of Lough Derg. And it was no Paradise. This was Devil's Island – for holy people. My three days of martyrdom – starvation, sleep-deprivation and kneeling on cold, wet stones – took place in 2008, just a week after I had romped naked in the rain with two thousand others for artist Spencer Tunick. But exposing just my feet was tougher! I may have saved my soul but I got blisters and bruises on my soles. Not even my strict convent-school childhood had prepared me for this. It was like the episode of *Father Ted* in which Sister Assumpta prepares the lads for Confession. Except this was not funny.

Still, I was in good company because there were 263 other penitents on the island with me – all practising Catholics who hadn't quite got it right yet. Now I'm normally at home in the company of sinners, but they're not usually the virtuous kind.

I confess I was tempted to cheat on the fasting bit. Well, I didn't want to destroy the body God had given me by starving it. So I thought I was canny booking into a nearby B&B the night before – until the owner's daughter guessed where I was going. With a pious smile, she said: 'Then you won't be wanting breakfast.'

Temptation struck again as I waited to board the ferry with a set of borrowed Rosary beads. I had planned to smuggle on a bag of chocolate, crisps and the ultimate forbidden fruit, an apple. But St. Patrick's statue seemed to be frowning at me, so, guilt-ridden, I left them behind as I took the boat to the austere island in the mist.

We were people of all ages – from twenties to eighties. Mothers, grannies, students and even a men's group from a homeless shelter in Liverpool – including Pip, a former cocaine dealer who had found God. He told me this was tougher than his stint in jail! The Liverpool lads were on their second pilgrimage – the year before some of them had gone straight to bed, only to be woken by the Monsignor, who booted them off the island!

Sadly, I also met some devout followers of high-living 'holy woman' Christina Gallagher. My good deed was to convince them that her House of Prayer on Achill Sound was nothing like this holy place, where pilgrims had been coming for more than one thousand years – including St Patrick himself. In contrast to the tens of thousands Gallagher asks her followers to 'donate' (or face eternal damnation), the €50 I had paid for three days on Lough Derg was a pittance. Mind you, I got very little in return. . . . The fee has since gone up to €70 but the spartan facilities are the same.

I fancied I was a medieval prisoner as I climbed the winding stairs up a turret to the women's dormitory on the third floor. The draughty corridors smelt of disinfectant and pepper – something that was to become a big part of my ordeal. There were no showers – unless you counted the rain. And no hot water. Not that we had time to wash properly. I had a bunk in a wooden cubicle, about seven-by-three feet, with no light-bulb, in a dorm shared with twenty-eight others. The narrow windows had frosted glass to preserve our modesty. Not that we would be doing much gazing out the windows. And we didn't get to sleep until after the twenty-four-hour vigil, which began at 10 PM. I had already been awake since 8 AM the previous day.

What we went through would test even a soldier to the limit, and yet there were octogenarians going thirty-six hours at a stretch, on only one basic meal a day – dry bread and black tea or coffee. To the tune of our empty stomachs rumbling, we marched for miles, barefoot, in circles, stopping every minute or so to kneel on hard rocks, all the time saying decades of the Rosary. Cruelly, the penitential sites were called 'beds'. We were forbidden to lie down, close our eyes or put on our shoes.

It was as if God was laughing at us. We even got complimentary postcards with free postage, bearing a picture of the miserable lake and the ironic caption: 'Wish you were here'. Being a Christian, I couldn't think of anyone I wanted to send it to.

Part of the penance involved turning our backs to St Brigid's cross, flinging our arms out and saying, three times, 'I renounce the world, the flesh and the Devil.' And certainly I felt I was leaving this world as my stomach burned from lack of food and I was dizzy. After a day of praying in the rain, we did the same in the basilica – all night. It was eerie to see eighty-seven zombie-like people walking around the aisles throughout the night, Rosary beads and scapulars dangling from their fingers. Some old men used the scapulars to lash themselves on the hips.

We were allowed breaks during the night to drink 'Lough Derg soup'. I was looking forward to this until I realised it was just hot water with salt and pepper. The most devout – or masochistic – forewent even this meagre comfort, including an ancient woman who remained in her pew, her back hunched and her head on her knees. For a horrible moment, I thought she was dead or dying, and gingerly put my hand on her shoulder, terrified that my touch might be the very thing to finish her off – she looked so frail. But she turned her face to look up at me, gave me a beatific smile, and I realised she was praying with her Rosary beads.

At the beginning of the all-night vigil, a priest had warned us, from the pulpit, not to fall asleep. He urged us to wake anyone we saw nodding off; we would be saving their soul. I didn't have the heart to wake up the pious priest from Nigeria who was snoring loudly on the back pew. But I felt guilty as dawn broke and his name was called from the altar; he was supposed to be taking part in the ceremony. All eyes were on the poor padre as another priest was despatched to the back of the church to shake him roughly awake. His loud snores changed to splutters, and he looked as if he wished the floor would open as he walked the whole length of the aisle and took his place alongside the others.

After Mass, we emerged, bleary-eyed from the chapel and were treated to the best ever performance of *Swan Lake* –with real swans. And for a while I forgot my discomfort and found something romantic in the idea of banishing my survival instincts for spirituality. The buzz lasted well into the morning. Deprived of any comfort, I found myself taking pleasure in the simplest things – the feeling of soft grass after kneeling for hours on hard stones, a tame bat and friendly swans, the subversive thrill of reading newspapers which had been smuggled over.

We endured a second day of prayer before we could take an eight-hour nap – which was really six hours because I just couldn't give up my grooming rituals. As I sneaked into the bathroom in the dead of night to pain my toenails red, I was surprised to find at least three others doing the same! We were like a secret society within the church – the Order of the Vain – as we dabbed away with our little pots of varnish, silent so as not to awaken the more pious. One of the other women in the dormitory was clearly referring to me the next day when she kept complaining loudly that 'someone' had switched on a light late at night during our eight-hour sleep period; unable to sleep on an empty stomach, I had been reading by the light of a torch – and anyway I knew I'd never wake up at 6 AM. The only way to manage it was not to sleep at all.

The bell for Mass rang at six on the dot, and a cold, miserable pre-dawn it was. It was followed by Confession, a sacrament of reconciliation, and then more penance. I was given the honour of carrying the huge wooden cross as the priest said the Stations of the Cross. I certainly felt crucified – and humbled. I nearly wept as I thought of poor Jesus.

But I felt even more sorry for myself. I grew so desperate for food, I tried to buy some of the tasteless Lough Derg biscuits in the island shop. Made from wholemeal flour with no raising agent or sugar, their only appeal was the fact that they were filling. However, the lady in the shop refused to help me break my fast. 'I don't sell food to pilgrims' was all she would say, but she made it sound as if we were lepers . Later, when the hunger pangs had given way to a burning sensation in my stomach, I pretended to be pious as I refused some broken biscuits offered by one of my fellow sinners – an ex-prisoner from the Liverpool men's homeless shelter. They were used to hardship – but even they admitted they found Lough Derg tough.

I felt like a total failure. In just three days I had managed to clock up three deadly sins – gluttony (I pigged out on the dry bread during my one meal a day), sloth (I felt my eyes close during Mass) and, briefly, pride – until I caught another glimpse of the frail old lady who was soldiering on while I wilted. I later told an ex-Army Ranger about her, and he said he had seen such people in war zones; their amazing strength and energy was fuelled by faith.

When it was time to leave, I couldn't get off the island quickly enough – partly because I had finally come clean and told the other pilgrims that I was a journalist. I even gave them a copy of the *Sunday World* – and they pored over it, drinking in the racy pictures and scandalous stories. I had forgotten that it included a picture of myself wearing nothing but a red trench-coat – open to the waist. Still, the other women regarded me as a bit of craic, and some of the men flirted as only shy, pious gents can.

We were in jovial mood as we enjoyed a sing-song on the boat. We had been good long enough – it was time to clock up the sins again. However, I resisted the urge to go back and plant chocolate biccies in the penitential beds.

But my fall from grace came within an hour of leaving! I was supposed to fast until midnight, but temptation called as I drove into the village of Pettigo and headed for the aptly named Garden of Eden – a chipper. Adam and Eve might have been content with an apple, but nothing short of fish 'n' chips would satisfy this sinner.

The Temple of Isis

They are witches, shamans, psychics – and civil servants. They all meet in an ancient castle several times a year to worship a four-thousand-year-old Egyptian goddess. Huntington Castle, in the village of Clonegal, County Carlow, looks like one of the many mock-Gothic castles dotted throughout the Irish countryside, but in its vaults is an exotic room adorned with hieroglyphics, colourful tapestries and gilt statuettes. Ireland's very own Temple of Isis looks like the set of a particularly lavish production of the opera *Aida*.

And its High Priestess would not look out of place in a Cecil B. de Mille movie. Lady Olivia Durdin-Robertson had just turned ninety-three when she gave me an exclusive interview in April 2010 – but she said she felt 'thousands of years old' as she performed a ritual dating back to beyond the time of the Pharoahs. Dressed in colourful robes and carrying an ornate gold staff, the leader of one of the world's most exclusive cults chanted ancient prayers as a handful of her followers re-enacted the crowning of the goddess Isis in the castle's throne room, to mark the Spring Equinox. As she resurrected a long-dead language and married it to modern English, in a rather robust, plummy voice, she seemed to transcend her tiny frame.

Then one of the priests, Fear McCabe, placed the sacred robe of the Temple of Isis on the shoulders of priestess Cait Brannigan, crowned her and handed her an ankh – a spear with a cross on top. 'The ankh is powerful because it symbolises balance between the power of the spear and the cross,' Lady Olivia explained. 'Our religion is all about balance, which you find in Nature – the balance between winter and summer, the dark and the light. The Equinox ritual is to mark the end of winter and beginning of the summer.'

Like most of the Irish members of the Fellowship of Isis, both Mr McCabe and mum-of-one Ms Brannigan were civil servants, Lady Olivia told me after the ceremony. But she said that they were a secretive lot in general and most did not want their names or jobs published – though they were happy to let our photographer, Patrick Browne, snap away during the ceremony.

The cult has incited some controversy over the years, with unfounded allegations ranging from cannibalism to witchcraft. Some of these claims are presented as fact on a website set up by a local man. Lady Olivia laughed when I asked her about the more bizarre rumours on the website. 'People say Isis is the Goddess of Destruction too, but it's not true.' She had mixed feelings about the 'witch' tag because of its creepy connotations, but she pointed out: 'Many of the [followers of Isis] would describe themselves as witches. We have thousands of witches in Ireland. There are more of them than ever these days. Most of them come from the Celtic pagan tradition. They recognise that Isis is also their goddess Dana. I might be a witch too – I don't know for sure. I do know that I'm psychic and I can communicate with animals. But I am definitely Christian. I believe in the teachings of Christ – and the Marian side of the Christian religion. I have been seeing apparitions since 1952, here in the castle. They are like the Marian apparitions you see at shrines around the country. I believe they are genuine. However, I believe that the apparitions here in the castle and its grounds are not the Blessed Virgin, but the goddess Isis and some other deities.'

She told me she had once heard an angelic choir of male and female voices chanting as the goddess appeared in the guise of the Celtic deity Dana. She said that the Celtic witch Morrigan had also appeared during a ceremony dedicated to her at the castle. 'She had long black hair and a red robe and she appeared to one of the priests of Rhiannon who was taking part in the ceremony.' On another occasion, she came face to face with a supernatural wolf. 'It was a lady wolf. She appeared when I was having a heart attack in bed – the moment this lady wolf appeared in my room, I got better. I believe she is my protector, and it is no coincidence that my family's coat of arms includes three wolves.'

Lady Olivia founded the Fellowship of Isis in 1976 with her brother, the late Reverend Lawrence Durdin-Robertson Baron Strathloch, and his wife Baroness Pamela Barclay. They set up a throne room in the thousand-year-old castle, which has been in the family since 1625. The cult now has about thirty thousand members in 132 countries – including thirty-one Arab countries. They even have members in China, where religion is forbidden. 'Word has spread about us. It's not always a good thing because people simply turn up at the castle uninvited. It's lovely that they're interested but our ceremonies are invitation only,' Olivia said.

She adds that anyone who joins the Fellowship may still keep their old faith. 'My brother was a Quaker who became an Anglican priest but he was also our High Priest of the Temple of Isis. He used to sit on the throne here in the castle during the ceremonies. After he died I continued to hold the ceremonies to mark the change of each season – but no one sits on the throne now. Ours is not a hierarchical religion.'

It may well be an ancient religion, but Lady Olivia came up with the idea of setting up its Irish branch when she was in her sixties. 'I wanted to express a female version of God. We have God the Father, God the Son and of course we have the Mother of God. But we had no Goddess. I found it fascinating that the ancient Egyptians and Greeks worshipped this goddess who was called Aset by the Egyptians and later renamed Isis by the Greeks. She can be found throughout history, in many cultures, and she appears under many names. We believe that everything in the world – every animal, plant, tree, stone, person – is born of this Mother Goddess.' She believes animals 'are just as important as human beings' and has been a strict vegetarian since she set up the fellowship in 1976. 'But I have lapsed on a few occasions and ate meat. I felt terrible because I believe animals have souls just like us. I can converse with them.'

Lady Olivia's 'spiritual awakening' had begun long before she set up the cult. As children, she and her brother used to visit a hermit, Daniel Fox, who lived by the River Slaney which runs past the castle. 'He was our Merlin. As he and I sat over a fire in his cottage, he would tell me of his visions of pagan people who lived by the river thousands of years ago. He would see and hear them, he said, as they rose at early dawn. They would drink from a well, bathe in the river and then assemble at an altar stone, high on the steep slope of the bank. There they would wait for the sun to rise across the river. Mr. Fox would show me the altar and well every time I visited him. He kept them clear.

When I was sixteen I painted pictures of the ancient ceremony as he had described it.'

Olivia believes the Slaney River and the 150 acres around the castle are sacred – and may have given her healing powers. 'I have the gift of seeing people's spirits and healing them,' she says – but adds: 'I would not claim to cure cancer or anything like that. I would say if you are sick go to your doctor. However, the healing I perform does make you feel better. And it's free, so you know it's genuine.'

While cults in general have been tarnished in the public mind by the scandal of pay-as-you-pray outfits, Lady Olivia points out that it costs nothing to join the Fellowship of Isis. 'A lot of religions are money-making rackets but we are not interested in making money. You can buy my book – but you can read it online for free. I charge for nothing. I believe spirituality should be free.'

She has never married and has no children, yet she is a kind of matriarch. She lives in the castle with her vast extended family, including her nieces and nephews, and their friends. 'I don't know how many of us are living here. We come and go and we don't get in each other's way. I suppose we are the original hippies.'

The Agent of the Devil

T abloid journalists get called all sorts of things, and we never take offence – we are the people millions of readers love to hate. Still, I was taken aback when I heard a reputable clergyman describe one of my colleagues as 'the agent of the Devil'. Fr Gerard McGinnity, the former Dean of St Patrick's seminary in Maynooth, also called our newspaper, the *Sunday World*, 'the work of demons'.

Investigative journalist Jim Gallagher had sent me undercover to report on the goings-on at the now-notorious House of Prayer on Achill Island. He had exposed its founder, Christina Gallagher, as a fraud who lived the high life while terrorising her followers with threats of hellfire and damnation if they did not donate their life's savings to her organisation. And one of her most devout apostles was Fr Gerard McGinnity, who had been widely admired after he exposed the abuse of young men at Ireland's top seminary, following the publication of the Ferns Report into the child abuse in the Catholic Church. He had been shunned by the church authorities for his brave stand, but was a hero to victims of clerical abuse. Yet there he was, attacking one of the country's most respected investigative journalists.

Fr McGinnity made the remarks the night before *Sunday World* hit the shops with yet more scandalous revelations by Jim Gallagher. Describing Jim's shocking expose of the previous week as 'gutter journalism', he denied that the 'Holy woman', who claimed to be impoverished, enjoyed the trappings of wealth, including an opulent mansion in Dublin. The pilgrims – most of them elderly – said they had seen the article and did not believe it.

The next day, the *Sunday World* published Jim Gallagher's latest exposé – including photos of the self-styled visionary's €4 million mansion in Malahide, in a gated complex known as 'Millionaire's Row' – her neighbours included Westlife's Nicky Byrne.

All hell broke loose as members of the House of Prayer Fraternity desperately snapped up the paper in an attempt to stop their neighbours reading it. In a newsagent on Achill Sound, I saw one of the women grab a bundle she could barely carry.

Elsewhere on the remote island (population three thousand) it was sold out. But, despite their best efforts to bury it, the story had spread around the community. After morning Mass in the real Catholic Church – whose priests do not recognise the House of Prayer – locals said they were not surprised. 'We've heard things over the years about Christine [*sic*]', a woman told me. 'Christine only wants cash – she won't accept cheques.' She nudged her husband. 'You'll have to start seeing visions!' He laughed: 'I'll have to get the stigmata too. That's what brings in the money!'

Most of the locals I met were disgusted that the House of Prayer was using a consecrated chapel for its money-making racket. The diocese had forbidden the organisation to say Mass in the little church, which used to be a chapel attached to the Sisters of Mercy convent and the school next door. Some people pointed out that Christina Gallagher was boosting the coffers of shops and B&Bs. 'You won't hear a bad word spoken about her in the B&Bs and shops – because without her, they'd have no business,' an Achill man said. 'Sure the place would be dead in winter without the pilgrims.'

At the island's makeshift golf club, Canice O'Sullivan said: 'The people who visit the House of Prayer are good people but – ah, I'd rather not comment about the organisation'. He added: 'I'm not religious anyway. When I want to feel God's presence, I just walk along the Cathedral Cliffs.'

But, as they pored over the *Sunday World* pictures of Christina outside one of her mansions, the keys to her €110,000 BMW in her hand, and read Jim Gallagher's damning evidence, the islanders realised they were being had – just like the pilgrims. A shopkeeper said: 'We're getting the business all right – but she's making more money than any of us out of it! All we're getting is crumbs from the rich woman's table.'

The pilgrims were mainly old and sick. They coughed and limped into the little chapel, in some cases aided by minders nearly as old as themselves. Most had grey hair – some long and wild – and a few men had matching straggly beards. Surgical tights, sensible shoes and Zimmer frames completed the picture of the typical pilgrim. It was as much a social occasion for these people as a religious experience – though the hardest tipple available was coffee. The toilets were the busiest room in the house.

I was one of the few under the age of sixty and, in my sweater and jeans, I felt as conspicuous as – well, a heathen in church.

With three coaches outside and a lot of cars, it was a typical Saturday afternoon. At least two hundred people crammed into the little church, and a further hundred or so into the café and shop where they could hear the Novena on loudspeakers. One gent told me he travelled every Saturday from County Kildare especially to say the Rosary. A local B&B owner's daughter told me there had been ten thousand visitors in July 2007 for the House of Prayer's fourteenth anniversary.

Inside the Church, Fr McGinnity preached through a screen on the altar. This was real fire and brimstone stuff – all directed at those who would dare 'attack' the organisation or Christina Gallagher. The *Sunday World* and journalist Jim Gallagher were the main focus of this wrath. Fr McGinnity spoke of a vengeful Virgin Mary, who was passing on warnings through Christina. These messages included: 'My Son's Hand is about to come over the earth in Justice . . . the chastisement . . . the purification . . . is on the way . . . Save us from the fires of Hell!'

It was all very Gothic, especially against the background of a brewing storm – but I feared most for the soul of Christina Gallagher, living in heavenly bliss at the expense of these pious people. It revolted me to think that these nice people were being codded, ripped-off and threatened with eternal damnation if they did not support Christina Gallagher morally and financially. They were gambling their life's savings – and the last years of their lives – on a promise of reduced Purgatory in return for funding a woman who must surely be thanking God for making so many fools.

Later that night, I slipped into the chapel. There were five people there, speaking in murmurs. As I entered, they began – or resumed –

saying the Rosary. The Sorrowful Mysteries, naturally. It was led by a very priestly lay preacher-cum-singer called John, whose surname the other staff could not tell me. Yet John was clearly a big player in the organisation; he led the Rosary at teatime, was back for the vigil from 11 PM to 1 AM – and was there before nine the next morning. John was omnipresent just like God – and, indeed, the House of Prayer itself, which seemed to be open all hours. I spent the night walking back and forth between my B&B and the House of Prayer, joining in the all-night vigil and rushing back to write up my observations. Every time I entered, the prayers got louder and an artificial scent of lilies was released into the air, drowning out the delicate fragrance of the real lilies.

The next day, one of their members, a kindly man called Eoghan, revealed just how suspicious of strangers the Fraternity had become. 'Anyone can just walk in and listen in on us. We don't know who they are. They could be the media.' Volunteer Paddy said the media was 'too powerful. You'd have to be very strong to take them on. That's why we don't bother reading the papers.'

But, clearly, some of the faithful had seen the paper – and rumbled me, because hushed discussions in the chapel quickly turned to loud Hail Marys as I walked in, a copy of the *Sunday World* in my hand. 'We don't take it seriously because we know it's not true – we have no comment,' a woman called Eileen, who worked in the shop, said. Other members of the Fraternity said they 'never read that paper' – but it was obvious that they had.

I was just as keen to read their literature, including a leaflet urging pilgrims to make donations to 'The Blue Ivory Trust', which it described as 'a legal Trust set up by the Fraternity to fund the work desired by Our Blessed Mother'. On a table in the shop, there were ring-binders full of typed letters which purported to have been written by satisfied 'cures', as the House of Prayer organisation officially labelled its customers. They thanked Christina for healing them emotionally, spiritually – and even physically. She was credited with five hundred miracles – including many cancer cures. But the names and addresses were vague – some were just initials. There was also a list of doctors who verified that patients had been inexplicably cured after they turned to Christina – but no one could give me contact details for these doctors. They're 'mostly in America,' Eileen informed me.

And it really was Pay as You Pray in the attached shop. Prices ranged from €2 for a souvenir pen to €500 for a brick in the church. Items on sale included Rosary beads (I bought a set for €8.50), statues of various sizes and styles (most around €10 but some for €50) and Mass cards for €5 – signed by Christine Gallagher's right-hand man, Fr McGinnity. And you didn't even have to be dead to get a Mass card. I asked for a card that was not for a dead person but one who was very much alive (my mum) – and they sold me one for a fiver, promising me that Christina and Fr McGinnity would pray for her. Pieces of cloth with 'Padre Pio's blood from his wounds' on them were touted from the pulpit by a Fraternity member after the Novena on Saturday night. At €5 a pop, visitors reckoned they were a small price to save them from the 'fires of hell'. The pews were studded with plaques devoted to various coach groups from all over the country. Volunteer Paddy said a woman visited once a week to accept donations for large items such as pews and I might be in with a chance if I put my name in the book.

I was also encouraged to buy a brick. It would have my name on it and 'Christina will pray for you,' a member of the Fraternity called

Paddy told me. Eileen in the shop said there were no more bricks available but I could simply make a cash donation. 'Do you take credit cards?' I asked. She baulked as if she was a bit shocked at my cheek, but quickly switched on a smile and said no, they didn't. So it was cash then. 'We'll put your name in the book and Christine will pray for you,' a helper promised. Would they put me in the dossiers along with the people who have been healed? I wanted to know. Yes, they said. I offered €100 cash, then realised I had only €50 cash; would that do? I asked Eileen. She blinked to hide what looked like disappointment, and said yes. She clearly wanted me to show her the money –and I wanted to see the greed, so, out of sheer devilment (well, my employers had been described as 'agents of the Devil'), I told her I could only donate €20. Eileen looked rather cross, but the man who worked with her was grinning as I paid up and Eileen got me to write my name and address in the book. I used my mum's maiden surname and an old address. 'What will my €20 get me?' I asked – apart from membership of the Fraternity of course, which entitled me to attend private meetings. Eileen seemed a bit flustered at this point, but trotted out the old line about helping Christina carry out the work of Our Lady. I pressed her further: 'Will it go towards this house – not the other ones that were in the paper?' She primly assured me it would be spent only on the upkeep and maintenance of the House of Prayer right there in Achill.

I was now officially a member of the Fraternity. But I didn't bother taking out a €30 annual subscription to the Fraternity's monthly magazine. At €2.50 a pop, it was 30c more than the *Sunday World* – and, since working for the paper made me an 'agent of the Devil' like Jim Gallagher, it was pointless paying for salvation. When I asked for a receipt for the contribution and some items I had bought, it was clear that the game was up. But Eileen and her helper went through the charade of trying to get the receipt machine to work. After a full fifteen minutes, they produced a receipt. Most of the people who visit the House of Prayer would never have thought to ask for receipts.

The staff and volunteers, mostly Irish, included a retired but aptly named private investigator called Dick, from Boston, who had first come as a pilgrim after reading about the House of Prayer. Dick was wearing a green fluorescent petard emblazoned 'Our Lady's Helper.' He said his old job hadn't fitted in with his morals. Dick was clearly clever – but so nice that he saw only the good in people. Local man Paddy volunteered at the centre and was paid in kind – with a free daily meal. A nun in full habit helped out by polishing the gate with a clean paintbrush.

Paddy, Dick, Eoghan and some of the other members of the Fraternity seemed genuinely good people. I hoped they would forgive me for deceiving them into thinking I was a pilgrim; I had done it in a quest for the truth. Though, after hearing Fr McGinnity's attack on Jim Gallagher and the *Sunday World*, I realised that the truth about Christina Gallagher was one Revelation that they didn't want to hear.

CHAPTER FOUR:
Good Sports

We Irish love a bit of sport. And the fun is not restricted to the field.

Effin' Eddie

He had earned the title Ireland's wackiest Gaelic Athletic Association commentator – for turning the air blue whenever he took the mic at Gaelic football matches. So, as a True Blue Dubliner, I was GAA-ging to meet Effin' Eddie Moroney. The milk-truck driver from County Tipperary had been a legend ever since he commentated on an Under-21s Gaelic football County Final in 1992. He got so worked-up, his false teeth flew out. His epic rant, which included calling the ref a 'bollocks' and unleashing a string of obscenities at the hapless Nenagh Town players, who were taking on a team from his home club, Aherlow, had nearly forty thousand hits on You Tube in just one month.

And, thanks to County Tipperary's victory over Kilkenny in the 2010 All Ireland finals, Eddie's notorious rant got a fresh airing – a documentary about himself. *The Legend of Effin' Eddie*, directed by his mate Mick Daniels, was released on DVD to raise funds for Eddie's local Gaelic sports club, Aherlow GAA. But, with bootleg copies of the original video turning up far away as China, the cheeky commentator was a household name everywhere from New York to New Zealand.

And he still didn't give a *puc* about po-faced GAA officials who had complained about his rather sporting turn of phrase. 'A few years after I did the commentary, the club here in Aherlow got a call from a senior member of the GAA to say they heard it was being shown on the big screen at the Ploughing Championships which were on in Wexford at the time. They said I was making a feck of Tipperary – only they didn't use words like that. They said I was "bringing the sport into disrepute. We're the laughing stock of the country", they said.'

But even the man Eddie called 'that bollocks of a ref', Jumbo O'Shea, had since forgiven him for the very public bollicking, Eddie pointed out. 'I met him last winter at a game and we went for a pint. I said at the time he needed wipers for his glasses because he missed an effin' penalty. Now he's a living legend – I made him.'

With revered Croke Park commentator Micheál Ó Muircheartaigh out of the way – as he announced his retirement in 2010 – it seemed that the way was finally clear for Ireland's wackiest commentator to take to the mic big-time, at an All Ireland final – if only those stuffy honchos would let him.

My own boss at the *Sunday World* had no such qualms about Eddie's foul language – and despatched me to Eddie's home in the hope that he would give me a few tips on how to report on hurling matches. I was off to a good start – since I know eff-all about hurling. Still, I half expected Eddie to tell me to eff off when I rang up asking for a chat. But he was a total gent. When he heard I was from the capital city, he even sang 'Dublin's Fair City' down the phone to me.

The dad of six and grandfather of nine was in top form when I caught up with him at his family's pub, Moroney's, in the picturesque village of Lisvernane. The tiny hamlet in the Glen of Aherlow has less than six hundred residents. With its storybook landscape, it's the last place you would expect to find a foul-mouthed effer like Eddie. But local residents are proud of the man who put the blue in the Tipperary's county strip of blue and gold. He may well be Ireland's most biased sports commentator, but he's also its ballsiest.

Eddie's own heroes include motor-mouth telly soccer pundit Eamon Dunphy.

'Dunphy would be a bit like meself – I'd like to meet up with him in a pub some time,' he told me. But it was hard to imagine Dunphy belching live on air and announcing to the crowd after the match: 'Oh Jaysus, I'm going to get sick after that . . . I had some feed of beer last night!' Eddie said he had 'just got carried away' during the 1992 match. 'You just get taken over by the passion. There was our little Aherlow team taking on the big, mighty Naynagh [*sic*]. The camera man standing beside me said: "Take it easy, Eddie – would you ever cool down?" I was grabbing on to him and I knocked over his camera. I couldn't help it – you get stuck into it. The passion takes you over.'

It was taking him over again as he relived the moment right in front of me in his family pub. His face flushed and his voice went up a few octaves as he explained what it felt like to be a commentator. 'The veins in your heart are coming through the flesh to the extent that every vein and blood-vessel in your body is bursting out of you! You couldn't describe the feeling you get when you see your own team out there and some bollocks of a ref is getting in the way of their victory!'

Commentators usually pretend to be unbiased, but Eddie says bollocks to that. 'I get a bit upset when we're losing – and go wild when we're winning. That's what the GAA is all about – that's the passion of sport. I am fiercely competitive. Aherlow is my life.'

And it wasn't just the ball that the spectators were watching during the infamous match in 1992. 'My false teeth actually did come out,' he said. 'I saved them – in me hand. It was the emotion, the excitement of seeing me own club in the final.'

He let rip again many more times, notably in 2010 in front of two thousand spectators who were in Thurles for the Tipperary Senior Football Championship Final. True to form, the sixty-one-year-old went mad with the mic when his beloved Vale of Aherlow beat Loughmore-Castleiney by two-four to one-six. Coming just two months after County Tipp won the All Ireland, the victory meant Aherlow was officially the best team in the best county.

On that occasion, Eddie wasn't content with turning the air blue – he had a True Blue helping him. 'Me brother-in-law, Paddy Donnelly, helped me out with the commentary. He's a real Dub, living in Dublin, with a proper Dub accent,' he said.

'And he used to play for a club in Dublin so he knows his football.' Eddie gave Paddy advice on how to commentate properly. 'You have to let it all out of you. You can't hold back when your lads are out there and the cup is at stake. You want them to beat those feckers – and you want the crowd behind them.'

He later explained: 'I do it for the Glen Boys – that's what gives me the passion. I had everything at stake in the match. My son Brian was in the goal. My other son, Michael, was on the selection board. Those were my Aherlah [*sic*] lads out there fighting for the honour of their parish. We are a small village with less than six hundred people. Imagine the pride I felt when we won. When our boys went up to collect the cup, I sang 'The Galtee Mountain Boy'. And I sang 'The Flying

Column' going back in my car, with me wife Kathleen beside me. It was a great end to a great day.'

But his finest moment was watching Tipperary beat arch-rivals Kilkenny in the 2010 All Ireland. The long-suffering Kathleen went to another part of the stadium to get some peace, while son Brian sat with his dad. Eddie laughed: 'A fellow beside us said "My ribs are bursting", because I kept digging him with my elbows. I couldn't help it. Brian said: "I don't think I'll be sitting beside you next time, Dad."

'For the after-party, I had to put on a suit and dickie bow – I thought I was strangled!' he laughs. 'And the water out of the hotel shower was scalding. I said to Kathleen: "Jaysus, me arse is on fire!" We're not used to hot showers here in the Glen of Aherlow,' he joked.

Eddie's entire family – wife, six brothers, five sisters, four sons, two daughters and nine grandchildren – 'live and breathe GAA', Eddie said as he introduced me to some of the clan. It was clear he was very much in love with Kathleen. He blushed a bit as he spoke about her. 'I met Kathleen after Mass in Aherlow. I said: "This could be my woman!" Kathleen's family lived in a remote cottage on the far side of the valley, but the love-struck youngsters used to meet up at the well. Their grandson Michael, at eight months, already had a fine pair of lungs and was clearly getting practising for the moment when he would take over the mic from his granddad. The baby was 'born with a hurley in his hand', Eddie said.

Eddie grew up in the pub, which was then the family shop with the house attached. Born in June 1949, the third of twelve children (five girls and seven boys), he just 'popped out. My ma said "Jesus he's bouncing already!"' He won the senior football medal in 1968 when he was eighteen, and managed Aherlow in 2010 when they won the

West Tipperary Intermediate hurling cup. He said he had been fascinated by Gaelic sports since he was a toddler. 'Sure there were twelve of us growing up – nearly a team! We were pucking and kicking a ball around as soon as we were able to walk. When we were children, you'd get a new hurley and a *sliotar* and it was like gold to us.'

But he discovered early on that he had a bigger *grá* for commentating. 'On a day when there'd be a match we'd be out in the garden acting [commentator] O'Hehir. I'd be doing a bit, Denis would do a bit and Pat would do a bit. My mother used to say, "Jesus, Eddie, would you ever be quiet!"'

Now he lives across the road from the old family home, in his 'ranch' – backing onto the GAA pitch. He has his own private walkway to the pitch. The local pitch is behind his house and the house itself is covered in Tipp flags. But what really marks it out as Effin' Eddie's house is the sign outside celebrating Tipp's All Ireland win over Kilkenny: 'Five in a row me arse!'

His next-door neighbour, schoolteacher Tom O'Shea, shares the passion and remembers how he and Eddie turned the field between their houses into a pitch. 'We were advised to plant corn in that field, but we said between us we'd fill it with children – and we did. Between my children, Eddie's children and all the pupils we could have a match every day.'

Eddie's top tips for a budding commentator are: 'If you know the players and what's at stake, make it exciting. If you've any little stories about them, share them with the crowd.' He gets requests to commentate at matches in Tipperary and Waterford, but has also been known to take the mic at greyhound racing – and even local beauty contests.

However, he dirtied his bib when he compered the Miss Aherlow contest in 2009 and announced over the mic: 'The fillies are now entering the parade ring'.

Eddie said he'd love to have been the commentator during the infamous World Cup qualifier in 2009, when the Hand of Henry dashed Ireland's dreams. 'If I'd been commentating I'd have said they should spancel him like a cow – he wouldn't be able to move his legs! But I blame the ref, not Thierry Henry. Wouldn't I do the same myself? But the goal should have been disallowed. It wasn't a nice thing to do in a penalty shoot-out.'

Eddie says the real beautiful game is hurling. 'It's the Lord of the Dance of sport.'

While the celebrations for Tipp's 2010 All Ireland victory continued back in the family pub, Effin Eddie revealed he was busily preparing for a match the following Sunday – clearing his throat, polishing his mic and soaking his false teeth. And while he's content with his life as a roving commentator, he has one big ambition – to take the mic at Croke Park during an All Ireland final. 'I wouldn't be in the same mould as Micheál Ó Muircheartaigh, but I'm in a mould of my own. I'm me own Effin Man.'

The Playboy of the Sunny South-East

As the star of *Tanya Tate's Tour of Ireland*, Greg Jacob left nothing to the imagination. But the hurler-cum-porn star got all shy when the *Sunday World* asked him to flash . . . his smile. It took Ireland's favourite red-top to bring a blush to the cheeks of the man who had appeared in a best-selling porn DVD, was in the process of filming a sequel, and frequently took part in swingers' sessions.

The horny hurler, who sported a number six jersey as he played for his native Wexford, had proved he was just as good at the number sixty-nine position in the video, which was seen by millions of viewers worldwide on Television X. He and twenty-nine other Irish men had been chosen from hundreds of Irish blokes to star in a raunchy flick with international porn star Tanya Tate. They performed for free in the two-part series, which was shot in a caravan at various locations in Ireland during 2009. And Greg was the star player. Tanya said he was good enough – or, rather, naughty enough – to make the switch from amateur to professional porn star. 'He even made me squirt!' the porn queen gushed in her blog. It was quite impressive, given that Tanya, a surgically enhanced former hooker from Liverpool, had won a SHAF-TA (Soft and Hard Adult Film and TV) award for her own athletic performances. She was earning a fortune from flogging the videos online, and bonking her way around the globe, visiting exotic locations such as Dubai and, eh, Dublin.

After her sporting encounter with Greg, Tanya declared Ireland to be one of her favourite places because she had got a 'big welcome'. Indeed, Greg had given her a Full Irish *céad míle fáilte*. He later flew out to London for a threesome with bisexual Tanya and her 'wifey', US porn star Jordan, to celebrate the success of the porn movie.

When my colleague Niall Donald broke the story, all hell broke loose in the conservative ranks of the Gaelic Athletic Association. Members all over the country called on the respectable organisation to boot the talented midfielder off the Wexford Intermediate Team, on the grounds that hurlers were supposed to be wholesome role models for children. But a handful of hard-core supporters thought the *Sunday World* was even more scandalous – for reporting the fact.

So I should have known what to expect when the editor sent me down to meet him in person. Posing as a lust-struck groupie, I asked for his autograph as he left the field following a minor match in Wexford Park, attended by about two hundred people. But the thirty-something super-stud, who had brazenly bared all in the porn movie, seemed to have turned into a tongue-tied teenage boy as I approached him on home turf. I wondered how he had ever found the *liathroidí* to star in a porno flick. Greg was the only member of the team to keep his helmet on after the match, which took place on a balmy summer evening. Hiding behind another player, he blushed and mumbled: 'I'm sorry, I can't, I can't', before walking away with another player. Another man rushed to his side, putting a protective arm on his back – while the crowd turned hostile towards me.

I was wearing a tight Wexford jersey with micro-shorts and a pair of high heels as a nod to the fact that I was getting my picture taken with a porn star. It was considerably more than Greg had worn as he got jiggy with Tanya in the porno flick. But clearly he couldn't handle a bit of cheek from yours truly – and neither could his loyal fans, who gave me stick as I left the stadium. They had just spent the evening shouting 'Up Wexford'. But it was more like 'Up yours!' to yours truly, as a small group of hecklers turned the atmosphere foul. What should have been a bit of harmless fun turned into an ugly situation as I was made feel less welcome than . . . well, a porn star at a hurling match.

A middle-aged man tried to get a rise out of me: 'He's only playing for his county. Leave him alone!' When I ignored him, he repeated it. He was soon joined by a woman who walked closely behind me, yelling every few yards: 'We don't want you here. We don't want your type. Go away!' Others called me 'filth' and 'dirt' as they dragged their bewildered children away. The kids had spent the evening watching porn-star Greg run around a field with other pillars of the community.

Some of the younger men saw the situation for what it was – a bit of fun. They followed me out to my car, whistling and calling 'Hiya, Tanya'. Others honked their horns. A group of teenaged lads asked me to pose for a picture with them. In true tabloid style, I made my excuses and left – though I was glad to have them as a shield from the older generation who, despite being prudes, did not look as if they were averse to violence.

Over the following weeks, the story gained legs. An anonymous correspondent in a local paper falsely claimed that I had grabbed Greg and that a rival local newspaper group, the *Wexford People*, had helped plan the 'tabloid ambush' in conjunction with my employers at the *Sunday World*, as part of a bizarre conspiracy by our parent company, Independent Newspapers, to give Greg grief. They also quoted the team's manager, claiming that Greg had 'feared for his safety' and had had to be escorted to his car. I didn't know whether to be flattered or offended to think that I had single-handedly scared a six-foot-something, super-fit sportsman, surrounded by his fellow hurlers and two hundred supporters. One woman wrote a letter to the same local paper in which she declared that I looked like someone she'd expect to see in a red-light district – though I wondered how many red-light districts she had visited where Wexford GAA jerseys were commonly worn. And I wondered if she had noticed that most of Greg's middle-aged supporters (male and female) were baring quite a lot of cleavage as they watched the match on that balmy night.

However, sporting fans from Wexford, and other parts of the country, contacted me to express their support, and to encourage the *Sunday World* to keep it up – just like Greg!

In a follow-up article, I pointed out that there were worse role-models than porn stars. The ageing yobs who had heckled and hounded me out of the stadium had set a far worse example to children. I could see the shock in the kids' faces as the adults turned into a pack of wolves. It was comforting to know that they represented only a minority of Wexford folk.

Tanya Tate continues to sing Greg's praises on her blog, which includes video footage of the hurler in action – as a porn star. And she was quick to post a public message congratulating Greg's brother, jockey Daryl Jacob, when he rode Neptune Collange to victory in the 2012 Aintree Grand National. She added: 'Both of the Jacob brothers are excellent riders.'

The Mammy of Cork Football

She had armed herself with Holy Water, Beamish stout, Barry's Tea – and Mars bars. And her main weapon was a glove blessed by Padre Pio. Noelle Feeney was back in business as the Mammy of Cork Football. And she was about to tell soccer bosses to FAI off – by bringing her beloved Cork City FC back to the top of the League in 2010. 'We had to change our name but we're still the same club,' the feisty mother-of-one said as the team unveiled their new jerseys with the Beamish logo.

It had been a rollercoaster in the history of Cork City FC. The club had closed down earlier that year after po-faced officials refused to renew its licence. Despite finding sponsors willing to pay their tax debts, they couldn't stop football bosses pulling the plug on the historic club. Months later, the supporters had set up a new club which was, in all but name, the same. And it was all because of Noelle and the *Sunday World*. The bubbly blonde said more than six hundred fans signed up after I wrote an article about her twenty-two years as the club's unofficial 'mother'. The new club, Cork City FORAS Co-op, was founded by the fans themselves. And, during their first season, they stormed up the league to reach sixth position, notching up twenty-one points. Within weeks of starting, they were just behind Dublin legends Shelbourne. As they celebrated yet another victory, Noelle said: 'We're starting at the bottom of the League of Ireland because we're a new team – but we'll rise to the top. We're the fighting rebels.'

She added that the Corkonians had the Man Above cheering for them. 'God gives us the grace. All the times I blessed that pitch and covered those boys in holy water – God will look after us,' she laughed.

Noelle had been in tears when the club was wound down earlier that year. They had weathered financial difficulties, paying off a tax bill, but still the Football Association of Ireland refused to renew their licence. Sitting in her living room surrounded by the team jerseys, scarves and flags, she had wept: 'My heart is broken. It's like someone put a claw in and ripped out my heart. It was like a death. I looked after my boys for twenty-two years. I was like their mother. Now it's as if none of us ever existed.'

Her terraced council house near Turner's Cross stadium had been the Club's unofficial headquarters. 'People would drop in at any time of the day – even Christmas Eve – to buy a jersey or scarf,' she said. Every room was decked out with bunting and plaques honouring her twenty-two years of hard work. She proudly showed me photos of herself with some of the biggest names in football – Alex Ferguson, Giovanni Trapattoni, Kevin Doyle, Roy Keane, Niall Quinn, Graham Souness, Sam Allardyce and Paul McGrath. 'Kevin Doyle was one of my babes. I looked after him when he played for Cork City. I was very proud of him the night Ireland played in Cyprus – the following day I got a text from Kevin Doyle looking for my address – he wanted to send me his jersey that he played in. And when Ipswich came to town Damien Delanay [another ex-Cork City player] gave me his jersey.' She pointed to Roy O'Donovan's jersey, which was displayed on a coat-hanger on her living room wall. 'I was heartbroken when Roy Keane took him to Sunderland'.

But she added that Keane was a great friend of hers. Indeed, whenever the legendary footballer comes home to Cork, Noelle greets him with a bottle of Holy water and Barry's green tea. 'When he was playing, he always loved a cup of green tea before he goes onto the pitch. He kept up the habit when he became a manager. The tea-lady in Sunderland told me, "He wouldn't take my tea. He took yours." He's my Roy.'

Pointing to another photo, she smiled. 'There's another two of my boys – the two Dans [Murray and Murphy] who went to Shamrock Rovers.'

Noelle was on the club's staff as Liaison Officer, but she went way beyond the call of duty. 'I used to make the sandwiches for my lads, and the visiting teams and supporters.' She travelled with the squad – but was too busy mothering them to see the sights. 'I remember once we went to Malmö and I spent three days just washing their clothes because they had no spare clothes with them. I asked the hotel to let me use their washing machines.' On a hot day, Noelle steeped their kit in cold water and wrapped the lads in bathtowels to keep them sweat-free before the match. 'I must have seemed mad. The doctor asked me "What are you up to?" But I knew my lads. I knew they'd play better if they were dry and cool.' Before every match, she'd rouse morale by singing the anthem of their native city, 'The Banks of My Own Lovely

Lee', on the sidelines – and sprinkling the pitch with holy water. 'I believe it helped them win all those games'. Noelle even devoted all her spare time to the club. 'On a day off, I'd go into the city and buy things for the team – food they might like for their lunch. And I designed their scarf.'

She had quirky ways of raising funds. 'Players used to be fined whenever they'd get a red or yellow card, so I suggested putting it in the kitty. Whenever we needed a new microwave, someone had to commit a foul!' She also found sponsors for the club – and was on the ball whenever the team changed sponsors. 'Sometimes we wouldn't have the new jerseys in time for a match – so I'd have to sew badges onto their old kit.'

She hired a train to take the team and supporters to Croke Park in 1998 for a clash against Shelbourne. 'It was a replay and I thought the lads and supporters couldn't have the hassle of making their own way. It was worth hiring the train for the sake of comfort because we won.' Noelle also supplied the ball boys. 'I'd go into the schools and find young fellas and little girls who liked soccer.' She is especially proud of a plaque she got from Sunday's Well Boys' National School for encouraging the kids.

Even the prisoners in Cork jail made her their soccer icon. She showed me a plaque they made out of lollipop sticks to mark City's victory in 1998.

The single mum said her own grown up son, John, had to share her with the soccer stars. 'He's not mad about football himself – he's more into his fishing,' she laughed.

It was only when the club went bust that Noelle discovered just how highly regarded she was among the fans. 'When I was on holidays in

Spain, I was in McGuinness's pub in Torremolinos and I heard this woman saying to her husband: "Isn't that Noelle Feeney from Cork City football club?" They recognised me from the *Sunday World.* From then on, her determination to save her club inspired people in all sorts of ways, and she was particularly chuffed when a woman told her: 'After reading about you I'm going to help out with the Special Olympics.'

She fanned the flames of the club's phoenix-like resurrection by setting up sponsorship deals with some of Cork's leading companies. Her old friends at Barry's Tea were among the first to get behind them – and Noelle promised there would be the usual cup of Barry's green tea ready for her friend Roy Keane if he dropped in. Beamish stout paid for the new kit. Other local firms who forked out for the footballers included radio station 96FM, Hummel Sportswear and Con Murphy's Fruit and Veg, who supplied fresh fruit for half-time.

But Noelle planned to rock on with the Mars bars regardless. 'I chop them up into bite-sized pieces. The boys don't have time to unwrap them at half time.'

It wasn't just footballers who got a taste of her kindness. 'The Cork City marathon goes past my house every year, and one year one of the runners knocked on my door. He said: "Aren't you the lady who hands out Mars bars at the matches?" I couldn't refuse. The next year, a whole load of marathon runners came to my door asking for Mars bars.'

When Noelle volunteered to help a suicide prevention charity, her motherly nature kicked in again. 'People used to call me at home at all hours. One night a young fella rang me and said he was thinking of killing himself. He had no place to go – so I told him to come and stay with me. I had him in my house for a month, until he was better. I can't turn people away.'

Kind-hearted Noelle continued to work tirelessly for local charities, including Cork's Marymount Hospice, while she was waiting for Cork City FC to rise again. But following an operation, it was her turn to put her feet up. 'I miss being able to run around doing things for the club, but it's nice to be looked after. I got the ambulance men to carry me into the hospital – I called them my two toyboys. And when I couldn't leave the house, my friend came from Waterford to give me a rub of his glove which was blessed by Padre Pio,' she said, adding: 'I'm going to ask Padre Pio to look after the team for the season.'

A few years later, Cork City FC got its old name back, and Noelle was digging out that holy water again.

Gaelic Football is in the Blood ... Pudding

He was the real Sammy Sausages – and a lot saucier than his namesake, a pantomime character played by TV3 presenter Alan Hughes, who entertains children every Christmas. Indeed, it was less like Dublin's Tivoli Theatre and more like the GAA-iety when I found myself in the midst of a real live panto farce in 2011, because the comic hero was an edible version of the Gaelic Athletic Society's Sam Maguire Cup – made out of blood pudding!

Never mind Sleeping Beauty and her spell, Cinderella and her pumpkin carriage, or Aladdin and his genie. It was like a sporty version of *Ali Baba and the Forty Thieves* when I uncovered a plot to 'steal' the All Ireland football cup – and turn it into a giant sausage!

Sausage-maker Kathleen O'Connor and her husband, John Paul, swore bloody revenge when Dublin beat their native Kerry in the All Ireland football final. They decided to make their very own trophy – out of blood! It sounded like someone was telling porkies, until I caught the couple with blood on their hands – literally! Of course, as a *Sunday World* reporter, I was well used to gory scenes, so I was not at all fazed when I stumbled on their secret lair in Cromane, County Kerry. The tiny fishing village is in the heart of the Kingdom of Kerry – where the real Sam Maguire Cup is the Holy Grail.

The couple's accomplice was local panto dame Declan Mangan, who interrupted his rehearsals for *Long John Silver*, down the road in Killorglin, to join in our game of hide-the-sausage. 'We took Sam back to Kerry because this is where he belongs,' a defiant John Paul said as I raided his fridge, where Sammy Sausages Maguire was chilling out. 'He's a bit cold, but we'll thaw him out in time for the football season. Then we're going to make the Kerry team eat him – so they'll bate the lard out of the Dubs!'

As a 'Jackeen', born just yards away from Croke Park, I could not let that happen. So I set off to Kerry to bring Sam home to the capital – and join in the fun. Since there was something Germanic about a cup made from giant sausages, I invented my own panto alter ego – Fraulein Saucy-ges – and wore a Bavarian butcher's maid costume in the Dublin colour. But I turned blue for real when I picked the giant pudding-trophy up – it was frozen solid! It also weighed a tonne – and, as a vegetarian, I couldn't even pig out on it! I felt like a right silly sausage as I struggled to hold it aloft like the majestic trophy it was supposed to be. Well, there was no dignified way to hold such rude food.

Meanwhile, Kathleen was waving a meat-cleaver at me, John Paul was brandishing a black pudding – and drag queen Declan was fluttering those huge false eyelashes in a menacing manner, as only a panto dame can. His wife Anne had dressed him to kill! And there was something very intimidating about a man in a red spangly bra and magic knickers to hide his own sausage! 'He's behind you!' snapper Eamonn

Keogh warned as Declan tried to lasso me with a string of sausages!
'Oh no he's not!' I yelled as I legged it – the ground was icy and his
stilettos were no match for my snowboots. I gave him the two-sausages
gesture and headed for the hills. But Kerry's panto stars are made of
tough stuff. And Declan, who is also the chairman of Puck Fair, had
clearly taken some tips from King Puck – because he head-butted me
with his stiff, curly wig! I nearly dropped the trophy.

Then a barking mad Jack(een) Russell joined in the chase, and for a
moment it was a real farce. All we needed was a horny old goat and it
would have been Kerry On King Puck.

After a few hours being chased around the by-roads of rural Kerry
in a hailstorm, I was Pucked – I no longer gave a sausage about Sam
Maguire. So I handed him back to John Paul.

The devout Kerry GAA supporter deserved all the luck he could
get, seeing that he was still waiting for the government to throw him a
sausage as he tried to get his business off the ground. The builder had
set up the company, Sásta Sausages and Puddings, after his work as a
sub-contractor dried up. 'Rather than sit around moaning, I created a
job for myself. I built this place with my bare hands, using our own
money because we couldn't get a government grant.'

The blood pudding was Kathleen's own special recipe. She had
trained as a sausage-maker thirty years previously, and had served her
apprenticeship in various parts of Britain and Ireland. 'It was something I always loved doing, it's very creative,' she said. Now she juggles
sausage-making with her day-job as a school-assistant for children with
special needs. But it's worth the hard work, she says. 'We're doing this
for our family too, our two daughters and grandchildren. We want to
leave them the business – we never want them to have to emigrate.'

And now the proof is in the pudding. Gourmands go GAA-GAA for the traditional fare, which is produced in the O'Connors' tiny factory-shop beside a fishmonger's. They also have a regular stall at the Glenbeigh Farmers' Market – and they dish it out every summer at Puck Fair, where, as anyone knows, a real Irish breakfast is part of the charm.

Racy Casey Rides Again

He made racing commentator Tracy Piggott blush as he told her, live on air, how he was going to celebrate a racing victory – by romping at home! 'It's unreal, I can't believe it. I'll have fuckin' sex tonight!' racehorse trainer Peter Casey said minutes after Flemenstar won the Arkle Novice Chase at Leopardstown in 2012. The next day, he told RTÉ radio interviewer John Murray that he had gone ahead with his celebration – and vowed to stop talking about his sex life in public.

But the galloping granddad just could not zip it, as I found out when I visited him at his north County Dublin stables soon afterwards. Racy Casey was raring to go when I turned up at his yard, The Palace, near The Naul, to ask for tips for Cheltenham. Since the festival was being held during Paddy's Week, I was hoping the luck of the Irish would hold out.

Ireland's randiest racehorse trainer certainly thought I was a bit of a ride in my Lucky Leprechaun outfit – but he stopped short of putting on a Darby O'Gill hat and stuck with his traditional flat cap. 'Sure I'm like a leprechaun anyway!' The minute I took off my coat, he offered to squeeze my boobs! I brandished my stilettos – but that didn't scare him off. 'Those are the best legs I've seen, on a woman or a horse,' he said to his stable-lads and son Francis. And he thought this fine filly was ripe for some schooling! He brought me into the aptly named lunging arena – and chased me around with a long whip! 'Come on, girl, you're not trotting fast enough!' he yelled as *Sunday World* photographer Conor O'Mearain ran after us.

I wasn't surprised when Peter told me that his female neighbours tended to bolt whenever he appeared. 'I can't walk down the road – women are afraid of me!' he confided. 'They cross the road to avoid me!' But wife Junie was taking it all in her stride. 'He's always been like this. We've been married fifty years and there's never been a dull moment. I knew what he was like before I married him. I never get jealous – sure who's going to take him off me?' she laughed.

Junie showed me the little thatched cottage on the land where they used to live when the children were young, keeping warm with peat briquettes – and each other. It was clear the romantic spark was still alive. The cottage had been converted into a tack room, but Junie still loved to walk around it, reminiscing about the early days of their marriage.

Since the infamous Tracy Piggott interview, Peter and Junie had been getting a ribbing from his three sons, one daughter and seven grandchildren, who all lived nearby. The youngsters, aged ten to sixteen, were chuffed to see that their granddad had 130,000 hits on You Tube after the live broadcast. And it was clear that Racy Casey was, above all, a family man. Sons Francis, Peter and Oliver and daughter Alison had inherited his passion for horses and all helped out on the 'ranch'. Peter Junior and Oliver had become jockeys, while Francis, who had been a promising jockey until he grew too big, now worked alongside his dad as a trainer – indeed, Francis had been largely responsible for Flemenstar's victory, his proud father said. While Peter had officially retired, leaving his sons to run the yard, he still gets up at the crack of dawn on race days, his wife said. 'He'd be up at five or six in the morning, making sure the horses were loaded and checking everything.' He could often be found on the beach at Mornington or Gormanstown, watching as the stable-lads galloped the horses on the wet sand. And, as I found out when he gave me a tour of the 140-acre farm, he was intimately familiar with the seventy horses in his charge, right down to their little quirks. 'Those ones there are all windsuckers,' he said, pointing to some pregnant mares who were gulping air while gnawing on their stable-doors.

Of course, I was particularly keen to meet Flemenstar – whose victory at Leopardstown had prompted Peter's risqué on-air announcement to Tracy Piggott. The horse, owned by Stephen Curran, lapped up the attention as he posed for our photographer. 'He knows he's the important one here,' Francis said, revealing that Flemenstar had to have his own separate paddock because he didn't like other horses! A week later, he was to win his next race, at Naas, taking the lead halfway to the finish and beating the favourite.

Another of Peter's pets, a randy stallion called Boss's Choice, had clearly picked up a few tips from the boss-man – even before I offered him carrots, he nuzzled my neck, gave me a kiss, then rested his cheek against mine. Peter revealed he had a special soft spot for his oldest stallion, thirty-year-old Geronimo the Teaser, a shaggy pony with the most frustrating job in the yard. 'Do you know what a teaser is?' he asked me. I did, but I wanted to hear it from Peter. 'His job is to get mares all excited – then he's pulled away at the last moment and we shove in the well-bred stallion to finish the job. Poor auld divil, it must be hard for him. We let him sire a few foals but he's had a lifetime of frustration. And now he's losing interest. A few years ago if there were mares in the next field, he'd be over the wall in a flash.'

And so was I, when I had a fall from one of one of Racy Casey's horses. He wanted to see me ride, and got Francis to give me a leg up on Inis Caitlin. In hindsight, I shouldn't have mounted a racehorse bareback, in her stable – wearing stilettos. I was careful to keep the heels clear of the mare's flanks, but she may have thought I was wearing spurs. And I sat too far back on her because I wanted to show off the leprechaun dress. Anyway, she wasn't keen on the girl-on-girl action; just as we were having our picture taken, she reared, bucked, spun and finally flung me sideways. I timed my fall to avoid hitting the wall, and landed on my elbow, rolling on the ground the way stuntmen had taught me. When Peter had suggested a roll in the hay, this was not what he meant.

Nor was I about to take him literally when he invited me to check out the horse spa – a stand-up bath for horses, with what looked like 1970s-style psychedelic disco lights! Peter switched on the infrared lights, and stood in it but didn't fill it up. 'I got into it the other day. I hated it, I don't know if the horses like it but the infrared light is good for their muscles.'

Then he got me to feed some week-old lambs. 'They'll get a right suck out of those tits!' he said – well, I was showing a bit of cleavage for the camera. I was relieved when he came back with bottles. One little speckled fella was just as cheeky as Peter – he nuzzled my legs and tried to climb up on my lap even before Peter handed me a bottle. Then he greedily grabbed it. Peter laughed: 'Now he's suckin' diesel!' The lambs, horses, sheepdog Jake and Junior the Jack Russell were all keen to get up close and personal – just like Peter.

And the atmosphere in their kitchen was lively as stable-lads, friends and family dropped in for a bit of ribald banter, Junie's home-made scones and mugs of tea. There was racing on the telly and one wall was covered with pictures of horses Peter has trained, passing the winning post in various races. 'Don't ask me how many winners I've had – I can't count them. I've had winners on every track in Ireland,' Peter said.

Neighbouring racehorse trainer Miley Caldwell dropped in for a chat – and to bum some Viagra! 'I asked Peter for some Viagra the other day but he wouldn't give it to me – he wanted to keep it all for himself!' he said as he rifled through Peter's pillbox. Peter said: 'The last fella I gave Viagra to was running around with a young one. Then he got her pregnant.' He added: 'I'm taking all sorts of pills. I'm falling apart, there's everything wrong with me. I've had a triple bypass, the hip done six or seven years ago, the lungs are gone – I got pulmonary fibrosis, I think I got it from shovelling corn-dust, I played Gaelic football and I'd have a fag at half-time'. He gave up smoking at sixty and doesn't drink. 'What would I be like with drink on me? I've never touched the stuff.'

Of course, Peter was entertaining enough sober. If racing was the sport of kings, he was its court jester. But any hopes of a Carry On Cheltenham were dashed when he revealed he wouldn't be going this time. 'I went for thirty years and now I'm too old.' He was coy about revealing his age – so I offered to do it the horsey way and look at his teeth. He chuckled: 'You wouldn't want to look in this mouth; you never know what you'd find. You will be looking at something else I have – but he's getting very small, you'd need a magnifying glass!'

But I did get to see Peter's cock. And it was huge! The feathered fella was roosting proudly in the hen house when I entered. He was fine until Junior the Jack Russell terrier entered, did a plop and just missed my leprechaun hat. Call it the Pluck of the Irish.

CHAPTER FIVE: Showtime – Showbiz, Showing Off and Showing All!

We claim to be modest – but the Irish are a nation of show-offs.

Losing his Shirt in the Recession

By day, he was the epitome of a respectable businessman, selling health supplements and body-building potions from his shop in Dublin's Square Shopping Centre. But at night, he toured nightclubs and pubs in the Carlow-Kilkenny area, wearing a fake New York cop uniform – and taking it off! Trevor McDaniel aka Jacque [*sic*] the Chippendale Cop, turned to a life of sin after he hit hard times in mid-2009, when four of his five shops went bust and he had to lay off eight of his ten employees. The electrical engineer had been a roaring success during the Celtic Tiger years with his Sports Nutrition shops around the country and website sportsnutritionireland.ie. 'Then the recession came along and I lost my shirt – literally,' he said. But while Jacque no longer had financial muscle, he still had his beefcake physique. The half-Italian, half-Irish hunk had won the Mr Ireland bodybuilding contest in 2008 and had gone on to represent Ireland at the Mr Universe Bodybuilding competition that same year. 'It was won by the likes of Arnold Schwarzenegger in previous years,' Jacque pointed out.

However, it was his striking likeness to Jean-Claude Van Damme that landed Jacque work as a stripper. A nightclub owner in his local town of Carlow spotted him working out in the local Olympia Gym – and promptly offered him work stripping at hen parties. 'He said girls were sick of skinny guys turning up. They ask for a male stripper and expect someone like Russell Crowe – and instead they get Borat.' He picked the name Jacques because it sounded sexy – then dropped the 's' because most of his clients would otherwise (mis)pronounce it. And it was this pragmatic attitude to making a living, coupled with a fair bit of cheek that had saved his ass. 'I get paid well for stripping – and I like showing off my body. Stripping is a career that won't last forever, but I'll do it for as long as I can,' he said.

His first ever gig was a hen party for a hundred girls at a club in Carlow. 'Five groups of hens got together and shared the venue – and the stripper. I got such a good reaction from them that I saw a niche in the market for a proper Chippendale cop – rather than a Skinnydale cop who normally turns up at hen nights. I decided to stick to the kinky cop routine because girls are turned on by police uniforms. And I have a few friends who are guards – they inspired me.' Indeed, Jacque was such a hit with the ladies that risqué telly puppets Podge and Rodge got him onto their show to 'arrest' pantomime star Twink. The diva is notorious for a tape in which she told her estranged husband: 'Zip up your mickey'. But she didn't tell Jacque to cover up! He also slapped handcuffs on comedienne Katherine Lynch on her TV show, *Wagon's Den*. And, given the hard times, he dropped more than his trousers – he also stripped down his rate to a recession-busting tenner a head.

But while he is keen to be known as Ireland's cheekiest cop, Jacque

has yet to cross the Thin Blue Line and do the Full Monty. 'I don't
need to. It's usually the skinny guys who take out their willies – because
that's all they have. There's more to being sexy than a big mickey. I'm
hot enough in my jocks!'

His wife Louise certainly thinks so. She goes along to the hen parties with him – to pick up his clothes. 'When I strip off, I throw her the
clothes. If I didn't, the hens would grab them and I'd never get them
back. I'd have to walk out in just my boxers! The girls go wild for me.
They grope me and try to rip the clothes off me even before I start.
Louise is very open-minded and it doesn't bother her at all that I'm
stripping off in front of loads of women and flirting with them. It's a
bit of harmless fun.'

But when I agreed to let Jacque 'arrest' me outside his local Garda
station, I worried that I might get nicked for real! He had offered to
teach me the art of stripping – and suggested I start off with an outfit
naughty enough to get me arrested. 'I have a few ideas for you as I
know you want a good eye-catching pic or two,' he said in an email. 'If
you're up for dressing up, maybe a lingerie-type Santa Claus outfit, suspenders, etc. I can get it for you if you want. I will wear my cop hat and
boxers and you can have my shirt pulled off in one hand and be pulling
down my boxers with your teeth. Or I can lift you up across by chest
and you can lick cream off my cheek'.

I passed on the licking cream bit, but, since it was close to
Christmas, I wore a 'Sexy Santa' costume, which I had bought in Ann
Summers. And that was how I ended up with a blush to rival Rudolph's
hooter, as I stood in front of Carlow Garda station in my saucy cossie,
complete with thigh-high boots, while 'police officer' Jacque slapped
handcuffs on me and brandished a big truncheon – and photographer

Dylan Vaughan took our pictures for posterior-ity.

It was a bright day, the ground was covered in snow and it was bloody freezing, so maybe that was why there weren't too many people around – though passing motorists gave us a fanfare of horns!

But instead of taking me down to the station, the 'cop' decided he was too sexy for his uniform – and stripped off to his jocks! Then he hauled my ass into the gym, which was empty except for the female owner, her husband and one of their regular clients. I tried to imagine how it must feel to strip in front of a drunken crowd. Jacque explained: 'You have to be fast. None of this burlesque stuff – they want to see you naked.'

I preferred his next tip: 'Always have someone with you to mind your clothes, and make sure to bring clothes you can throw on quickly. When the crowd gets too excited, you want to leg it – and not in the nip!'

As we went through a series of poses for the photographer, Jacque's muscle-bound mate, who was working out alongside us, offered me a grand to strip to the buff – in front of the Garda station! It was tempting, but I wasn't ready to be arrested by a real cop just yet! However, I decided that, if all policemen were as kinky as Jacque, I'd turn to a life of crime.

Ladies' Night at the Red Cow

Whatever about female strippers, who require nothing more than a g-string to kick-start their routine, it seems the male variety need a uniform of some sort. And when the manager of Dublin male stripper troupe The Chain Gang offered me a ringside seat at their sellout show, I got an entertaining insight into the mass hysteria generated by the flash of a fireman's hose or a US Navy pilot's sparkling white blazer.

The air was thick with the scent of perfume and lust as six hundred women packed into Hush Nightclub at the Red Cow Inn in west Dublin to see the lads in action. The crowd ranged in age from twenty-something to sixties – a demographic you'd never expect to find in the same place on a night out, bar a family occasion. The young women, including a hen party, giggled and screamed in mock-shock. But it was the older ladies who went wild – indeed, the burly security guards were kept busy ushering some of the more enthusiastic cougars back to their seats.

It was the ultimate girls' party – but it was more a lads' night out as the guys whipped off boxers, g-strings and towels in front of the shrieking mob. This was not a case of 'Willy or won't he?' – total nudity was guaranteed. 'If they didn't take everything off, there'd be a riot in the club,' their manager Tommy Egan explained as he instructed his bouncers to keep the ladies off the stage until they were invited up.

These guys were not only too sexy for their shirts – they were too raunchy for breakfast TV too, as they had found out when they offered to wake up the nation's early risers with a bit of sausage. Tommy had offered to bring his troupe onto TV3's *Ireland AM* programme but he kept getting turned down. 'We have been offering to go on the show for the past seven years, but, every time, we get a message back saying we're "not suitable". Ireland is still in the Dark Ages as far as male nudity is concerned. We got a better reception on British TV. Richard and Judy loved us when we appeared on their show – they treated us like royalty. Their viewers voted our lad Rocky the sexiest male stripper in the world.'

Tommy had been managing the troupe since the late 1980s, with a long succession of strippers playing the roles of fireman, *Top Gun* officer, cop and biker. They had spent twenty years playing pubs, nightclubs and private parties throughout Ireland and the Continent, and a brochure to mark two decades on the road sold out immediately – they had to print a second run of one hundred thousand copies for Ireland alone. The original troupe, including Tommy himself, had been replaced several times by lads in their twenties. And while the first lot were The Full Irish, the current line-up when I met them had just one Irish lad, Dubliner 'Rocky'. He later left to join a rival stripper troupe and was replaced by a Lithuanian guy who had a day job – as the manager of a plush Dublin hotel. The others were American, Russian and Hungarian. Tommy pointed out: 'It's easier to strip when you're a foreigner. The Irish lads used to be afraid someone would recognise them. If you knew anyone in the audience, you'd be mortified.'

While they were coy about revealing their real names, the lads were happy to pose for photos with the fans in the interval– for €10 a pop. They should have been terrified of being mobbed by lust-crazed ladies, but they just struck smouldering poses for celeb snapper Brian McEvoy, as the girls sat on their laps.

Dublin ladies Sandra Kearney and Dorothy O'Connor, who were at the show with colleagues from Superquinn in Lucan, said they'd happily fight over these blokes. New Yorker Six Pack was Dorothy's favourite. 'He's so fuckin' sexy!' Dorothy said . It made her night when the hunk came over and let her stroke his chest.

'The more you scream, the more they take off!' compere Johnny Sonic promised, his inner city Dublin accent adding a surreal touch – it was a voice you'd expect to hear flogging fresh fruit in the market, yet there he was, tempting the local ladies to check out the prime Irish beefcake. 'Who wants to take him home? Go on, ya good thing!' he said as one lady sucked the banana Six Pack was brandishing – then bit it off, to squeals from the audience.

Next, burly blonde Blade from Moscow had all the women Russian onto the stage as he stripped off a three-piece suit to reveal rippling pecs. Moscow had just won joint-second place on Europe's worst dressed list in an international survey – but who cared, when the men had bodies like that? Meanwhile, cheeky Chico from Hungary took off his US Marines suit to reveal his own *Top Gun*. He got a hard time from twenty-something Tallaght girls Jennifer and Laura Bracken,

Amy Miley and Tina Cole, who had never seen the show before and were a bit boisterous. 'We told our boyfriends we were going but they don't mind. They know it's just a bit of fun,' Laura (aged twenty-seven) giggled. After the show, there was a rowdy hen party in the VIP room – but the din outside was louder as gangs of girls queued for a chance to get close to their hunks.

Tommy had banned all partners from the venue on the night. 'These guys need to be available because women fantasise about them. It wouldn't look right if they had girlfriends coming along to the show.' But I later met one of the lads – with his toddler son! He had brought the little lad along to one of their twice-weekly rehearsals. Not that the kid would have seen anything shocking; the lads kept their clothes on as they practised their dance routine with their choreographer, Des Allen – who's best known for his work on *Riverdance*. The rehearsal was gruelling; it had begun as usual at seven and due to finish around midnight. In between rehearsals, the lads were expected to go to the gym four times a week and were on strict diets.

Tommy admitted he had got some of his ideas from the Chippendales – and had even sat in the audience, among the women, 'to pick up a few routines for our show'. And when the Chippendales suddenly pulled out of a tour of Ireland in 2009, the Chain Gang filled the gap for a lot of Ireland's Desperate Housewives.

And I had another scorching hot date with the Chain Gang two years later, when they got me to take off my bra! Not any old boulder-holder but the Emergency Bra – its cups doubled up as his'n'hers gas masks which could even filter out nuclear particles! It had won the Ig Nobel Prize (a spoof award) for Best Public Health item in 2009, and its designer, Ukrainian doctor Elena Bodnar, was thrilled when I got the Chain Gang to help me test-drive it. It didn't matter that Chico and Co. were fake firemen and the blaze was just a smoke machine – these lads were used to ladies flinging their undies at them. And as Chico and I fled the fire, with the bra cups over our faces, I thought it was rather cool to find myself on a hot date with a cross-dressing hunk!

However, the Chain Gang were too hot to handle for *Big Brother* star Georgia Salpa, when she was hired to promote the nightclub Hush Hush in 2012. The Irish glamour model had got fans all over the UK and Ireland steamed up as she posed for lads' mags, and clearly had an eye for ladies' men when she dated Calum Best. But when strippers Leo and Chico offered to carry her into the Dublin nightclub, she went all shy and refused.

Naked Nation

The Irish have traditionally tended towards the prudish when it comes to nudity or even partial nudity. Irish girls may go topless on holidays abroad, but, back home, even our lingerie models are wary of posing bra-less, never mind starkers. And while nudist beaches have been dotted around the coastline for many years, they are regarded as a dirty little secret by the moral majority. Even the people who dare to bare for charity calendars tend to cover their 'naughty bits', in keeping with the standard set by the genteel ladies of the Women's Institute in the English comedy *Calendar Girls*.

But all that changed, briefly, in June 2008, when four thousand Irish people did something that, just a year before, would have been regarded as gross obscenity – they went starkers in public. Not in some far-flung holiday resort, among strangers, but in Ireland, in front of their friends, neighbours, families – and the world. They even allowed a film crew to capture their nakedness for posterity – and art.

Just how the controversial New York artist Spencer Tunick managed to convince Irish men and women of all ages, from every part of the country and all walks of life, to pose in the buff for his video installation was anyone's guess. Tunick had been arrested five times and jailed three of those times for 'indecency in a public place' in New York, during the reign of 'zero tolerance' mayor Rudy Giuliani. And now he was coming to Ireland to photograph the nation in the nip, first in Cork, then in Dublin.

Some people thought it was a rebellious thing to do – and this appealed particularly to the Corkonians, given that theirs is nick-named the Rebel County. Others said it made them feel part of their community since their neighbours were taking part too. Some did it because they wanted the pictures as souvenirs of their youth or even middle age – it would be something amusing to show in the future at the active retirement club while everyone else was passing around snaps of grandkids.

I took part because it was part of my job as the *Sunday World*'s up-for-anything roving reporter. But I was, for the first time in my career, overcome by something akin to stage-fright. The moment the event was announced, readers contacted me to suggest I take part. So I was expecting a call from the boss, and switched off my phone until I had got my head around the idea. 'You don't have to do it if you don't want to, but it might be a bit of craic', the news editor pointed out. He was right. And I could think of worse reasons to expose myself – such as money. Unlike celebs who wait until 'the price is right' before they bare all in a movie or magazine, Tunick's models do it free – for art, for exhibition, or for whatever reason. I would be paid no more than the usual rate for my job as a reporter.

Still, the bottom line was that I knew I'd be making an 'arts' of myself. Because I would not be one of the anonymous flesh-coloured dots in Tunick's snapshot – I was expected to write about it, to literally expose myself. In my case, I was wearing a suit to work – my birthday suit.

Of course, vanity was a big factor in most people's decision whether or not to strip. And I was no different. It bothered me that Tunick's pictures rarely showed their subjects in a flattering way. After all, this might the only time I had ever bared all in public, and I didn't want to be snapped at a bad angle. And it was no consolation when the boss said the people in Tunick's pictures would be 'tiny – you won't be recognised in the crowd.' I knew people would pick me out if the picture was published with the article. So I was relieved when he added that it might be an idea to do an advance piece about my intention to strip for art – because I knew the pictures taken by our own photographers would make me look my best. It was one of the nicest things about working for a tabloid paper.

Luckily, I was assigned top snapper Val Sheehan – a veteran from the days when the *Sunday World* used to have a Page One glamour girl, as well as a total gent with an irreverent sense of humour. If anyone could put a first-time nude model at ease, Val could. He was a total gent, and we spent most of the photoshoot having a laugh, and taking breaks for tea and biscuits. Val took a few 'arty' shots of me in his studio, wearing nothing more than a smile and the merest hint of fake tan – well, I wanted to look as if my skin below the neck occasionally saw the light of day. The uneven marks made it all the more natural – I didn't want to look like some airbrushed celeb. Val also snapped a few saucy shots just in case the editor wanted to revive the *Sunday World*'s old-school tabloid style. I had fun posing in classic glamour girl style – boobs and bum to the fore. These pictures never made it into the paper but no doubt they will some day.

There was no 'money shot', as they say in the glamour modelling business – but Val decided we needed a funny shot. 'Since you're going to be a flasher, we need a pic of you in nothing but a rain mac – on the street!' My red trench coat was perfect for the job; I belted it tightly but left the top few buttons undone to show a bit of cleavage, and we drove to the Dublin docks near Jurys Inn. Tunick had dropped some hints that he'd film his work of art in the docklands, but kept the locations a secret until the last minute. As it turned out, the actual event took place on the docks all right, but much farther out to sea – the East Wall. Still, as I struck a saucy pose on the quay, I got a taste of what was to come – I felt brazen! We had to interrupt the shoot when some people walked by on the Liffey boardwalk, and I realised that I had not quite got over my shyness. My blushes were enough to paint the town red.

As the big day approached, I worried about more practical matters – it would be a bummer having no pocket for my notebook and recorder. Still, I doubted that I would forget any details. Being naked in public is one of those things that's supposed to happen only in nightmares.

After my advance piece appeared in the *Sunday World* alongside four large photos of me in the nip, I got a mixed reaction. There were loads of the expected ribald comments, as well as a few praising my gumption and some spiteful comments posted anonymously on the web. I was inundated with requests from guys I barely knew (and not barely . . .) to flash the flesh again – but only in private. I also got invited to join naturist groups – my news editor advised me to ignore them, as they seemed dodgy.

Meanwhile, randy men were flooding the web with requests for female body-buddies to take part in the event. Clearly they were too shy to ask women they knew. Some were not quite ready to strip off in front of the neighbours. One wrote anonymously on Boards.ie that he was thinking of taking part in the Dublin event rather than the one in his native Cork, because 'Cork's a small and nosey place, there are going to be a lot of folks turning up "for the craic" and just to have a gawk at who's doing it . . . What if you're the guy that's visible/recognisable in a photo that's going to be immortalised in Cork? Things tend to retract and shrivel when they're cold.' The aptly named 'Strange Guy' replied: 'I'm really excited about this. I have a perfectly shaped and discreet hot water bottle which can be wedged right in between my cock and balls. I will look absolutely spectacular in the freezing Irish weather.' Fellow contributor Franco spelled out the potential drawbacks for another guy who was having qualms: 'A rabid dog could bite off your lad. . . . Spencer Tunick could decide to go with a close-up of just your balls and face. . . . You could touch off some naked dude by accident and "it" could move.' Other men expressed fears that they would be booted out for ogling naked girls or that they would have embarrassing moments of 'morning glory'.

Size apparently mattered a lot to the men taking part; the biggest fear expressed was that their willy might be smaller than some other lad's. And Dublin cosmetic surgeon Patrick Treacy told me he had noticed an increased demand among his female clients for a treatment in which a synthetic substance called macrolane is injected into the breasts. There was no way of knowing if these ladies were getting it done so they could get their tits out for Tunick. And beauticians revealed that they were inundated with people coming in for spray-tans – and no doubt countless more were going down the DIY tan route.

Women who might worry that they would be scrutinised had their worst fears confirmed by one message on an internet forum aimed at women: 'There will always be someone fatter/ with more cellulite/ saggier boobs/ saggier bottom/ too scrawny etc. there than you, so it'll make everyone feel good!' Scarier still was the message from one Cephalopod on the aptly named website Thumped.ie: 'I'm gonna do this and I'm gonna have an erection.'

Meanwhile, website Sapphic Ireland posted an open invitation for the lesbian community to get out and proud. And on Queerid.ie forum, one member suggested that they prolong the craic by doing a Gay Pride march naked too.

The event was even advertised on the Labour Party's Dublin South-East constituency blog – and I wondered if we would finally get to see if they were hanging to the left or just showing some barefaced cheek.

Those who warned that it was against the law were quickly silenced – the consensus was that, even if we all got arrested, there would be no shame. One flasher may be regarded as a pervert, but a thousand streakers in the slammer would be just a bit of craic.

So there was no excuse to back out. And, four days after 1,100 people stripped off in Cork, I joined more than two thousand who flashed the flesh in Dublin.

It all happened at sunrise – but it was more like the rising of the moon as two thousand bare bums appeared on the horizon. For one blissful morning, we were all beautiful – from the lissom young people to the old ones with lived-in, loved-in bodies. It lent a whole new meaning to the 'crack of dawn'.

We met up at 2.30 AM at various locations in the docklands, to be picked up by specially laid-on buses which took us to our top secret location – at the very end of the harbour wall on the south side of the docks. I hooked up with a friend who had travelled from Mayo. We had both registered under fake names – in his case, out of shyness, whereas I didn't want the organisers to know I was a reporter. This was to be an undercover exposé – literally.

I had expected trouble of the kind you usually find when large groups of people meet. So I was surprised to find that everyone around me was courteous, calm and friendly. Maybe it was because we would soon be exposing our most vulnerable parts. The stewards, dressed in fluorescent petards and warm clothes, had no trouble keeping order, as far as I could see. As we huddled in padded anoraks and layers of woollies, it struck me that this was going to be a very strange striptease. As we waited for dawn, we lost some of our shyness and started cracking jokes. But as the sky began to redden around 4 AM, I felt my face do likewise. Minutes later, we all had a chance to cool down –and there was a collective gasp as the brisk breeze smacked everyone's skin at once. But I soon found myself giggling along with my new friends, including a Dutch mother and her daughters who had travelled to Ireland especially for the event.

Naked, we trudged a mile along the harbour wall to our location and were told to stand on the Xs chalked on the flagstones. They should have been triple-Xs, I thought as we went through a series of Kama Sutra-style poses. First Spencer asked us to stand facing the sun, then the other way. Then we had to sit on the ground, legs straight in front, arms back and our heads strained towards the sky. Next was the foetal posture, which should have been comfy only we were doing it on hard, cold, wet stones – and, as I bent down, my face was just inches from a hairy bum. It's not in my nature to obey orders when they don't make sense, and I had to fight the urge to storm back to my nice, warm car. I felt ridiculous, powerless and very, very naked. But as the wind and rain whipped up into a mini-storm, I was determined not to chicken out. Others did, and I didn't know whether to envy or pity them as they scurried back to their towels and the safety of the Red Cross ambulance where they were handing out hot drinks. Spencer, sitting atop a cherrypicker with a microphone, thanked them – then thanked us especially for sticking it out.

The artist, who kept his black T-shirt and jeans on at all times, had to cope with exposure of another kind – to the Dublin wit! Some lads with an inner-city accent were determined to take the mickey out of him as he got us to perform the sun-salute. 'Hey, Spencer, show us your willie!' one piped up. 'Jaysus, me knob is gone tiny,' his mate said. Everyone sniggered and the lads continued to entertain us. Spencer politely asked them to leave – but the stewards could not find them in the crowd. The farce continued for a few minutes – it was like the scene in *The Life of Brian* where Pontius Pilate tries to find out which soldier is laughing at him – only there was no Biggus Dickus in this crowd because it was too bloody cold!

But the joke soon wore thin, as the sky darkened. Our dawn backdrop was gone. Some people pleaded with the lads to shut up. 'Let the man take the picture,' one guy chided. Trying to choreograph two-thousand first-time models is no mean feat in any weather, and Spencer finally lost his rag. 'Look at the sky,' he yelled. 'Look. At. The. Sky! LOOK AT THE SKY!' I had my moment of shame when he pointed me out: 'Hey, you, blonde woman in the front. Turn your feet towards the sun!' The sun had just disappeared, so I checked the position of the feet closest to my nose and tried not to look at other things. The funniest moment was when two ferries passed, each with passengers staring out of the windows in shock. I wondered if they realised how privileged they were. After all, we couldn't have given them a better céad míle fáilte.

But the Irish weather was not so hospitable. It began to pelt hail, and about half the crowd chickened out. At this point, we were all so cold that Spencer told us to put on our clothes while he set up the camera for the next series of poses – ankle-deep in the freezing water. Spencer even suggested we give up – he said he didn't want to put pressure on us, since it was a lot to ask and we were clearly freezing. Our teeth were chattering, our toes numb and I noticed that everyone around me was turning blue! I had turned a vibrant shade of orange, thanks to my fast-developing fake tan. However, I wasn't cold enough to accept a hug from a hairy Canadian guy who kept talking about the benefits of 'shared bodily warmth'. It could save me from hypothermia, he said. I told him to go hug someone who looked as if they needed it. 'What's wrong with Irish people?' he said as others rejected his offer. As we ran on the spot to keep warm, I felt my heartbeat slowing, and my legs losing power. Maybe I shouldn't have got a bikini-wax before my strip – after all, the hairy guy didn't seem to be suffering the cold at all. But I couldn't decide which was worse – being snapped in the arms of a stranger while naked in public, or dying of hypothermia in the nip.

The bravest person there was a guy in a wheelchair. While we were jumping up and down to keep warm, he was just sitting there, freezing. His minder, a young Asian woman, was naked too – and didn't look as if she wanted to be there.

Suddenly the sun burst through the rain, our goosebumps disappeared and Tunick finally got the healthy flesh tones he wanted. Our

Rebel TD Ming Flanagan lent a new meaning to 'turning the sod'. Here he is, breaking the law on the bog near Roscommon, with yours truly. Image © Mick McCormack

Size matters – when you're measuring pot-les. Cavan man artin Hannigan invited me to check out one the size of a wimming pool. age © Lorraine Teevan

I was taking no chances when Ireland's 'worst driver' took me for a spin.
Image © Billy MacGill

I'm not the 'damsel in distress' type, so when Lanesboro's knight in
shining armour galloped to my rescue, I knicked his sword!
Image © Mick McCormack

Lanesboro's
Paddy Farrell is
fond of the birds.
Images © Mick
McCormack

Misty the Mare and I hit it off at Maam Cross Fair.
Image © Hany Marzouk

It was feeding time at Lough Owel Organic pig farm, and I was about to make a silly sausage of myself. Image © Mick Flanagan

The Sunday World's Pub Spy sent me on a special mission – to serve a pint to a bull.
Image © Rory Geary

I did my best to look like a farmer's wife, but like most Irish males, these calves were only interested in filling their bellies.
Image © Pat Moore

I was all set to play milk maid to the cows travelling to Dursey Island – but they were banned from the cable-car. Image © Billy MacGill

St Patrick looked as if he had given up on this sinner before I boarded the ferry for his penitentiary on Lough Derg.
Image © Mick McCormack

The High Priestess of the Temple of Isis, Lady Olivia Robertson, in full ceremonial garb. Image © Patrick Browne

Effin' Eddie put the blue in the Tipperary strip.
Image © Emma Jervis/Press 22

The Mammy of Cork Football, Noelle Sweeney, shows me how
it's done. Image © Clare Keogh/Provision

All those Elvises and just one groupie! I was spoilt for choice in Bundoran.

Image © James Connolly

The dress code for Sunday World journalists was getting ever more lax.
Image © Charles McQuillan/Pacemaker

Cavan's farmers are close to nature.
Image © Lorraine Teevan

For once, I was wearing more clothes than the people posing with me!
Enjoying the harvest with Ireland's Naked Farmer Calendar Boys.
Image © Mary Browne

Spot the imposter at the Redhead Convention!
Image © Billy MacGill

The traders in Cork's English Market had some fishy tales to tell
about their encounter with the Queen.
Image © Billy MacGill

For some, the Royal visit was a load of auld tripe.
Image © Billy MacGill

The power of a picture. After the Sunday World ran this photo, the Queen's itinerary was re-routed to avoid the Ann Summers sex shop.
Image © Billy MacGill

Honouring the US president's visit the wacky way. The Bar-ack Obama chocolate. Image © The Chocolate Garden

Alas poor Yorick – how the hell didst thou end up haunting Hook Head lighthouse?
Images © Mary Browne

mood changed from stoic to playful, and suddenly it was like a holiday camp, with the artist yelling orders over the megaphone and everyone playing Simon Says – only naked.

As the artist got us to display our delicate bodies against the harsh backdrop of the city, I wondered why we Irish had for so long been afraid of showing off. That day, we made up for lost time. While I was taking part, it felt wild, bonkers, racy – and yet when I look back on it, it was just an innocent romp. As I reluctantly put on my clothes, I felt like a child who didn't want to get dressed after a day at the beach. My new friends whipped out cameraphones and we all struck silly poses. Then I caught the eye of an ambulance man who was staring at us in shock. He clearly thought we were stark raving mad – and we were. It was time to leave the Garden of Eden.

But I was to bare all once more within twenty-four hours. As I had run up the strand towards the bundles of clothes, shaking hands with the artist as I passed his cherrypicker, some of his helpers had given me a slip of paper – an invitation to take part in another, smaller photoshoot. It said 'You have been chosen by Spencer' – how could I refuse?

The chosen few met at Dublin's Alto Vetro building the next morning at dawn. They only wanted women or couples, but quite a few men had got wind of it and turned up alone. Tunick wanted the mixed and gay couples to pose together on a bridge, and the men who had arrived alone desperately canvassed us women – once I heard it involved hugging, I said I'd stick with the other group who were going to pose on the balcony. We were divided into mixed groups of men and women, spread throughout the apartments in the building, and told to strip off. We spent about half an hour lounging around the empty apartments, making conversation – in the nip! I had one of those uh-oh moments when a man recognised me; he was a film producer who had taken part, alongside me, in a protest against a development proposed for Dun Laoghaire seafront. 'Last time I saw you, you were wearing a bikini,' he pointed out. As if I needed reminding that I was wearing a lot less! We all made awkward conversation as we waited for Spencer to set up his cherrypicker outside the building. Then a girl with a clipboard told us to go out onto the balconies in small groups. I ended sandwiched in between the film producer and another man. Spencer got us to face the camera, then show our bums. In between poses, we chatted, carefully maintaining eye-contact – at least when we were close-up.

Just as I was about to put my clothes on again, I was given another slip of paper – inviting me to join a ladies-only nude shoot, for women aged twenty-to-thirty. I was chuffed that they thought I was under thirty, so, even though I was tired, I agreed. This time, there was a different atmosphere – the other women all seemed to know each other, and I felt awkward as I lay down among these strangers. I had to move several times as some places had been earmarked for friends. Spencer took a few group shots, then walked among us with his hand-held camera, snapping us individually.

Tunick inadvertently broke the ice when he was moving some planks off the floor. 'I just wanna shift some wood here,' he said – and we all burst into laughter.

As we left, one of his assistants handed me yet another slip of paper, but this time I said 'No thanks', explaining that I was tired and cold. The reality was, the novelty had worn off nudity. Surrounded by people who felt it was normal, I no longer felt naughty.

But I still blushed when I saw the front page of the *Sunday World* – far from being a dot in the middle of the crowd, I was in the forefront, running across the page. A wire agency snapper had captured the image. When the picture editor, Gavin McClelland, had shown me the photo, to check if it was in fact myself, I had initially wondered if it was someone else; my face looked different as I grimaced into the driving wind and rain. But there was no mistaking the freckles, fake tan-marks, matted wet hair – and two friends, whom I had met on the day, running behind me. When the paper came out, they were the first to ring. Later, we found ourselves on the official video of the event. And quite a few papers carried the picture of my bum on the balcony.

It seemed an eternity since I had first convinced myself that baring all was no big deal. Now it was just another event in my increasingly bizarre life. Others who had 'stripped for Spencer' wanted to make it part of their lifestyle. Shortly after the event, they emailed members of the unofficial Spencer Tunick website inviting them to join up and 'enjoy being naked in a non-sexual setting'. I would still have preferred the sexual setting – or at least the artistic one. So I passed on the offer to become an official nudist. There didn't seem to be any point showing off my body without getting something – a picture or romance – in return.

I was flattered when an art photographer who took part asked me to pose for his portfolio – I have yet to take him up on his offer, but for the first time in my life I didn't agonise over his reason for asking me. I didn't care whether it was a chat-up line or a simple request.

Surprisingly silent were the prudes – it was as if Spencer Tunick had lifted the veil off Ireland.

A few weeks after the big strip, I got a handwritten letter from an elderly farmer in County Kerry's remote Magillycuddy Reeks mountain-range, who wanted to bare all. He said he regretted having not signed up, and wanted to know if the artist planned to return to Ireland. I put him in touch with Tunick's Project Director, Jonathan Porcelli, who offered to give him the VIP treatment if he wanted to travel to New York to take part in a future event.

Later I tracked down some men who had turned stripping-for-Spencer into a sort of hobby – flying around the world to take part in the mass nude photoshoots, blending in with the locals in places as diverse as Mexico, Amsterdam, Barcelona, London and Rome. Some of these men had been Tunick Tourists long before the artist visited Ireland – so he could be forgiven for thinking that naked people the world over looked the same.

After the Spencer Tunick strip, Ireland went nuts for nudity. It seemed every town had a bunch of flashers dying for an opportunity to show off their bits. And charities benefited tremendously from the slew of nudie calendars, strip shows and skinny dips.

The death-knell for the Irish prude came in June 2009, when 180 ladies held a Dip in the Nip in Sligo to raise money for the Irish Cancer Society's Breast Aware campaign. It became an annual event and even got the seal of approval from legendary broadcaster Terry Wogan, who did a piece to camera in front of them as part of his documentary on Ireland. Wogan wrapped up well in an overcoat and woolly scarf as the women ran starkers into the sea behind him. Since quite a few had had mastectomies, they didn't want to be filmed full-frontal, and the Irish Army guarded the beach from gawkers while the event was taking place. The following year, men signed up, so the beach was divided into three parts: male, female and mixed. The numbers taking part have more than doubled since the initial event, and there have been copycat events around the country.

Irish men, in particular, shed their traditional shyness as they stripped off to raise funds for all sorts of good causes. While most of these lads proudly sported beer bellies and hairy white legs, it was a hunks-only affair when a bunch of farmers showed off some prime Irish beef in the first ever *Irish Farmer Calendar*. It was in aid of Third World charity Bóthar, and publisher Ciara Ryan said the farmers were happy to pose for 'the price of a good night's drinking'. Indeed she had to turn away a few who were too enthusiastic about stripping off. 'A few weirdos applied to model for the calendar – one guy from Kerry sent me a picture of his bum. I emailed him back asking him for a pic of his face and I realised his bum was his best asset.'

Ciara, who had no background in farming, 'wanted to find out if farmers were as shy as everyone said they were.'

But while they were happy to lose the image of the bashful country lad, one of the lads proved Irish farmers were still big mammy's boys. 'Mr March brought the mammy along to the photoshoot to make sure nothing happened to him. And two of the others brought their girlfriends to watch.'

All five hundred copies of the calendar sold out straight away after it was launched at the National Ploughing Championships in 2009. And while they had cowgirls wanting to ride 'em, some of the other male farmers were jealous! Ciara revealed: 'Some men came up to me and said: "Those are not proper farmers. A real farmer would be getting his hands dirty." But I can assure everyone these are all genuine farmers. And they're 100 percent Irish beef!'

The *Irish Farmer Calendar* has gone from strength to strength since then, and the hunks who posed for it in 2011 were happy to strike a few extra poses for the *Sunday World*, with yours truly as a 'farmerette'.

Meanwhile, Cork was the place to let it all hang out. Shortly after the Spencer Tunick event, eight cyclists took part in the city's first-ever Naked Bike Ride – but the following year fifty-seven took part. In 2012 there were more than one hundred. It was meant to be a protest against car-culture, but some of the people who took part arrived in gas-guzzling jeeps and modified sports cars. They also happened to be members of nudist groups. Clearly the real appeal was baring all in public – though many cheated, wearing body paint.

And I got to bare all again in the name of art in summer 2012 when I wrote about an attempt to break the world record for the biggest gathering of people wearing body paint.

TV3's Paul Byrne had done a report on the world record attempt a few weeks in advance, and contacted my news editor, John Donlon, to suggest sending me along to try it out and write about the experience.

So that's how I found myself standing naked (except for a Dunnes Stores g-string) for six hours as two artists painted red butterflies all over me, then finished it off with an intricate design that looked like a gently flowing blue stream.

Artist Stephanie Power had spent the morning and night before designing my 'costume', and began painting me in the afternoon. Halfway through the session, another artist, Niamh Leonard, arrived to help out. Only then did I see myself in the mirror and was amazed to see a half-human, half-alien creature staring back. They had been painting steadily for three hours, so I thought I was well-covered – but one side of my body was still naked. Still, the artists and I were happy to let photographer Daragh McSweeney capture the work of art in its unfinished stage.

'We love it when people take photos of the work – we want to preserve the image,' Stephanie said. 'But some people don't want to be photographed; they just want the experience of being painted.'

I enjoyed being a blank canvas and the brushstrokes felt like a gentle massage. But, towards the end, it wasn't just the paint that was making me blue, and they had to turn on the heaters.

After six hours, I looked like something out of the Fauvist period in French art, crossed with a bit of Gustav Klimt. I had always wanted a masterpiece to hang on my wall – now all I needed was a mirror.

So I wasn't looking forward to seeing it vanish down the plughole! 'As soon as you take a shower, it'll be gone,' Stephanie said. 'But this is pure art – a moment in time.'

Former US President Bill Clinton was in Cork the same day, and we were tempted to help him paint the town red. 'If Monica Lewinsky's red lipstick drove him wild, imagine the effect of a female body covered in paint!' Niamh laughed.

Anyway, I felt bold enough as I went outside to pose beside a post box and against a graffiti-covered wall for photographer David Hegarty, who was to take the official photos for the world record attempt. My article, with pictures, was spread across two pages of the *Sunday World* a few weeks before the world record attempt.

I was happy to give them a bit of free publicity. I was even happy to pass on their details to the many readers who contacted me to say they wanted to take part, having seen my article.

However, shortly before the event, when I invited them to pose for photos to illustrate another feature I was writing, I discovered that, far from being grateful, the organiser had resented my article because it hadn't mentioned their website or the venue where the event was to take place (they had asked me to keep it a secret to deter voyeurs). She added that I was welcome to take part – but only if I did not report on it.

I immediately put a message up on Facebook telling readers I was not taking part after all, and was promptly bombarded with messages asking why not, and stating that they too would pull out even though they had signed up for the event.

In her email, the organiser had also told me they were banning reporters from the event. But closer to the time, she continued to seek publicity from other media, though most of this appeared in the *Cork Independent*, for which she worked. The *Examiner* quoted her pointing out that she was inviting people 'of all shapes and sizes' to take part, in an attempt to change the media's 'warped' idea of beauty. So I wondered if she blamed the likes of yours truly – i.e. the tabloid press – for the insecurities of everyone who felt they didn't measure up. I made no apology; we save our ugly pictures for the crime pages. And, while we sometimes print pictures of celebrities whose surgically enhanced bodies conform more to the porn industry, the nubile models whose images grace our fashion and beauty pages are in keeping with an ideal of beauty rooted in ancient Greece, Egypt and possibly further back. While mature people can be very attractive on a personal level, no one wants to look at pictures of saggy old folk any more than they want to see decrepit nags racing in the Grand National. Blame Nature, not us, I felt like saying to the right-on brigade.

In the end, the body painters allowed a male journalist from Irish-language channel TG4 to take part, though it didn't make the evening news on any channel.

They claimed to have broken the world record but didn't get the 'nearly 600' who had registered; instead just 317 turned up (a record of 264 had been set in New York five years previously).

However, they provided some amusement for passersby in Cork city that afternoon when they took part in the city's third Naked Bike Ride. It should have been renamed the Painted Bike Ride, as nearly everyone was covered head to toe in body paint – with hairspray over the paint to stop it washing off in the rain. They looked as if they were clad in their usual lycra suits, only with matching balaclavas.

The most surreal moment was when the painted people surrounded the Deputy Lord Mayor of Cork, Jim Corr, on the steps of City Hall and got him to pose for a photo with them. In his smart suit and chain of office, Cllr. Corr looked strangely vulnerable. He had clearly been taken by surprise and his expression was a picture, as we say in Ireland. His unpainted face made him the most naked of all.

It was a different story back in 2003, when the members of Dunmanway Football Club in County Cork scandalised their rural community – after they posed in the nip for a fundraising calendar. 'Their own mammies were ringing up the local radio station to say it was disgraceful!' manager John Buckley laughed. 'But the young women went mad for the calendars!'

John took the picture himself. 'I was just taking a shot of them for a calendar, and I thought I'd liven it up a bit, so I asked them: 'Would ye mind stripping off?' Half of them walked away, a few just took off their shirts – and the boldest lads took off everything. It was a bit of craic.' While they covered their modesty with football boots for the naughty pose, the picture which appeared on the calendar – and in the *Sunday World* – was the Full Monty.

But red-headed Timmy O'Donovan was showing a few hairs too many for the tastes of the *Examiner* – so they airbrushed him. The cover-up only added to demand for the real pic, his manager revealed. Unlike Ronaldo, these lads don't believe in Brazilian waxes or fake tan, left-back Declan 'Vidgie' O'Dwyer pointed out. 'We're not into all that girly stuff. We're real men down here.'

Vidgie and his mates made 'nudes' again nearly ten years later, when the mighty Liverpool sent over a team to play a friendly match against them. They didn't realise they would be taking on Manhood United.

Calling Elvis – to Bundoran

I t's not often a girl gets to meet the greatest rock star of all time. So when I was invited to hang out with Elvis, I was All Shook Up. Never mind that he was supposed to be rockin' on Heaven's door these days. Millions of fans insisted that the King was Alive, well, and appearing in all sorts of places. So I put on my blue suede shoes and headed off to meet my idol in Las . . . Bundoran.

Now, the County Donegal town is not the first place to spring to mind when you think of Elvis. But my Suspicious Mind was put to rest when I discovered that, not only was the King in town – he was all over town. Blokes in sideburns and rhinestone-studded suits were to be seen in every shop, pub and hotel, as hundreds of Elvis impersonators flocked to the town for the annual Elvis Festival in 2008. The festival has since moved to Dundalk, but, for those who attended that first amazing event, Bundoran will always be the Irish Graceland.

They had come to compete in the All Ireland Elvis contest, to keep his memory alive, to raise funds for the festival's charity Down

Syndrome Ireland – and to simply strut their stuff. And, having watched those old Elvis movies where the King is mobbed by admiring girls, I felt immensely privileged to be the ultimate groupie – surrounded by a bevy of Elvises!

Professional Elvis impersonator Craig Parker (from Texas) wanted to make sure I would not be Lonesome Tonight – so he pulled me onto his lap, gave me a kiss and crooned 'Love Me Tender'. Priscilla and Ann Margret, eat your hearts out, I thought as I Got That Lovin' Feelin'. And, with so many Elvises in town, photographer James Connolly and I were spoilt for choice.

As they belted out his hits for three days and nights, they all sounded uncannily like Elvis. Better still, they were a lot younger than the King, who would have been 74 that year – and not looking so hot, unless those rumours of his survival were true.

Anyway, I was so impressed by these guys that I was tempted to ask a visiting clergyman from Wales, the Reverend Steve Caprice, to marry me off to one of them in the Little White Chapel, which had been set up in the town for the weekend. Steve, aka. the Rockin' Reverend, sings Elvis hits to his congregation in a caravan park in Hull, Yorkshire. He married his own sweetheart at an Elvis festival in Porthcawl, Wales – and their ceremony was a re-enactment of the wedding scene in *Blue Hawaii*. And he was happy to play matchmaker for me as he checked out the Irish Elvises, who, he said, were all the better for having the gift of the gab.

But I wanted a Little Less Conversation, a Little More Action. So the following year, I challenged some of the impersonators to a game of golf. Elvis may have the pelvis – but did he have the balls? I wondered, as local photographer Matt Britton 'putt' us through our paces on the soggy course in the grounds of the Great Northern Hotel. If there was one thing worse than stepping on Elvis's Blue Suede Shoes, it was getting his flares wet. They were soon Caught in a Trap – and there was a Whole Lotta Shakin' Goin' On as the sea breeze threatened to whip off their sideburns.

Back on stage, Wexford Elvis Dan Kirwin put the roll in rock 'n' roll as he did a hip-swivelling routine in his wheelchair. And G.I. Elvis, aka Dubliner Martin McCluskey, got everyone's morale rockin' as he sang hits from Elvis's G.I. days. Martin, who had a day job with a Dublin security company, had long been an Elvis fan, but had begun impersonating him only the previous year when he came to Bundoran during the finals of the first ever All Ireland Elvis Contest. 'I was helping push a milk float around Ireland to raise money for Down Syndrome Ireland, when I came into this town and I saw all these Elvises. I wanted to try it myself.' Martin's mum and sister had come along to cheer him on but he gained a lot of new fans too – most of them female.

But it was Heartbreak Hotel for Martin and six other finalists when they were pipped at the post by Dubliner Tom Gilson in the All Ireland Elvis Contest that year (2008). The dad-of-three from Lucan, County Dublin, had been honing his act for a year-and-a-half as he played at weddings and in pubs. 'I'm only working two days a week [as a bookbinder] so I have time to practise my routine in between gigs. The recession has closed one door but opened another,' he said as he celebrated his win.

Tom, a very youthful-looking thirty-nine, said he had first become an Elvis fan when he was a child, watching his films. 'I always admired Elvis because he was this cool guy surrounded by girls. He was a real gentleman too – he was the good guy who always won his fights and got the girl. I wanted to grow up just like him.' Luckily for Tom, he already had the Elvis look. 'I'm afflicted with this hairstyle. I've always had sideburns, my head is shaped like Elvis's and my hair just sticks up naturally. My mother has the exact same shape head. So I was born to be Elvis,' he laughed. And he revealed that his biggest supporters – wife Gillian, kids Megan (then aged ten), Rhys (seven) and Ben (two), his four brothers and three sisters – were all 'Elvis heads!' To them, Tom was Daddy Cool.

He went on to beat rival Elvises from twelve countries, including the US, England, Wales and Australia, when he came third in the finals of the 2009 Elvis World Cup in Wales. He also teamed up with 2008 Bundoran Elvis winner Ciaran Houlihan to form an Elvis double-act, gigging all over the country.

However, for many Irish Elvis fans, the best impersonator yet is Mark Leen, aka. the Emerald Elvis. The Tralee man broke hearts when he announced his plans to retire in 2013 on his forty-second birthday – 'because Elvis died at that age'.

But Ireland's most devoted Elvis fan has to be Kilkenny man Myles Kavanagh, a drag queen who has a life-sized statue of the King in his garden in Kilkenny. The rockin' granddad has even named his Yorkshire terrier Priscilla. His wife Mary, daughter Sharon and grand-kids Tadgh (nine) and Faith (five) have had to get used to sharing the house with Elvis. The statue of Elvis shares the tiny garden with a man-nequin adapted to look like legendary Kilkenny hurler Henry Shefflin, complete with team jersey, hurley stick and ginger wig.

And when he's not dressing up his dogs in Kilkenny jerseys, singing along to Elvis records, posing for local photographer Pat Moore, and giving yours truly tips on where to buy the best nylon tights, Myles is flying over to Wales to take part in drag contests.

I believe Myles was dead serious when he told me: 'My biggest fantasy, to be honest, would be to meet Elvis – while I'm dressed as Priscilla.'

There's No Show like a Joe No-Show

They were Ireland's original groupies. And none was more loyal than Limerick lady Ann Joyce – who held a wake for crooner Joe Dolan in the sitting room of her council house, shortly after he died in 2007. 'All my friends and neighbours came round to pay their respects. We had no buzz in our lives when Joe died – it was like a death in our own family,' she said.

Ann also organised an anniversary Mass in Limerick's St Mary's Cathedral, attended by 150 people, and made a 'pilgrimage' to his home city of Mullingar. She said the only sour note was the fact that the bronze statue of him, which had been erected in the town, was 'not a bit like him – but you couldn't make a statue of Joe anyway, unless it was a moving statue! He was always very lively!'

Ann was one of five thousand fans who flocked to Killarney's Gleneagles Hotel for the Official Joe Dolan Reunion Show, to hear Joe sing 'Make Me an Island' and 'Good-Looking Woman' once more. Nearly two years after his death, the legend was still pulling the ladies

– many with husbands, kids and grandkids in tow. They had come from all over Ireland to the Irish National Entertainment Centre (INEC) theatre for two nights of nostalgia. Photographer Eamonn Keogh and I were hit by a wall of perfume and hairspray as we arrived in the middle of it; these ladies were still blinging it up for Joe. Decked out in scarves bearing his photo, they wept openly as six big screens showed footage of Joe in his youth, while his brother Ben told the story of his life. Behind Ben, an image of Joe in his trademark white suit appeared, that big smile lit up the room and suddenly it was as if Joe had never gone away. After the show, fans hung around the hotel lobby to swap Joe stories. And while it was clear the star had touched the lives of everyone there, Joe's groupies confessed they had been keen to touch Joe too!

Dublin granny Maura Dolan (no relation of Joe's) admitted she was a bit of a Joe 'ho'. 'I was one of the girls who used to throw knickers at him,' she told the *Sunday World*. 'I used to buy them in Penneys to throw at Joe. He used to bless himself every time he'd see me in the front row.' The Rathfarnham woman was just six years old when she met Joe at Dublin airport. Joe posed for a picture with Maura and her older sister's friends. 'He was going off to England to record *Make Me an Island* – but he still found the time to talk to us.' She was fourteen when she finally got to see him on stage – thanks to her sister, Kay Sutton. 'She was supposed to be minding me and my cousin, but she wasn't going to let us cramp her style. She said 'I'm not sitting in minding you two little bitches'. She put make up on us and made us wear bras with tissue stuffed into them so we'd look old enough to get into the Crystal Ballroom [in Dublin]. We looked like two Dolly Partons.'

Maura's crush on Joe continued after she got married. 'My husband has learned to live with Joe. Tough luck if he does mind. It's Joe or no show!' Daughter Rebecca and grandson Dylan (eleven) are also 'mad about Joe,' Maura added.

Marie McGrath from Limerick had first started going to Joe's shows as a teenager in the 1970s. 'We used to go up to his room. We followed him up – he'd always let you in.' But she added that he never took advantage of the star-struck young girls. 'Joe was a real gentleman. He'd just talk to us. We were delighted this big star found the time to talk to us. It made us feel grown up.'

Gwen Whitehouse had the ultimate Joe story – he had serenaded her on her sixteenth birthday. Gwen, a gypsy whose family had settled in Bettystown, County Meath, later struck up a friendship with the star. 'When he was on stage, I'd go over with a glass of water and hand it to him and he'd say '*Sláinte*' [Irish for 'Cheers', literally meaning 'Health!'] on the microphone. 'If you went up to his room he'd sit there, drinking a glass of water, listening to you. Water was all he drank when he was doing a show. He always had time for people. He'd talk to gypsies, people in wheelchairs, children.'

Gwen's boyfriend, John Brady, admitted he had ulterior reasons for following Joe Dolan around the country. 'Myself and a gang of lads went to see Joe at a barn dance in the Knock Cross [near The Naul, North County Dublin] in 1980. We knew there'd be lots of girls there. My sister came along too of course. She was mad into Joe – all the girls were. What I liked about him, as a fella, was his personality. He wasn't stuck up. And he was a good performer.' John had been chuffed when Joe singled him out from the crowd. 'Joe was looking at my silk tie and said: 'I'd say that cost a good bit,' so I just gave it to him and he gave me his scarf.'

Dubliner Iris Mooney (seventy-seven), insisted Joe was 'a real Dub. Although he wasn't from Dublin, he was like our own.' She and her sister had first seen Joe in Raheny on the north side of Dublin, where they grew up. 'We used to save all our pocket money to go and see Joe,' Iris said. 'There was a big gang of us, all girls. Did we fancy him? Course we did!'

One of the youngest fans at the reunion was Mark Doyle (twenty-seven) from Tullamore, who was there with his mum, Catherine Galvin. Mark said he had grown up listening to Joe's music.

Joe was famous for his gentlemanly behaviour towards groupies – but his crew had a tough time protecting him. His former bodyguard, Denis Mee, told me: 'The women would pull the shirt off him and tear the neck off him when they had a few drinks. There was no harm in them but Joe drove them a bit wild.'

However, while thousands of country women had thrown their knickers and bras at Joe, it took a city gal to get into his bed! I couldn't resist a romp in the singer's king-sized scratcher when his friend gave me the real Joe Show. Unlike his other sex-crazed fans, I kept my underwear on.

'Joe's probably spinning in his grave now!' his pal and promoter, James Cafferty, laughed as he let photographer Philip McCaffrey and me loose in Joe's plush penthouse suite at Bundoran's Great Northern Hotel. Room 212 was where the star rested, ate and got dressed in between sell-out gigs. 'He used to leave his costumes here so he wouldn't have to unpack,' James said as he showed me around. And it was quite spooky to find some of his flamboyant spangled suits still hanging in the wardrobe.

They say there's no show like a Joe show, but I was glad it was a no-show this time – because he had been dead nearly a year. Staff at the Great Northern Hotel had left his room intact and some believed it was haunted!

James now stays in the lavish open-plan suite when he's in Bundoran. He was the first person to sleep there since Joe passed away. 'No one else was allowed stay in it when he was alive. It's always going to be known as Joe's Room. But I know he'd like me to have it,' James said.

The Showtours boss even persuaded Joe's brother Ben, nephews Ray and Adrian and other former bandmates to form their band, The Dolans, which has been playing sell-out gigs ever since.

James says putting on the shows helps him cope with the heartbreak of losing his friend. 'I miss Joe an awful lot. I can't believe he's not here. It's a bit strange sleeping in his room. But it's a nice feeling too. I'm hanging on to it for him! Joe used to have all his meals in his room – otherwise he'd never eat! He loved people coming up to him and asking for his autograph. 'But he never acted like a star, even though he had fans all over the world. He was very humble.' In private, the superstar was 'a very shy man', James said.

As his friend and promoter, James got to see a side of Joe no one else did – but even James wasn't allowed talk about Joe's age. 'That was the only thing that would annoy Joe – someone asking his age.' Joe kept everyone guessing right until the end.

CHAPTER SIX:
A Wacky Irish
Welcome for VIPs

It was the week when two of the world's most powerful leaders visited Ireland. And what a wacky welcome we gave them. . . .

A Royal Nosh-up

It was the Royal salute that nearly didn't happen at all. When nervous honchos saw what the traders in Cork's English Market were putting in the Queen's hamper, they were in a right royal tizzy – they insisted on removing local delicacies tripe, pigs' feet and drisheen, aka black pudding – a pungent giant salami made of sheep's blood. The rather rude-looking food was hastily taken off the list of items to be presented to the royal couple on their visit to the historic market. But Cork is not called the Rebel County for nothing. Traders decided their drisheen was fit for the Queen. And while the pigs' trotters didn't get to make their debut, they managed to sneak in some tripe.

The man who had filled the hamper, Rory McCann, struggled to hide his disappointment as he waited for the Queen and Prince Philip to arrive at the market. 'It's traditional Cork food, but Bord Bia [the Irish food authority] got onto us and told us not to include it,' he told me. 'They didn't give any reason. They just said it wasn't a big seller on the international market and they said the main thing to promote was Irish beef. But they let us include buffalo mozzarella, which we've only recently started producing in Cork. They didn't actually tell us to

NOT to put anything in that would offend the Queen. But they said they wanted to give us, in their words, "guidance so as to create a good impression of Cork", and they gave us their own list of products to put in the hamper.'

Rory and Stephanie Moe of Bord Bia were surprised to find that the centrepiece of the hamper did in fact include a packet of drisheen with a bit of tripe on the side, courtesy of butcher A. A. O'Reilly and Sons, who have been in business since 1910 – a year before the Queen's grandfather, George V, visited Ireland.

It's not known if the King tried the traditional food, but Queen Elizabeth didn't bat an eyelid as she came face to face with the crude food, which was tastefully arranged so it wasn't pointing straight at her. Nor did she flinch at the freshly killed pheasants, quail, duck and rabbit hanging out of a pole as she entered the central aisle of the market. Indeed, the Queen is not squeamish and has been known to eat the odd bit of haggis when she's in Balmoral Castle.

Prince Philip hovered over the hamper, and was clearly gazing in wonder at the tripe and drisheen. But he didn't mention them, and the delicacies he picked up to examine were more . . . well, delicate. A carton of mussels caught his eye. Then he spotted the Queen's favourite Irish cheese, Milleen, and studied the packaging while his wife chatted with Lord Mayor Michael O'Connell and his wife Catherine.

Butcher Tom Durcan was chuffed when Prince Philip picked up one of his beef patties. 'He asked me what it was, and I told him: "That's my spiced beef". Then he said: "How do you cook it?" I said "You boil it." He seemed very interested – and hungry! You couldn't buy that kind of advertising. Our market is going to be known all over the world.'

Once it was clear that the Royals had not taken offence at the contents of the hamper, not even the bosses at the food authority could quibble. Stephanie, who represents Bord Bia's Small Businesses section, laughed: 'The rebels got their own way in the end!'

She added that there had been fierce competition among the traders to have their wares presented to the Queen. 'They initially gave us a long list, including lots of fresh meat, but it wouldn't have been manageable, so we got together with City Hall and drew up a much shorter list. We couldn't include anything that might go off on the plane or anything that wasn't familiar to the English market. We included Frank Hederman's mussels because his salmon was served to the Queen on her eightieth birthday. He exports a lot of salmon and eels to the UK.'

Other non-controversial items in the hamper included porter cake, tea-brack, a side of Irish beef, smoked salmon and eels, apple syrup, Wexford honey, Bandon butter, handmade chocolates and Turkish Delight – made using a Cork recipe!

But the hamper never made it to Buckingham Palace. In keeping with Royal protocol, it was donated to the traders' chosen charity – Marymount Hospice, a local nursing home for the terminally ill. Meanwhile, a replica hamper was on sale the following weekend, costing €300-400 depending on whether or not you wanted the drisheen, tripe and trotters. Smaller versions ranged in price from €70 to €140.

However, the Royal seal of approval did not extend to a badge on the hamper, Rory McCann said. 'We wanted to call it "The English Market Queen's Hamper" and put a badge on it, "By Appointment to Her Majesty Queen Elizabeth II", but the Palace said we couldn't. They didn't explain why not.'

Stallholder Paddy McDonnell said the hamper took the shine off his majestic array of fresh fruit 'n' veg. 'The Queen and the Prince didn't come near me. But they smiled over. They were very, very nice. I got a lot of slagging from people when I told them I was going to meet the Queen today, but it was worth it. She's a lovely lady.'

Meanwhile, the Queen's footwear got the nod from Francis O'Connor, whose shoe shop is just outside the market. 'There was a nice little heel and they looked both comfortable and stylish.' He had a pair of shoes just like HRH's in his shop. 'I'm going to call them the Queen's Shoes from now on!' he laughed. But he added: 'I was hoping she'd come into my shop and buy a pair of soft slippers! Her feet must be killing her, walking around all day.'

Of course, she was also the Queen of Bling on her Irish trip, and she was most impressed when Cork's Lord Mayor Michael O'Connell handed her a beautiful brooch.

But butcher Paul Murphy gave the Duke a bit of cheek when the royal couple stopped at his market stall, Coughlan's Meats. 'He remarked that it was odd that we were selling honey with meat, and I said: "Your Highness: red meat and honey – you'll live for ever. My mother is ninety-six – nearly your age!" 'He laughed at that. He can take a joke.'

Eight-year-old John St. Leger wangled a place behind Tom Durcan's counter for the day and got to present the Duke with two books – *The Coast of Cork* and *Serving a City – The Story of Cork's English Market*. And little Julie Anna Higgins presented a posy to the Queen as she arrived.

Trader Peggy Murphy went a bit further – and gave the Queen's security guards a fright! As the Queen and her entourage made her way down the aisle, Peggy, who runs the Roughty Fruitcake stall, stepped out in front of her bearing a home-made cardboard placard, on which she had scribbled the name of the Queen's champion racchorse, Carlton House. 'The Queen laughed her head off! She said: "My horse!" She was lovely. But then her security guards moved in. I did it because my husband is a bookie so we're connected with horses, and the Queen loves horses. Carlton House won the Epsom Derby for her. I thought I'd make her feel at home, greeting her with her favourite horse's name. It was just an idea I had this morning.'

Peggy's daughter Harriet laughed: 'I got a fright when my mother did it – the security guards were quick to react. They just surrounded her! But I'm glad she did it. My father [Michael Murphy] would have loved it. He would have been here today but he's not well.'

Peggy, who is the Market's longest-serving trader, said: 'This was my proudest moment in over fifty years on the stall.' She and Harriett had glammed up for the occasion. Harriet said: 'The Queen is very stylish, so we wanted to look our best. I got this dress for the Galway Races last year, so I thought it would be appropriate meeting the Queen, who loves racing.' Peggy and Harriet loved the Queen's aqua-marine outfit. And some wags joked that the stylish lady was in fact actress Dame Helen Mirren, who had played her very realistically in a movie.

But there really was something fishy going on when the Queen stopped off at Kay O'Connell's stall, where the late fishmonger's sons Paul and Pat O'Connell were brandishing some fearsome-looking hake. 'She smiled. But she didn't pick them up. She had her lovely little gloves on, so I suppose she didn't want to get them dirty,' Paul said. 'She was on, asking about the gurnard and the monkfish – but,

Jesus, I can't remember what she said. She was very interested. She's a sweet lady.' The Duke was fascinated by the John Dory, hake, oysters and salmon, Paul added. 'He said he was very impressed that there was so much variety in Irish seas.'

Paul said he was surprised the Royal couple looked so young for their ages. 'For eighty-five and ninety years of age, they're in fine shape. She wasn't feeble, as you'd expect. And he stands very tall and upright.

'I was delighted when they went out and met the people in the market and on the street – it went better than Dublin in that regard. They didn't need as much security in Cork – we are still the Rebels, but we gave the Queen a right Royal welcome!'

A Raunchy Royal Tour

They call it the Real Capital of Ireland – and in 2011 Cork was the Royal Capital as its residents not only laid down the red carpet for Queen Elizabeth II, but got to meet her in person. The city's historic English Market was one of the highlights of the Queen's visit down south. But of course Cork is also the Rebel City. And the market traders (gently) broke Royal Protocol to give me and photographer Billy macGill our own Royal Tour before the security clampdown. They couldn't resist having a last-minute laugh as they braced themselves for all the pomp and ceremony. And, while the Queen herself couldn't resist a giggle with fishmonger Pat O'Connell, and didn't blink when she came face-to-face with some conger eels, giant sausages and freshly killed rabbits hanging up on a pole, some cheeky Corkonians were really looking forward to the Queen and Prince Philip passing by a shop selling creatures with a lot of life in them – rampant rabbits!

The Ann Summers shop on Prince's Street is located directly opposite one of the entrances to the English Market. And while the naughty shop was not on the Royals' itinerary, it would have been impossible to hide it from their view as she passed – or stop the snappers taking pictures of her in front of it. 'She'll either walk past it on the way in or walk out the door and see it right in front of her,' a local businessman said. 'We won't know until the last minute which way she'll enter and exit, but, either way, there's no way she can avoid passing Ann Summers.'

The saucy shop had a gigantic ad for a push-up bra in its window when I visited it just days before the Royal visit. Even if City Council chiefs had got the firm to cover up their shopfront, there would have been no way to avoid an enormous boob – and it would certainly have excited the curiosity of the foreign media who were combing the city, looking for exclusive stories.

But, as the big day loomed, HRH's minders finally managed to Save the Queen from a royal flush – at the last minute they changed the itinerary. Maybe they had read the *Sunday World* – because we spoiled the sexy surprise a week early. As I posed for a picture in front of the shop, I gave a Royal salute – with two of the sexy toys. The Royal purple rampant rabbit would look rather regal in her boudoir at Buckingham Palace, I suggested in my article. And I was sure she'd be amused by the leprechaun-sized bullet vibrator in a nice Irish shade of green.

Readers who contacted me after the article appeared said it was a shame that the Queen would not get to take home those souvenirs to commemorate her first ever Irish trip. Meanwhile staff at the English-owned shop were keeping a very British stiff upper lip on the subject.

The Royal Wee

Dubliners were just as flush with their céad míle fáilte to the Queen – and none more so than plumber John Lawlor. Thanks to him, Elizabeth II felt right at home when she visited Dublin Castle, where she was given her very own Irish throne. And her Number Two, Prince Philip, also got to enjoy John's, ahem, john. The plumber was flushed with success when his employers, the Office of Public Works, gave him the rather important task of refurbishing the toilets which were to be used by the Royal couple during the State dinner.

And, instead of blinging up an old loo, John took his job so seriously that he built a new one, especially for the Queen. 'I took it apart and built it again from scratch, to make sure everything was right. I put in the pipes and checked it was working properly. The toilets in this place are ancient – you wouldn't want the pipes to back up while the Queen was doing her business!

'It's something to tell the grandchildren about! One hundred years from now, this will be in the history books and maybe someone will remember my name as the plumber who did something practical for the Queen. Even the Queen needs to go to the toilet.'

Meanwhile carpenter Dermot Curran was busy building platforms and stands at the various venues on the Queen's itinerary, including the Irish War Memorial Garden at Islandbridge. 'There were lots of little jobs to do to make sure she was comfortable. She's a tiny little lady, so I had to make sure the steps were small enough for her to climb.'

Just like everyone who got within a mile of the Queen that week, John and Dermot both had to undergo rigorous security checks coming into work. 'They scanned our bags and checked our tools were not weapons! We were vetted by the Gardaí. It was a bit of excitement for the week,' John laughed.

The lads, who were in the room during the banquet, said they were delighted to see that the Queen had brought a bit of Buckingham bling to Ireland. 'It was great to see her wearing the tiara,' Dermot said. 'And her diamond necklace. It was dazzling,' John joked: 'We were looking down on the ground, hoping she'd drop some of it! And yeah, I was half hoping she'd lose her wedding ring down the toilet and I'd have to get it back for her!'

Bar-ack of Chocolate

It was the sweetest tribute to a head of state. While Queen Elizabeth has her face on coins and stamps, Barack Obama was a-head of her – on a bar of chocolate!

An Irish couple, Jim and Mary Healy from Tullow, County Carlow, came up with a novel way to celebrate the US President's visit in 2011, when they produced the 'BAR-ack Obama' at their small chocolate factory in Tullow. The President's face was engraved into the chocolate and his picture was on the wrapper, which was decorated with American and Irish flags.

'Now anyone can take a bite out of the President of the United States,' Mary said, adding that it was the nearest most people would get to the President.

Shortly after he visited the country for just twenty-four hours in May 2011, Mary and Jim sent a batch of the novelty bars to his ancestral village, Moneygall, so the locals could try it out. At €2 each, the chocolate Bar-ack Obamas were a lot cheaper than a trip to the White House.

'We wanted to give it to the President but for security reasons were weren't allowed. It's a shame,' Mary said. But the couple plan to send a batch to the White House. 'They can run them through security, x-rays, whatever, and they'll see that there's nothing in them but very good Irish chocolate.'

CHAPTER SEVEN: Wild Things

Ireland is an unspoilt country – and even Mother Nature behaves like an Irish mammy. She refuses to mollycoddle us, and tends to interfere – even when we treat her with the utmost respect.

Invasion of the Giant Rhubarb

I t had all the ingredients of a slasher flick. Monsters, heroes, a community under siege, gory scenes in which giant mutants are hacked to death with a range of sharp tools. . . . The massacre took place on a windswept island. But this was no movie. The action was real – and so were the monsters. And, like a real horror heroine, I was expected to fight them to the death! Armed with an array of deadly weapons, I joined thirty brave islanders in a war against . . . the Giant Rhubarb. The ten-foot high, ten-foot wide plants, which had taken over Achill Island off Mayo, looked like something you'd expect to find in *Jurassic Park* – or a Hammer House of Horror version of *Jack and the Beanstalk*. And, just like the mutant plants in cult 1980s' TV series *The Day of the Triffids*, the fast-growing plants had been terrorising the inhabitants – breaking through walls, bursting out of tarmac and even imprisoning people in their own homes.

It was clearly a job for the RRR: Rapid Rhubarb Response unit. That was the nickname I gave the intrepid group of volunteers who decided to tackle the terror in the summer of 2010. The crack squad, made up of islanders aged from eleven to over sixty, and a few scientists from the National University of Ireland, Galway, swung into action with axes, saws, chemicals and gardening shears as they waged war on the plants for more than a fortnight in an attempt to exterminate the giant rhubarb – or *Gunnera Tinctoria* as it's officially known.

They were all gunning for *Gunnera* when local photographer Keith Heneghan and I joined them for the start of the battle – it was D-Day for the Devil Plants. Our Field Marshal was local gardener John Sweeney, who, along with wife Noreen, Mayo County Council's Heritage Officer Deirdre Cunningham and plant extermination expert Andy Booth of Conservation Services, were determined to rid Achill of the pests. John had been waging war on the giant rhubarb all his life. 'For years, we were hoping to find some practical use for the plants, but they are just pests,' he explained. 'They kill everything else because they take over all the ground. They spread a canopy over the land and the other plants just wither and die in the dark. You can't farm the land they're on.'

Originally brought to nearby Curraun Island 100 years ago by a landlord called Dickens as an ornamental garden plant, they had spread all over Curraun Island and were rapidly colonising Achill. In their native Chile, the Air Force had been called in to blast them with poison from the air! And, while some desperate diners in Chile had eaten them, John said he wouldn't risk making a rhubarb dumpling out of them. 'They grow so fast, they'd probably burst through your stomach like the creatures in *Aliens*', he joked.

His neighbours, too, had plenty of horror stories about the plants. Breffeney Harris had had to hack her way into her house when she first moved in. 'The house was buried in giant rhubarb. We couldn't even get in the front door – we had to chop our way through to the back.' She had opened an art gallery in the house – but spent much of her time fighting the giant rhubarb which threatened to surround it. 'After I had been away for the winter, I came back to find the stuff had grown back. A house nearby is completely covered in them – they'll never free it. It has been abandoned.' Breffeney's daughters Jessica (eleven) and Laura (sixteen) took part in the 'war' on the plants. Their nineteen-year-old brother, Greg, slept it out the first morning – and his mum joked that he might wake up to find himself imprisoned by rhubarb! 'He'll have to hack his way out,' she said.

Neighbour Mary Lineen McNulty said she was 'living in fear' that the plants would trap her in her house – after they had ripped through the freshly laid tarmac on her driveway. 'I built a new house seven years ago and disturbed the soil – that's what woke them up. I had tarmac put down last December, and the contractor had sprayed the plants in October and November, so I thought they were all dead. But by Easter they were back. The tarmac just bubbled up – it happened over a period of two weeks. There were little hills under the surface, then it popped and the plants burst through.'

Rampaging rhubarb might sound like a tall story, but the islanders had not been exaggerating, I realised when I joined them at the Rhubarb Forest in the grounds of Kildownet Castle. The fortress, which was once the home of pirate queen Granuaile, aka Grace O'Malley, had been under many a siege – but nothing like this. John Sweeney said the pirate queen would have approved of the battle to free her castle from the giant rhubarb. 'She fought off the British in the fifteenth century – now we're repelling an even tougher invader,' he said. But, unlike the British, who now returned as tourists, the giant rhubarb had remained hostile.

Before we got to work, Andy gave us a demo and supplied us with a range of vicious tools – Japanese pruning saws, loppers and bill hooks. Our biggest weapons were bottles of Round Up, a plant-killing chemical – mixed with a fluorescent blue dye so we'd know which plants we had poisoned. Andy told us to lop off the leaves – then squirt the poison into the open cut within twenty seconds so that the plant would have no chance of survival. 'You need to put poison on every single leaf and every single stem,' he said. He warned us not to split the plants or leave unpoisoned shreds of them around because 'It will create another plant'. He also told us to poison the plant's protective mucus, which looked like blue-veined cheese. It was too windy to spray the poison, so we squirted it. It was like a water-pistol fight – only this one was for real.

And the plants were fighting back! As we grasped their stems, they whipped us with spiky branches and swatted us with their leaves – which had spikes underneath and a surface like sandpaper. Their stems swayed under the weight of the three-foot-long knobbly seed-pods. 'Once those little balls turn red, they're ready to pop,' Andy said.

The birds flying in and out of the plants were already spreading the seed. And so did the farm machinery Mayo County Council had initially used to eradicate the plants. This only made them stronger, Deirdre Cunningham said. 'Machines break the plants, seeds get lodged in the wheels and spread. We've been experimenting on them for three years, to find the right herbicide.'

Giant rhubarb is just one of many 'aggressive' plants and animals invading the Irish countryside. Others include giant hogweed, which can cause a deadly allergic reaction, Japanese knotweed, zebra mussels, grey squirrels and big trout. Achill is also plagued by rhododendrons, which hog all the soil, leaving other plants to die. 'But people are reluctant to destroy them because they look nice,' Deirdre said.

Not so pretty was the area around the castle after we had finally cleared it. All that remained that night was a field of decapitated plants – and the eerie blue glow of the poison dye. But Andy warned: 'Just because you've got rid of the *Gunnera* doesn't mean it won't come back next year. The seeds are still viable in the ground.'

And indeed it did return, the following two summers. The locals accepted that they might never rid the island of it, and there was even talk of holding an annual rhubarb-killing festival. 'We might even advertise it as an adventure sport,' John Sweeney said. 'It would attract tourists looking for something a bit different.'

Puckering up to the King of Kerry

Most girls kiss a lot of frogs in the hope of meeting Prince Charming. I went one better and nabbed myself a goat – who turned out to be a King. This was my first time to kiss royalty. Our date took place in front of thousands of the king's subjects – right under his throne. Because this wasn't just any old regent, but King Puck – ruler of his very own fair in the Kingdom of Kerry.

Normally, rugged outdoor types wouldn't stand a chance with yours truly – because they tend to be total animals, but King Puck was a perfect gentleman, so I didn't mind when he gave me a friendly nuzzle. He might have spent all his life in the wilderness until now, but his perfectly groomed beard would beat the Puck off Colin Farrell's goatee. Unlike most wild beasts, he didn't even stink – because his cage had been disinfected.

The crowning of the goat is the highlight of the bizarre festival. The ancient fair has taken place on the same three days, 10-12 August, every summer for more than four hundred years in the town of

Killorglin, County Kerry. Ever since King James I granted the licence for the fair in 1607, it has been a right royal knees-up. It has survived many a recession and even the Great Famine. But some historians claim the fair started as a thank-you to wild goats for unwittingly warning the townsfolk that Cromwell's soldiers were on the way. Frightened by the troops, the goats bolted from the hills and galloped into the town. Another legend has it that the fair began more than a thousand years ago as a pagan festival. Back then, the goat was regarded as a god and a symbol of fertility. The pagans prayed to him for a good harvest. And, nowadays, the harvest comes in the form of forty-to-sixty-thousand visitors from Ireland and abroad. But, while most Irish festivals have become multicultural affairs, with Samba dancers and African drummers calling the tune, there is no sham-roguery about Puck Fair. This is hardcore Irish. Here the bodhrán is king and the foreign visitors are all tourists. The festival includes a horse-fair, carnival, stalls and sing-songs in the pubs.

There was even an imposter one year – and I was there to meet him. Just like this Dubliner, King Puck 2009 was a blow-in from the far side of the land. Unlike previous holders of the title, who had been captured in nearby Macgillicuddy's Reeks, he had been caught near Fair Head, in Northern Ireland, by a posse from another old festival, Lammas Fair in Ballycastle, County Antrim – to mark the thirtieth anniversary of the time the Puck Fair festival sent a goat to Lammas. Killorglin locals told me that King Puck 2009 was a descendant of that very same goat, who was released in the hills near Ballycastle – and who was I to argue? 'When I look at him, I can see the likeness to pictures of the other goat thirty years ago – and he has the look of some of the local goats in Macgillycuddy's Reeks', Puck Fair's chief goat-catcher Frank Joy said.

King Puck of the North even had his very own passport – the first ever issued by the British government for a goat. His date of birth was only a guess but, in keeping with agricultural practice, all animals are officially 'born' on New Year's Day, so his star-sign was definitely Capricorn. The passport also bore his picture and his name – which was given as 'Liam 'Billy' O'Malley'. 'We chose the surname in honour of the pirate queen Grace O'Malley, because he has the air of a pirate about him,' Frank said.

Like any royal dignitary, King Puck had a team of minders, including members of the Irish Society for the Prevention of Cruelty to Animals, who took it in turns to stand guard under his plinth over the three days, while he munched leaves and generally just lounged on his throne of straw. Indeed, the captive king did Puck all; he was quite the pampered monarch. He was entertained by dancers, clowns, stilt-walkers and musicians, including top Irish bands Aslan and Onora, who played a gig on the second night of the fair. After his not-so-busy stint reigning over the festival, Puck relaxed in a shed on Frank's farm before he was brought back north in a trailer – and released where he had been caught.

Puck Fair's first ever Northern goat-catcher, Ballycastle councillor Seamus Blaney, said it had been a tough job catching the King. 'It took fifteen men six weeks to find and then capture him. We found him high up in the hills with a big herd. We knew immediately he was the leader – he was our King Puck. He was the biggest, toughest, oldest goat.' At six years old, His Majesty was fully grown – and very well-endowed. So it was no wonder that he had found it hard to tear himself away from his herd of nanny-goats. After all, he was already king of the hills – and he hadn't yet seen the Kingdom of Kerry.

Seamus confessed that they had resorted to bribery. They built a mound of grass and heather, laced with ivy – which is apparently every King Puck's preferred poison. 'They love the stuff. It's a delicacy for goats.' Having a net thrown over you and being driven in the back of a trailer from one end of the land to another may be a form of kidnapping – but, before his trip, the wild goat spent ten days in a shed on Seamus's farm, where he was treated with kid-gloves. And he seemed to enjoy the break from minding his flock.

But he had no shortage of female company. Luckily for the Queen of Puck, twelve-year-old schoolgirl Cassie O'Grady, and her ladies-in-waiting, they were not sacrificed to him as young girls might have been in pagan times. Still, lady-in-waiting Sophianne Horgan made sure to keep the crowd sweet by singing 'Spancil Hill'. The townsfolk brought up 'offerings' to their regent, including his favourite treat, ivy, and a kind of muesli for goats, supplied by Kerry Co-Op. As if on cue, King Puck nodded and the rain stopped.

But it was clear that he was coming to the end of his reign when a disrespectful man climbed up to have his picture taken with his Highness. After three days of being noble, the King simply turned his back on the crowd and mooned. Giving the order for him to be dethroned, festival chairman Declan Mangan announced to the crowd: 'He's a handsome goat and he has fulfilled all his royal duties.' He then formally declared King Puck free. As we stood around the scaffold looking up at the horned king, it was easy to imagine we were islanders in a scene from yet another remake of 1970s' horror flick *The Wicker Man*. As Queen Cassie removed his crown, and the cage was lowered to the ground, Billy gave a defiant shake of his head. But before he could hoof it, he had to oversee the procession. Looking bemused, he turned to watch the pipe band, floats and people with banners marching past. As he was towed away on a cart, he turned his back on the procession.

Two years later, I joined chief goat-catcher Frank Joy, his son Francis and a posse of mountainy men on the hunt for King Puck 2011. I had been warned that it would be a tough day in the wilderness of Macgillycuddy's Reeks. They would not give up until they had found the perfect Puck. 'If we don't find a billygoat, there'll be no Puck Fair', Frank explained. Not any old goat would do. This was the Rose of Tralee for goats! 'They have to be chosen from among the feral goats of Kerry. They've been roaming Macgillycuddy's Reeks for hundreds of years', Frank said.

By the time I arrived, they had found a likely candidate in the foothills above Killorglin, and were holding him captive in a meadow at the back of Frank's farmhouse. I was bound on oath to keep his location secret until the festival began.

Frank was impressed by his captive: 'This fella has the royal lineage, no doubt – look at the size of him! Look at those massive horns!' But he added: 'We're going to round up a few more goats and pick the best one. This fella is a contender, certainly, but I'm still on the look-out for the perfect King Puck. To wear the crown, and preside over the Fair, a goat would have to show a certain nobility – and this fella seems a bit too wild!' he added, as the feisty creature tried to head-butt him. Still, while the billygoat was acting the yob, he looked quite regal, with a lovely long beard, a magnificent mane and his very own, natural crown – a huge pair of horns.

Of course, it's not every day that a *Sunday World* reporter gets involved in a kidnapping. So, while the men did the rough stuff, I played the role of a racy goatherd. Never mind Heidi or Little Bo Peep looking for sheep – I was on the hunt for a horny old goat, after all! Declan, who doubles up a pantomime dame with the local drama group when he's not too busy organising Puck Fair, was more of a Big Bo Peep as he stood back and let Frank do the hard bit – grabbing the goat! Frank's Springer spaniels were supposed to be helping out, but they clearly knew that they didn't stand a chance. Instead, they practised their herding skills on yours truly! And Frank's wife, Maureen, had a good giggle at the rest of us as we chased after the animal. 'I've had to get used to my husband doing this every year. Puck Fair is part of our lives,' she laughed.

Like all the best kidnappers, we surprised our victim while he was off guard. He was standing up on his hind-legs, eating a hedge, when Frank sneaked up behind him and slipped a horse's head-collar over his neck. All hell broke loose for a few minutes, as Frank wrestled the goat. Hanging on to the horns, he suddenly leapt sideways like a matador as the goat took a run at him. We had to call for a neighbour to help him hold the creature, which Frank reckoned was about four years old – a randy buck in the prime of his life! 'He's a very big goat. Steer clear of his forehead,' he warned us. 'Even if you hit him between the horns with a truck, he wouldn't feel a thing. That's where all his power is.'

The goat calmed down only when I presented him with a meal fit for a king – a bunch of tasty leaves. Being a total gent, he didn't gobble them all up at once, but stopped in between bites to make conversation – or, rather, little groaning noises. Then he suddenly took a shine to me. Maybe it was because I'm a Capricorn – and I was wearing my lucky Zodiac pendant. He let me pet his face, play with his ears and stroke his beard. With his luxurious fur and big, soft eyes, he looked more Disney than dangerous. As the wild beast nuzzled my nose and blew into my nostrils, we thought he looked a bit puckish – in a not-so-regal way. But I reckoned I had just been anointed a Dame of the Realm of Puck. Then I got the royal seal of approval – a kiss! It was not as romantic as it should have been, because there was a right bang off him – and I don't mean his horns. His Majesty was a bit, well, mountainy. He certainly lived up to the name of his birthplace, Macgillycuddy's Reeks. A team of royal attendants would have to clean up this dirty old goat if they were going to put a crown on him, Declan admitted. He was keen to point out: 'This is the only festival in the world where a goat is crowned King – and the people act the goat!'

Of course, the wacky fair attracts more than its fair share of *craic*-pots. Bearded bodhrán player Colin Synon, from Sligo, usually comes dressed as a monk for the occasion. 'I've been coming to Puck for thirty years. The fair is my spiritual home,' he said. Ian Barber from Terenure, Dublin, is another annual visitor – though he prefers to think of himself as a Viking on the rampage, and looks the part in his metal helmet. 'I have two hundred Vikings waiting on the other side of the river to invade the town,' he roared when I approached him. But first he had to shift some Goth ornaments. The creepy skulls and dragons looked perfect for the mantelpiece of the kind of person who likes pillaging and plundering.

Retired local Garda Pat Healy gets his motorbike Pucked up especially for the fair every year. 'It's one of those big tricyles like Billy Connolly's. It had massive lights on it, but I've replaced them all with skulls.'

In Kingston's pub, musician Joe King of trad band The Puckaroos sang a song he had written in honour of King Puck, accompanied by his brothers and their mates on the banjo, bodhrán, accordion and guitar. The band, which performs only at Puck Fair, is made up of Dublin men who have sworn allegiance to King Puck and have been coming to the fair for thirty years. Puckish Joe claimed he and his four brothers were 'the real Kings of Puck Fair!'

Their sisters, Angela Byrne from Rathfarnham and Emily Elders from Beaumont, wandered around the streets paying their own tribute to King Puck with a bodhrán – and a pair of bones. 'They're the bones of my dead husband, Paul,' Emily insisted. 'They were all that was left of him after his cremation.' Angela and Emily recognised me from the *Sunday World* – and made me feel like royalty when they sang a song, which they had composed on the spot, in my honour.

That crowned my perfect day in the court of King Puck.

Sharks and Stingrays

When former Miss World Rosanna Davidson was pictured swimming with stingrays in Bray's Sealife Aquarium at Easter 2012, it brought back memories of my own close encounter with the creatures –and their scary cousins – nearly thirteen years before.

The moment a smooth-talking man offered me drinks by a pool, I knew there was something fishy going on. Seconds later, Kevin Flannery summoned two men in black – who flung me into a tank full of sharks! Moments later, I was to find myself in the middle of an underwater riot involving sharks, stingrays, triggerfish and a shoal of mackerel.

Surrounded by some of the ocean's most feared creatures, I was terrified as I sank to the bottom of the tank at Ocean World in Dingle, County Kerry. As the five sharks bared their huge teeth, I hoped they were just smiling at me and my companions – aquarist T.J. Scanlon and diving instructor Mike Shanahan. The seven-foot-long, 180-pounds monster circled us, and I tried not to wriggle like a baby dolphin or an injured fish; I had watched enough wildlife documentaries to know that, at the first sign of weakness or panic, the sharks might attack! Subduing my fear, I began to enjoy the view – and the thrill of being an intruder in the world of these powerful hunters. Beautiful and beastly in equal measure, they certainly commanded respect. The sharks ruled this underwater realm and, to survive, we had to obey their laws. To them, we were just three more creatures in the tank – or an option on the menu. In their world – the wild world – no one cared whether or not we had health insurance. We couldn't call the police if someone decided to turn us into their version of fish 'n' chips. And we were only alive because they weren't hungry enough – or we weren't tasty enough. Experienced divers had told me that sharks were not adventurous diners, and I was glad to find that these ones were not gourmands. I was sure the wetsuits helped to make us unappetising – biting a diver covered in nine-millimetres-thick neoprene rubber would, I imagined, be like eating a sandwich wrapped in clingfilm.

But they were certainly curious. As we lay flat on the gravel, they swam lower. I saw a huge shadow on the sand beneath, and turned on my back to look up; it was the biggest male sandbar shark, swimming slowly over me. One of the others brushed off my hair – I felt the strands snag slightly on the creature's sandpaper skin. I looked up and saw that it was one of the female sand-tiger sharks. Her mouth was open and the rows of gnarled teeth, curving in all directions, looked as if they could do some serious damage. There were three sand-tigers and two sandbars, which looked marginally less ferocious, but were considered dangerous in Australia, according to Mike's wife, Helena. She had heard plenty of scare stories from the tourists who hired scuba equipment. Yet the creatures did not harm us. 'Food or foe,' they seemed to be thinking as they gazed at us, their black eyes gleaming, at once soulless and full of manic energy – or so I fancied. I had only seen eyes like those once – in a newspaper photo of Charles Manson. At that point, I'd rather have entered his cell – these killers were a lot bigger!

It was one of my scariest assignments ever, as the *Irish Daily Star*'s daredevil reporter in 1999. When news editor Bernard Phelan told me I would soon be swimming with the fishes, I thought he was about to put me on the gangland beat. But these predators would make mincemeat out of even the toughest thug.

The sharks shared their tank with two giant stingrays, a friendly turtle called Spike, a shoal of mackerel and a school of triggerfish, who survived because they were both cunning and inedible. One of the triggerfish bit Mike, and they nibbled my hair. Later, I was amazed to hear that Mike's finger had bled slightly under the water – yet the sharks never bothered him. 'I must have poisonous blood,' he joked. It was proof that these creatures were not as dangerous as their reputation would suggest.

I was warier of the two huge black stingrays. They were like playful puppies – only with poisonous tails! It was all very well playing with them at the water's edge, when the most they could do was chew my fingers. Underwater, they were fearsome fighters, able to take on the sharks – and occasionally win. Kevin had told me that one of the biggest sharks has lost an eye when a stingray attacked him a few months previously – but the eye was growing back! And when I saw them circling frantically on the glass in front of me, as if they were polishing it, I thought another fight was about to break out . The sharks were nowhere to be seen, but I felt their presence.

Keeping an eye on the stingrays, I knelt on the gravel, in between

Mike and T. J. I felt a current dragging me sideways, and grabbed some rocks which, mercifully, were heavy enough to hold me down. But my legs flew up, backwards and sideways. For a horrible moment, I was afraid I'd shoot up to the top of the water – the worst thing a diver can do when there are sharks around. As the water swirled, I imagined I was a crouton in a bowl of soup. I breathed very slowly to calm my nerves.

After what seemed like an eternity, the water calmed too. Mike put a hand on my shoulders, we gave each other the thumbs-up signal, then he gesticulated to me to follow. Staying close to the ground, we made our way to the ladder. The men made me go up first; a gallant decision, and probably not the wisest, since I was the one most likely to panic and block the exit route. Anxious not to churn up the water too much with my fins, which would attract the big fish, at the same time I had to make it snappy – otherwise the sharks would! As I scaled the rungs, using the tips of my fins (there was no time to remove them) I was worried sick that I'd hear a gurgle from below and see blood. . . . Kevin was waiting at the top of the ladder and yanked me out of the water while the other two emerged calmly and swiftly – no bother to them!

Kevin later told us what had happened; he had seen it all from the front of the tank, along with a large crowd of spectators. Four of the sharks had been circling the tank clockwise, as they tended to do – but one of the sandbar sharks had gone anti-clockwise and bumped noses. 'They went apeshit,' he said. The crash triggered off a mass frenzy, and the frightened fish swam fast, in tight circles. A shoal of mackerel which had just been released into the tank went into defensive mode, wheeling and twirling to confuse the predators. Not that it would save them – sooner or later, they would be eaten by their bigger cohabitants.

Kevin told me one of the sharks had recently devoured half a shoal – forty mackerel in one gulp! 'They were lucky this time, but not for long,' he said.

And I felt as if I was tempting fate when I had to get into the tank again, just two days later – because we had no pictures of me with the sharks. Tabloid journalists don't enjoy the automatic respect given to their broadsheet counterparts; every story must be accompanied by photographic evidence. And if I had no pictures, I doubted that the *Star*'s readers would believe that I really had swum with sharks. Our snapper, who was on the other side of the glass, had been jostled by the crowd of spectators and had lost the roll of film (this was in the days before press photographers used digital cameras).

The *Star* had sent me down on a plane the first time, but, second time around, I had to take a train and bus. This might have had something to do with an embarrassing incident – airport police had confiscated my diving knife, which I had forgotten to take out of my dive-bag. In fairness, it looked like something Crocodile Dundee would have carried, and I should have realised that it was in there with the wetsuit and diving-mask.

Anyway, I had plenty of time to work up my courage again on the long rail-and-road journey, and was so psyched-up that I was afraid I wouldn't look scared in the photos! Kevin obliged by showing me some photos of people who had been attacked by sharks – one glance at the picture of a surfer with a chunk out of his torso was enough. I was ready for the fright of my life – again!

Kevin added that he had not fed the sharks since the first time I had been in the tank, because the food would cloud-up the water. So they had been three days without food. . . . 'They'll be nice and lively,' he joked, adding: 'Fish can go a few days without food. They'll be OK' – which was all very well, I said, but what about us?

Mike and T.J. were macho about the whole thing. They said they had lost the fear long ago – because they regularly entered the tank. T.J. usually cleaned the glass and checked the filters, while Mike was the 'cover diver' – watching for signs of trouble. When you provide room service to these creatures, you do not wait for a tip.

Later, I helped them feed the sharks from dry land, with some freshly killed mackerel, mixed with vitamin supplements, attached to a pole. I had another scary moment as one of the powerful creatures grabbed and shook the pole. I released my grip and let him have his takeaway meal!

It had all begun as a hobby for Kevin, a fisheries officer with the Department of the Marine. 'I had been collecting rare fish for years, and giving specimens to the Natural History Museum in Dublin. But seeing them in a jar, dead, is not the same as seeing them alive.' So he built an aquarium with the help of his friend Declan Quigley, and opened it to the public. They had bought the five sharks, for €5,000 each, just five months before my close encounter with them; they had been caught wild off Miami four months previously. They were among the few foreign fish in the aquarium – and they quickly showed the other creatures that they were top of the food chain, Kevin said. 'There was an Irish tope in the same tank – a big enough native shark, about six foot long. It was charcoal grey – but when we put the sharks in, it turned white! It was as if the tope was a local gangster, and now the big boys from the Mafia had arrived! It looked petrified – we had to move it to another tank. Even then, the tope took a few days to recover from the shock and it wouldn't eat for a while.'

Meanwhile the Miami sharks were reeling in the visitors. Of course, not everyone appreciated their finer points – that didn't bother Kevin. 'Sharks are scary – that's why people are fascinated by them. They are malevolent, and no one should ever trust them,' he said, adding that their violent feeding frenzies seemed to suggest that they got excited by the blood of their prey. Savage mating rituals only added to their mystique for Kevin – and me. I was hooked.

CHAPTER EIGHT: Irish Pride

Woe betide anyone who tries to prick the pride of an Irish person.

The Real Craggy Island

It sounded like the plot for an episode of *Father Ted*. But there was nothing fake about the bitter rivalry between the real 'Craggy Island' and a little village on the mainland. Both were holding festivals in honour of the cult comedy series.

But, while one was a tremendous success, attracting thousands of Ted fans from around the world, the other was a rather amateur effort of the kind you'd expect from Ted and Dougal. And, while the hugely successful Tedfest, which has taken place every February since 2007, has always been organised with the kind of attention to detail that would do credit to Bishop Brennan, the fledgling Father Ted Festival in 2011 was closer to an Irish dancing session in Father Noel's caravan.

Asking a national newspaper to supply him with a float so he and his mates could do a Pat Mustard was something only the likes of Ted would have tried. But Father Ted Festival organiser John Morgan claimed to be up to the task of turning the village of Kilfenora, County Clare, into Craggy Island for three days. As he and his mates prepared for their event, Morgan (no relation to the late Dermot, who played Fr. Ted Crilly) insisted: 'This is the ONLY *Father Ted* festival'. He added:'Tedfest is run on an island off the coast of Galway, where there is nothing connected to *Father Ted*. I believe the organiser of Tedfest lives in Wales and holds the festival in Kilronan on the Aran Islands. This is the same as holding The Rose of Tralee in Kilfenora.' He pointed out that not a single scene of *Father Ted* had been filmed on any of the Aran Islands ('only the opening scene from a helicopter passing by'), adding that he had helped the producers select locations and find locals to take part as extras. He even claimed to have a member of the cast on site – the horse that had appeared in Ted and Dougal's video for their Eurovision attempt, 'My Lovely Horse'. 'The horse is still alive and kicking more than fifteen years on.' It was fighting talk indeed.

It wasn't the first time for the festivities to be torn apart by rivalries; back in 2007, the islanders on the largest and smallest of the Aran Isles, Inish Mór and Inis Oirr, each claimed theirs was the 'real Craggy Island'. They settled it with a football match between rival teams dressed as priests – and got football legends John Aldridge and Tony Cascarino to captain them. Cas won, making Inis Oirr the official Craggy Island.

But, this time round, Tedfest organiser Peter Phillips was not willing to play Rugged Island to his rivals, Craggy Island. The former Channel Four producer, who organises Tedfest on Inish Mór and Inish Oirr every February and March, as well as an Australian version and various spin-off events, said: 'I'm aware of it [the Father Ted Festival]. It's nothing to do with Tedfest but we wish them the best of luck'. Peter later branded the rival festival 'Naff Fest'.

But of course the naffness is all part of the craic at both festivals. Still, Father Ted Festival appeals more to the anoraks who want to see the exact spot where Ted kicked Bishop Brennan up the arse, and have tea at the actual Craggy Island parochial house.

The 'Ted House', as it's known locally, has become a holy shrine for fans of *Father Ted*. And in March 2012, its owners finally reaped the benefits when they threw open the doors to paying guests. I was happy to hear that they were inundated with bookings from hen parties.

I even forgave them for their sinful treatment of me when I had knocked on their door back in 2007. I had been commissioned to write a piece for the *Sunday Express*, and the woman of the house, Cheryl McCormack, had seemed friendly enough on the phone – at the very least, I expected 'a nice cup of tea' and a plateful of sandwiches. Instead, I got the kind of céad míle fáilte that would not be out of place in Sister Assumpta's convent during Lent.

My pilgrimage had taken four hours from Dublin to the remote location, eighteen miles from the tiny hamlet of Kilfenora. Locals directed me to the house. As I drove for miles up a grassy, mucky, bumpy boreen, I thought I was lost. But suddenly it appeared – it was unmistakeably the Ted House. It glowered down from a bare, bleak hill. The short, overgrown drive wound up to the front door just for the hell of it. A pack of dogs roamed the muddy field. Curious hens stopped rooting to look at the stranger. The white paint on the wooden door was peeling and the knocker looked as if it was about to fall off.

I spent more than fifteen minutes in the rain, until Cheryl finally opened the door – just a crack – and peered out. The smell of dampness hit my nostrils. I half-expected Father Jack to throw a brick out. She barked: 'Did you not get my message? I'm not interested!' It turned out that she had texted me to call off our chat, about six minutes before – around the same time I was trying to open her rusty gate at the end of the long drive, in full view of the house. . . .

There was no point trying to persuade her – 'Ah go on, go on, go ON!' was no use against a door slammed shut. Such was her hostility, and the baying of the dogs, I decided to get the hell outta there. But my car got stuck in the mucky gravel in front of the house. No one came out to help me dig it out, and it was another fifteen minutes before I finally finished my penance at the Ted House.

Meanwhile, Tedfest continued its reign as the world's biggest gathering of 'Tedheads'. Thousands of revellers from all parts of the world turn up every year dressed as Ted, Jack, Dougal, Mrs Doyle and others from the series. Every year, 250 fans fill the guesthouses of Inis Mór to bursting point, others camp on the land and still more celebrate on the mainland – all the hotels for up to twenty miles around are booked out a year in advance.

The wacky fun on the island includes a Lovely Girls contest, speed-dating with Pat Mustard the Milkman, an All Priests' soccer match, Riverdancing in Father Noel's caravan, a tea-making contest, a Lovely Girls contest judged by Dermot Morgan's son Rob – and penance doled out by Sister Assumpta! For those who can't get accommodation on the island, the organisers also lay on a few events in Galway city pubs, including the Toilet Duck Award for stand-up comedy. The experience is like taking part in the closing sequence of the *Benny Hill Show*, a *Carry On* film and the wackiest ever St Patrick's Day parade – all at once.

The sixth Tedfest, in 2012, happened during Lent and the Recession. There was also a funeral on the island, as I later found out. But the misery was banished in favour of madness as I arrived on Inis Mór to find moustachioed milkmen chasing buxom, aproned housewives down the street, dishevelled old women sprinting behind them waving teapots, a few nuns tripping over their habits as they tried to catch up...and priests – lots of them. Gangs of dog-collared men roamed the countryside shouting 'Arse!', 'Feck!', 'Drink!', and 'Girls!' There were even a few bishops in full ceremonial garb, brandishing their mitres.

I wasn't ready to take a vow of poverty just yet, so I arrived in style – on the Airway to Heaven, Aer Arann. The six-minute flight was like the opening sequence of *Father Ted* as I got a bird's-eye view of the real Craggy Island. Pilot Denis Collins was kept busy from dawn to dusk bringing revellers over in his nine-seater plane. With 250 Tedheads on the island, every B&B was full.

And it was like *Carry On Clergy* as Inis Mór turned into a den of iniquity. The festival theme that year was 'Clerical Lingerie', with adult party games and a Pyjama Party keeping the Tedheads hot under the collar. And, when they spotted me in my naughty nun costume, I was nearly defrocked!

Given that it was Lent, this sinner was ready to do penance. But when stern Sister Assumpta and her saintly sisters spotted me cavorting with the clerics, they took a no-nonsense approach – and joined in the craic! And there was no shortage of dishy Bishops and Holy hunks to lead us into temptation.

Most of the diehard fans come from England, Scotland, Wales and Ireland itself. And it seems that Tedfest has done what centuries of diplomacy have failed to do in Northern Ireland, because there's always a large contingent of Northern Protestants who are happy to 'go Catholic' for the craic – people such as Norman Coates and Peter Miller, from Holywood, County Down, who gleefully described themselves as 'Protestants being naughty'. Peter even sings in the church choir back in his Anglican parish. But he and Norman turn Catholic every year for Tedfest. They have formed their own rock 'n' soul band, the Christian Brothers, especially for Tedfest. Both men are real Fathers – Norman a dad of three and Peter the father of two girls. Peter's eldest daughter was on the organising committee for Tedfest a few years back, and it was she who converted her dad to the joys of running amok in a dog-collar.

Other Nordies who made the pilgrimage in 2012 included Martin Lynch and his mates – who got some funny looks on their 'pilgrimage' as they cycled from Omagh dressed as priests and cardinals.

But brother-and-sister Louise and Isaac O'Neill from County Antrim went a bit further to celebrate their first trip to Craggy Island – they got matching tattoos! Belfast tattoo studio Skinworks had etched the huge cartoons of the Holy Stone into Louise's thigh and the side of Isaac's torso – and they were happy to show them to photographer Hany Marzouk, who snapped them for the *Sunday World*. IT-worker Louise came dressed as a lady priest, while salesman Isaac got to be her real 'Christian brother'. Louise explained: 'We're Tedfest virgins – so we have to prove ourselves worthy.'

Dermot Morgan's son Rob was there in the name of the father – dressed as a sister! And he was in good company – there were lots of bearded nuns! But local granny Mary T. Burke (originally from Belfast) pointed out that she was the first cross-dressing cleric on Craggy Island. 'Before Tedfest, when Dermot Morgan was still alive, we put on our own amateur dramatic play based on *Father Ted* – and I was Father Jack. I borrowed a dog-collar from the parish priest, Fr. Ciaran Blake.'

Louise Kiernan made her debut at the first ever Tedfest in her wedding dress, with her fiancé in his morning suit. 'We got married – but it didn't last,' she sighed, putting it down to the 'Curse of Tedfest – you arrive as a couple and you leave single'. She went as a nun every year from then on – and once won the Lovely Girls contest.

Friends Gary 'Dougal' Quinn and Karen 'Sister Assumpta' McCulloch, both from Glasgow, brought temptation to Tedfest when they arrived with chocolate Easter eggs. Karen said she wasn't giving up anything for Lent. 'I did Anti-Lent – I detoxed from Hogmanay until today, but I'm back on the drink now for Tedfest. I'm on the holy water – with vodka!'

And there was no shortage of like-minded revellers in local pub Tí Joe Watty's once it had been renamed The Parochial House.

Engineering students David 'Dougal' Foy, Paddy 'Father Damo' Moynihan and Johnny 'Ted' Campion, all from Loughmore, County Tipperary, confessed they were on the prowl for some Lovely Girls – and had started their very own drinking society in honour of Father Jack at NUI Galway.

Of course, there is always plenty of drink, feck, arse, girls – and a big queue to give Bishop Brennan a kick up the arse! And my Cardinal Red stilettos were Tedly weapons as I gave him a bit of Bish-bash! In my black PVC nun's habit, I soon drew a congregation of not-so-devout followers – including an American man who followed me around, snapping pics of my bum.

Organiser Peter Philips said: 'The funniest thing about Tedfest is seeing the reaction of tourists who don't know what's going on. One year an American couple were walking to their B&B when they suddenly came across all these priests and nuns walking down the road.

Then a bunch of guys on segways passed them on the road – dressed as Nazis, in honour of the episode where Ted is mistaken for a racist.'

A funeral took place on the island during Tedfest 2012, so we had to avoid one of the pubs as the cortege passed. Peter was anxious not to repeat the previous year's gaffe. 'We were on the other island, Inish Oirr, and there was a funeral on – but the Tedheads thought it was a spoof funeral! They were all following the coffin, shouting 'Drink, feck, arse, girls'. We had hired a plane to fly low over the island, and the pilot buzzed the funeral as the coffin was being lowered into the grave – everyone started shouting 'Mind yourself!' and 'Go on, go on, go on!' It's just as well we don't hold it on Inis Oirr any more – there's probably a fatwa on us!'

But Tedfest has spread far beyond Craggy Island. There was an Australian version, which erupted in controversy one year, after they discovered they had no drink licence – not that that bothered the hardcore Ted fans, who simply headed to the nearest pub. And Peter organised a special Tedfest Tour for the Irish soccer fans travelling to Poland in the summer of 2012. He described it as 'an invasion of Poland – like Hitler in reverse.'

Ravin' Redheads

They are born here, bred here and RED here – just like my employers, the red-top *Sunday World*. But Ireland's red-heads were in a flaming rage in 2011 with the news that a top sperm bank had banned gingers! They saw red when Mr Ole Sehou, the boss of Cyros International, which supplies sperm to women in sixty-five countries, gave the red light to gingers. He said carrot-topped donors who dared turnip didn't stand a flaming chance alongside dark-haired Latin lovers. While semen donated by red-headed men's 'sold like hot cakes' in Ireland, he said that Italian, Spanish and Greek women wanted sperm only from men who looked like their own – dark-haired and dark-eyed.

Of course, it's easier for an Irish couple to pass off a red-headed baby as their own, because ten percent of our population is ginger. We are second only to Scotland, where one in eight babies is born with a tinge of the ginge.

Meanwhile the host of American TV dating show *Millionaire Matchmaker*, Patti Stanger, said: 'I can't get my millionaires to date a redhead. The only men who like redheads are Irish.'

No wonder anthropologists predicted in 2011 that the ginger gene would die out in a hundred years.

But the organisers of Ireland's annual Red Head Convention, carrot-topped brother-and-sister Joleen and Denis Cronin are on a mission to 'save the redheaded race before it's too late' – by encouraging redheads to mate! One of the most popular events at the festival in the village of Crosshaven, County Cork, is a 'red-hot dinner-date night' for single redheads. Lonely gingers, who might have been more familiar with the cooking of Ronald McDonald, get all hot under the collar when Denis, a qualified chef, cooks them a spicy meal using only red ingredients such as chillies – which are said to be aphrodisiacs!

Denis was a bit red-faced himself in when his sister revealed he was dating a brunette. 'I'm disappointed in him,' she joked, adding: 'There's nothing wrong with having red hair – I'm proud to be a redhead!' The single girl said she'd happily date a red-head and would love to be a blushing bride some day. 'But I might have to go to the sperm bank now!'

Growing up ginger, Joleen had been teased by her schoolmates. 'I got a lot of slagging because I had a very tight haircut like Annie in the musical – my friends used to call me 'microphone head'. But I got loads of compliments about my hair too – especially when we went abroad. I've never dyed it.'

The Cronins inherited their Titian tresses from their Dutch mum, Thecla, but their dad, local publican Seán, was dark before he went grey – and, during the festival, he has to wear a red wig to get into his own bar!

I too had to go ginger to get in when the *Sunday World* sent me to report on the event in 2011. Having a red-headed granny wasn't enough, the organisers told me – I had inherited the freckles, but not the hair. But my red wig did the trick – they even gave me a Certificate of Foxiness!

Joleen came up with the idea in 2010, as a fun-raising fundraiser for the Irish Cancer Society – and a birthday party for Denis. 'I suggested inviting every redhead in the country so he'd have plenty of company. We were amazed when 350 redheads turned up.'

The following year they reckoned that they had doubled the (red) head-count. The streets were a sea of orange as Titians from all over Ireland, north and south, and as far away as Germany, blazed a trail to the tiny coastal village, to take part in a range of activites including carrot-throwing contests, lawn-bowling with oranges instead of balls and red balloon races. There were prizes for the best red eyebrows or beard, longest red hair, most freckles per square inch, and, for baldies who insisted they were once red, the Best Ex-Redhead. Cafés served up strawberry cupcakes, the chippers give discounts on portions of fish 'n' chips and the local amusement park, nicknamed The Merries, was merrier than ever as the redheads frolicked on the carnival rides for an 'blushingly low price'. Revellers sipped Red Bull, Bloody Marys – and a special tipple, Sunburnt, which was invented especially for the occasion by the Eight Degrees Irish Beer Company in Mitchelstown. Cork band The Red Herrings played some 'red-hot hit' at the harbour. Every genuine redhead who attended also got a can of Cork's red Tanora lemonade and a gingerbread man made by Mags Curtin – a mother of three redheads who is herself blonde.

And, this being the 'Red-bellion', there were Reds Under the Bed – or at least in it. 'The B&Bs for miles around are busy and we've had loads of enquiries since we put it on the web,' Joleen said.

But not everyone answered the call. Taoiseach Enda Kenny politely declined, citing other engagements. 'He's more of a strawberry blonde anyway,' Joleen said.

She hopes to eventually lure some red-headed celebs, including retired RTÉ puppet Bosco who has probably gone grey since his heyday as a star of Irish children's TV in the 1980s, *Riverdance's* Jean Butler, TV presenters Hector Ó hEochagain and Bláthnaid Ní Cofaigh, singers Linda Martin and Red Hurley, Munster rugby star Paul O'Connell, economist David McWilliams – and movie legend Maureen O'Hara. But there'll be red faces for sure if they are joined by another fiery Cork celeb – Channel Four's *Embarrassing Bodies* host, Dr Pixie McKenna.

Meanwhile, 'gingermen' enjoyed a sudden surge in sex-appeal shortly after the Royal Wedding, when Prince Harry was voted 'the most desirable picnic date for Irish women'. Never mind the sperm-bank – hot Harry was living proof that redheads are best enjoyed in their natural form.

Keeping it Culchie

As a tabloid reporter, I'm always up for a bit of muckraking. So I was ready to get down and dirty when I heard about a place famous for its self-professed 'muckers'. Kiltimagh in County Mayo had just earned a place in the 2011 Oxford English Dictionary as the source of the word 'culchie' – which it defined as 'an unsophisticated country person', adding that the term originated in the 1950s to describe people from 'Kiltimagh, a country town in County Mayo'. While the common word, which is said to have been coined in the 1940s, had appeared in Bernard Share's *Slanguage – A Dictionary of Irish Slang* – in 1997, and had been in the Oxford dictionary for at least a decade, this was the first time the prestigious lexicon had named the town as the source. And while it used to be an insult hurled at country folk in general, the one thousand residents of Kiltimagh were now proud to call themselves 'culchies'.

Local music mogul Louis Walsh could rock 'n' roll all he liked over in London – back home in Kiltimagh his old neighbours were keeping it country, and the music blaring out of the cars was more likely to come from country 'n' western crooners Daniel O'Donnell or Patrick

Feeney. And even though a local lady, Mary Davis, was at that moment vying to become Ireland's first citizen and take up residence in the Presidential mansion, Arás an Uachtaráin, her old neighbours said they would rather go around with the Arás out of their trousers than follow her to Dublin. Never mind the bright lights of Castlebar just up the road, or the buzz around nearby Ireland West International Airport, and the crowds of pilgrims at Knock Shrine; for the people of Kiltimagh, the real centre of the universe was 'the arsehole of the country', as some natives put it.

The name Kiltimagh comes from the Irish *Coillte Maith* – good woodlands. But the town's Culture Maith comes from its sculpture park, museum, exhibition centre and its most famous sons: the blind poet Raifteiraí, boxer Gene Tunney, athlete Seán Lavan and Apollo space-shuttle engineer Mike Hogarty. But the locals were just as happy to keep it their own little secret.

Barber John Regan described a culchie as 'a gentleman like myself. We're always friendly towards visitors and each other. We make people feel welcome. And we have a sense of humour.' The dapper bachelor said that the hallmark of a culchie was 'loyalty to your own people'. He described himself as an ardent supporter of the Mayo footballers, local woman Mary Davis, who was at the time running for president, and Taoiseach Enda Kenny 'because he's a real culchie, even though he's from up the road [in Islandeady, near Castlebar].

'And I'm a traditional culchie when it comes to food – I'm a bacon-and-cabbage, spuds kind of man. I like my beef, onions and broccoli.' Surely he meant cauliflower, I suggested. But the dapper bachelor pointed out that he was a 'cool, cosmopolitan culchie', who frequently left Kiltimagh to run marathons in cities around the world.

His country cottage on the edge of town looked like something out of *The Quiet Man*, but he had converted his front room into a swish barbershop. He had got the city slicker out of his system in London during the Swingin' Sixties, while he was learning his trade from celebrity crimper Vidal Sassoon, but it was clear that he still had fond memories of his days in the big smoke – the walls were festooned with pictures of John hobnobbing with football legends, including Georgie Best, Man. United Manager Tommy Doherty and Tottenham Hotspur and, later, Arsenal goalie Pat Jennings, as well as glamorous actress Nina Baden Semper.

But his hard-earned sophistication was not the reason John had just turned down an invitation to compete in a contest to find Ireland's most genuine culchie. 'A true culchie doesn't have to prove it,' he said, adding: 'A culchie would never show off.'

Another local, Noreen Dyra, was more qualified than most to comment on Kiltimagh's entry in the dictionary – she had two houses in Oxford! 'And I have a load of Oxford English Dictionaries. I'm delighted they've given Kiltimagh a mention – so we're officially muck-savages!' she laughed as she tucked into a hearty carvery lunch in the Cill Aodhan Hotel. The mum-of-four had moved home to Mayo to send her kids to school in Kiltimagh, and described herself as 'a culchie at heart.'

Neighbour Jimmy Fleming was catching up on the gossip in the hotel's lounge – where, he said, 'swanky culchies would hang out during the day'. The place was full of solicitors and accountants in smart suits. 'You'll find the same people in the pub at night,' Jimmy said. 'We love a bit of chit-chat. That's what we do for entertainment in country towns. We're very nosey.' Married to a Kiltimagh woman and working as a carer for local elderly people, Jimmy rarely left the town. But he was looking a bit too suave to be a peasant. And he revealed that he might just be related to 007 creator Ian Fleming. However, he insisted: 'I'm a genuine culchie.'

Judging by the rails of posh frocks and suits waiting to be dry-cleaned at the local launderette, this was clearly a fashionable town. The sign above the door said Kiltimagh Launderette, but it used to be called the Culchie Launderette until owner Evelyn Martin renamed it, part-time assistant and 'culchie chick' Cassandra McNicholas said. 'But everyone knows it by its old name,' she added. 'We're proud to be culchies!'

The people of Kiltimach were not the only ones to lay claim to the title culchies, as I had found out two years before, when I attended the Culchie of the Year contest. The annual knees-up, which takes place in a different country town every year, is a bit like Miss World – only the contestants are smelly, scruffy, hairy men!

Dubliners – even from the rural parts of the capital county – are barred from entering the contest. Ironically, festival founder Paddy Rock was originally a Dub, but had moved to 'the country' – Galway city! He admitted his neighbours in the cosmopolitan city were a bit put out to hear themselves described as 'culchies'.

As a wannabe country girl, with a mother from Wexford (town), I wanted to enter the contest myself – but women were forbidden, Paddy said. 'We will drop the ban when the Irish Countrywomen's Association lets men join,' he promised.

But I got a warm country welcome in the pungent form of an

invitation to the highlight of the 2009 event, the Bacon and Cabbage Ball. Until then, the little town of Ballyjamesduff, County Cavan, had been best-known as the homeplace of songwriter Percy French. Now, instead of singing French's 'Are you right there, Michael?' ten thousand visitors were greeting each other with 'Howya, horse?' and 'Up ya boyya!' Indeed, anyone visiting the place could be forgiven for thinking they had wandered into the auditions for a remake of 'Eighties scarecrow show *Worzel Gummidge* crossed with a zombie flick. The place was full of dishevelled blokes in straw hats, tweed jackets belted with pieces of string and, of course, wellies, all staggering around and slapping car roofs.

Of course, I was expecting a bunch of sweet, innocent country lads. But, while they may lead the Good Life, some of these boyos were a bit, well, mucky. Faced with a city slicker, all they could think about was Sex in the . . . Country. Some of these lads had clearly taken flirting lessons from rustic rogue Richie Kavanagh or from his British counterpart, comedian Roy Chubby Brown.

One of the organisers, Tipperary man Brendan Morrissey, explained: 'the culchie is the guy sitting at the back of the class with a woolly *caipín* on him, who is not afraid of being laughed at.' He said the criteria for being a culchie had less to do with where you lived than the way you lived. But there were some strict rules, including a ban on pyjamas (culchies apparently prefer to sleep in longjohns if it's cold, or the nip if it's hot), being either a heavy drinker or a Pioneer (Culchies don't do things by halves), smoking a clay pipe rather than fags, and wearing your best suit for Sunday Mass.

Potatoheads

We Irish love our spuds. And, for us, a single potato is more romantic than a dozen roses on St. Valentine's Day – especially when it comes out of the ground shaped like a love-heart! When my mother found one such spud in a sack of Dunnes Stores potatoes on Valentine's Day, she said it was her lucky charm. And it was – because she was pictured in the *Irish Sun* the next day, holding the unusual vegetable. It summed up traditional Irish romance – because she spent that evening cooking bacon and cabbage for my dad.

And there's apparently no limit to the things Irish people do with the humble spud, as I found out when the *Irish Mirror* sent me down to the swanky K Club in 2007, to try out the latest fad in their spa – the potato facial! Now, I'll admit I'm fond of mashed potatoes – but not when they're mashed into my eyes!

K Club Spa manager Mona Carberry assured me it would work wonders for my skin, I hoped she didn't mean I'd end up looking like Golden Wonder crisps – in fact, I didn't want potato-skin at all! And when Mona said the potatoes would also be good for my eyelids, I fretted that I might end up with the kind of eyes you'd find on a Kerr Pink or Rooster. But Mona reassured me that it would all be just like the crisps – Hunky Dory.

At €75 for a session with the spuds, this was taking our national obsession a bit far, I thought. But, as I was to find out, it was worth every cent. The potatoes were first peeled, then grated, and applied raw in a gauze poultice to my closed eyelids. It felt cold, clammy and heavy on my eyes – and I hadn't realised until then just how pungent raw potatoes were. They smelt like the soil they had come out of which gave me a feeling of being buried alive. As the cold potato-juice seeped into my eyes, nourishing them, I had a sudden urge to get some properly cooked spuds – in the chipper. With photographer Barbara Lindberg pointing her lens at my freshly scrubbed face, it was anything but relaxing.

But Mona said they would drain away toxins from my skin –and I must have been quite toxic, because I was there for more than an hour.

After my bizarre treatment, which also included a Swedish massage and pedicure, I felt like one hot potato.

CHAPTER NINE:
Dodgy Dating

Those who say the Irish are sexually repressed are in for a rude
awakening if they ever come here.

Love, Lust and Laughs at Lisdoonvarna

When singer Sinead O'Connor turned up at the Lisdoonvarna Matchmaking Festival in 2011, she changed its image forever. Another singer, Christy Moore, had put the quirky annual event on the map many years previously with a witty ballad. But Nothing Compared to 2012, when Sinead and her entourage descended on the tiny village in the wilds of County Clare.

And when the singer agreed to hook up with yours truly on a manhunt, she got more Man-dinka than she had bargained for. 'I know I said I wanted hairy men, but not like this, eeuwww, no-no-NO!' she laughed as I introduced her to 'Elvis', aka Kevin McCormack. Kevin's sideburns had poor Sinead All Shook Up. 'Where did you find him?' she shrieked. I had picked him up on the street. Well, it was hard to avoid picking up an Elvis impersonator at Lisdoonvarna – the place is a magnet for them, and indeed impersonators of all kinds.

But the busker from Cavan was not the pushy kind. He had been coming to Lisdoonvarna for two years, but said he'd never find true love there – because he was still pining after his first love from fifty years ago. 'I was going out with a girl for a year-and-a-half when I was twenty-three and she was twenty-one. We broke up, she came back to me three times, then she married someone else. She's my soulmate. Once you have your soulmate, you'll never be free. I've had a lifetime of girlfriends but she's the only one for me.'

Next up for Sinead was another Cavan man, Mick McManus from Glangevlin. But he turned out to be a bit of a love-rat. 'My girlfriend is at home. She's working, so I came here with a few friends,' he admitted.

Sinead then tried to fix me up – with her male nannies, Luke Barber and Jamie Wilson. 'Have you got a boyfriend? They're sick of sixteen-year-olds coming up to them in all the bars.' Luke and Jamie were taking a break from minding Sinead's kids to look for their own bit of Irish romance. The 'mannies' and Sinead admitted it was a culture shock. Sinead explained: 'They're from England, and this is the first time they've been outside Dublin. It's like *Father Ted* crossed with *Ryan's Daughter* for them.' But unlike Sinead, who has a *grá* for the older man, these lads were grossed out by Lisdoonvarna's grab-a-granny culture. 'They're horrified looking at all the grannies on the dancefloor,' she said as the lads hid in the snug of the Matchmaker Bar, where the real business of Lisdoonvarna was in full swing.

Sinead didn't find a man – but she did find a willie! Matchmaker Willie Daly's phone had been ringing all day, every few seconds, as he waited for Sinead to arrive. I couldn't help eavesdropping as Willie told one man: 'I'll give you an introduction but it's hard to say what she's after – she'll know her man when she sees him. She's still got a good figure – she has fairly decent breasts. . . .' Hanging up, he turned to me. 'That was a man of seventy-four. She should never have said she was after an older man. I have every auld fella from here to Donegal coming to Lisdoonvarna.' He added: 'There's twenty-nine-and-a-half men to every woman west of the Shannon.' I warned him that the feisty singer would raise hell if he tried to fob her off with half a man.

Willie and festival organiser Marcus White arranged for Sinead to be squired around town by a real auld cowboy – Tennessee man Mark Flanagan. The twice-divorced, fifty-something Tom Jones lookalike from Memphis, Tennessee, who has been a regular at the festival since 1983, spent a week growing his chest-rug, beard and mop of curls as he got ready to be Sinead's dream date.

And Mark was not the only one, Willie revealed. 'The local shopkeepers told me they haven't sold a razor since Sinead went on *The Late Late Show* to announce that she was coming here in search of a man. There's a right bunch of dirty auld fuckers at Lisdoonvarna this year!'

Bachelor T. J. Nagle hoped Sinead would lose the hair. 'I think the bald head suited her,' he said, though he confessed he also had a thing for blondes. And he admitted he'd love a threesome with Sinead and yours truly! He added that he was a good catch: 'I've a big house with seven rooms near the Cliffs of Moher – and I'm a real bachelor. I used to be a big farmer, now I'm a cattle-dealer. And I've plenty of time on my hands for the right woman.'

However, years before Sinead declared that the festival was the perfect place to find 'a hairy man', it was clear that Lisdoonvarna's quaint, twee atmosphere had been booted out of bed for a much raunchier – and more realistic – image. Because the people who go there every year are bonkers – in more ways than one. They come looking for love, lust – or a quick grope.

The annual event was set up more than 150 years ago, to arrange marriages in rural communities, and has always attracted large contingent of Americans looking for love while they search for their roots. So, when the *Irish Mirror* sent me to report on the festival in 2006, I expected to find a cross between the Rose of Tralee and *The Quiet Man*. But there was nothing quiet about the men I met at Lisdoonvarna that year, and every year since.

Orgies, illicit affairs and quickies are all part of the fun and frolics at Lisdoonvarna these days – and always were, according to veterans such as Mark Flanagan. He was twenty-seven when he first made the trip from Memphis, Tennessee. 'I came looking for a nice Irish girl – I found lots! It's getting better all the time.' He first came to take part in a barbecue contest, but he soon forgot about his sausages and now works on the organising committee.

And while some locals poo-poohed the rumours of orgies, Mark said a bit of dirt did no one any harm. 'There are people who come here every year and meet a different person every time,' he said. 'And that's why I like it!' He said he worked his way through 'about 330 women every festival. Two a day is about average for me. I haven't found any this weekend, so you're in luck,' he added with a wink as he pulled me – onto his lap.

Mark also meets a few old flames every year, and has noticed that couples meet up just for the festival. He said: 'This is what young people do every weekend – but Lisdoonvarna has no age-prejudice. It's not unusual to see couples who are carrying on twenty-year affairs. They never contact each other the rest of the year but they know they can just pick up where they left off. There are people walking into rooms they never booked, groups of people getting together – it all happens here. It's a very open-minded place.'

I thought he was joking until I overheard a receptionist in a local hotel telling a chambermaid how to prepare a room for a regular guest. She said: 'He always asks for two extra beds, two extra pillows – a room for four.' Mark said that was one of the better hotels. He added: 'Some of the others are a bit prudish and wouldn't let you bring in extra people. But there are fields, ditches and plenty of bushes around.'

Mark had given up all thoughts of settling down. 'I've never married anyone I met here, but I've had plenty of affairs with women. It's great. There are dances in the hotels around town from 11 AM until late at night, all month. It's easy to pick up a woman after she's had a few pints. These dances are crowded. Everyone's bumping into everyone else, know what I mean? I've seen men and women going in [to a dance] long-faced and coming out with great big smiles.

'Some of the women come looking for a man who'll give them a home, but more often they'll be offered a pint of Guinness, a takeaway burger – and a shag. And, guess what? They like it. That's why they come back every year.'

Indeed, when the *Sunday World* sent me back to the festival in 2008, I met a bunch of randy Irish women who confessed they had left their hubbies at home – to hunt for sex. The sneaky cheats at first pretended they were single and looking for true love – then admitted they just wanted to shag strangers at the annual month-long bonkfest. And while some said they were inspired by *Sex and the City*, it was clear they were really looking for Sex in the Country.

But not everyone got lucky. 'The men are all tanked up,' a Kerry housewife told me. 'Take any of them to bed and all you'll get is the auld brewer's droop!'

Self-confessed 'cougar' Levina Walshe, from Rathdowney, County

Laois had been coming to Lisdoonvarna every year for the past twelve years and said: 'I always find a man. The best was the fella I met just after I got divorced. I met him in the Matchmaker Bar. He asked me for a dance. Then he asked me would I like to meet him the next day. And that was it – we were in love,' she sighed. 'He lasted for seven years – then he just fucked off. The good ones always fuck off.'

In 2010, she brought a 'chaperone' – her twenty-one-year-old daughter, Orla. 'I'm only here to mind my mother!' Orla laughed.

The men I met were like Dan the Man in Irish showband singer Brendan Shine's song 'Catch Me If You Can' – 'awful shifty for a man of fifty . . . off for the craic, the women and the beer'. Posing as a lonely lass looking for love, I prowled the town. I wasn't looking for a husband – but I found plenty. The love-rats claimed to be single – yet I couldn't get a single home phone number. But while they were bold enough to chat up strangers, the cheating spouses got shy as soon as I mentioned that I was with the *Sunday World*. 'My wife would kill me if she knew I was here,' forty-something Brian from Meath told me – moments after he had invited me to go dancing. Another admitted: 'I'm terrified of the wife. If I get my picture in the *Sunday World* with you, she'll throw me out and keep the house. I need some poor eejit to take her off my hands,' he said, turning to the matchmaker. 'Willie, if I bring her here will you get rid of her? Can I just dump the bitch here?'

He was the quintessential Irish man – brazen and shy at the same time. Rather like the festival itself. While it does attract swingers, it's more like the Irish band Crystal Swing – naff and proud of it.

Chat-up lines are not too complicated in Lisdoonvarna, where a stranger can walk up to a strange woman and propose marriage. Or ask her to go to bed with him – and not expect a stiletto heel in the whatsits. Some blokes take their cue from Father Ted's side-kick, Dougal, and ask a girl: 'What age are you?' And 'getting to know you' is meant in the Biblical sense.

The matchmaker had told me that I needed 'someone with a bit of life in him'. And the men were certainly fresh, I thought as I ran the gauntlet of gropers in the Matchmaker pub. So, after I had posed for a few photos for the *Sunday World*, I slipped into a loose pair of jeans. Never mind the fact that hotpants came of age in the 1970s – so did some of the men at this festival of the ancients. And they were of a generation that did not do 'look but don't touch'.

While the matchmaker couldn't find Mr Right for me or Sinead O'Connor, 2011 was his most successful year ever, when he got 237 couples to tie the knot. The divorced dad-of-seven has been putting couples together since the 1960s, when he took over from his dad and granddad.

He's busiest during the festival, which runs for the whole month of September every year, but he operates his matchmaking service all year round, from his ramshackle cottage on his dairy farm.

But anyone who thought matchmakers were like Mickileen in *The Quiet Man* is in for a surprise. While the art of matchmaking was once about marriages of convenience, these days it's just as much about quickies, and Willie was keen to move with the times. In 2009, he sexed-up the snug in the Matchmaker pub where people signed up for his service. Explaining why he had plastered the walls with pin-ups of naked women, he laughed: 'It gets the auld lads going – and the young lads. Not that they need any enticing!' Willie said the action was extra-sizzling that year – thanks to the weather. 'The warm nights are a great boost to the festival, because the girls are able to wear skimpy clothes and the men can appreciate them better.'

A bevy of local beauties, who would not have looked out of place in the Miss Ireland contest, were helping him take down names – but they coyly refused to sign up themselves. Nineteen-year-old Katie Linnane, from Milltown Malbay, and Amy Bradley (eighteen) from Lisdoonvarna were under strict orders not to nab all the male talent for themselves. But they admitted they'd keep an eye out for 'hot blokes'. Unfortunately for them, the young dudes were unable to get past the hordes of drunken auld fellas who were queuing up to sign the book – and grabbing any woman who tried to pass.

Pensioner Michael McNamara wanted the matchmaker to take note of his best asset: 'I've a big willy! Write that down in your book – it will improve my chances. I'm looking for a good woman to be my wife.' But Michael thought yours truly was a cheap date – he pushed a fiver on me. 'Take it because you're a lovely girl. I want to show my appreciation,' he urged me as I forced him to put it back in his pocket. The retired Council road-worker from Feakle, County Clare, was convinced women were only looking for men with money. 'I was married a few times and they all left me because I hadn't enough money. But I'd spend every penny on the right woman.' He took a set of rosary beads and some prayer leaflets out of his pocket. 'I'm praying to find a woman here tonight. I've been coming here for twenty year [sic] or more. Willie set me up with a few women but they all said I was too old for them. I'm in my eighties but I'm fit and I can go all night – and all day if you like,' he said, adding that he regularly ran marathons. 'To be honest, I spend most of my time these days running after women!' And he was certainly fast. As soon as I had turned my back, he was off chatting up another girl.

Later that night I saw Michael heading off on a proper date with probably the most eligible woman in the town – oil baroness Jan Carr. The busty blonde widow from Aspen, Colorado, has been coming to the matchmaking festival for the past five years. 'I have been looking to Willie to find me a boyfriend. If he's the right man, I'll move to Ireland. But I'd have to give up my two houses and my oil well in Texas – and all my animals. I have deer, horses, and a few bears living on my land.'

As she checked out the wildlife in Lisdoonvarna, she confessed that she was falling in love with the matchmaker himself. 'Willie is my friend for years and he's the most romantic man I've ever met.'

Willie revealed the secret of his popularity with the ladies: 'There are two things I never ask a woman – her age and has she children. A man has to tread carefully. Irish men need a bit more sensitivity. Some of them are more used to talking to cows.' But the matchmaker insisted he would never pick a woman for himself at the festival. 'It wouldn't be ethical for a matchmaker to be matching himself up. I'm here to make other people happy.'

His sons, Henry and Rory, have no plans to follow him into the business – they'd rather check out the talent! Rory said: 'I have the craic talking to the women who come in to see my father. They don't expect to see someone my age here. I've met loads of girls – a lot of them older than me. It's hard when I can't ask them out.' Henry said: 'I often felt like flicking through my father's matchmaking book and picking out someone, but I'm only messing.'

Willie's matchmaking book is full of letters from desperate would-be housewives, who write in all year round. At the festival in 2006, the women who had paid €65 to sign up included a Dublin pensioner who described herself as 'not fussy', and a sixty-seven-year-old Cavan lady who was looking for a husband. The men, surprisingly, included a few young Dublin lads in their twenties. Willie said: 'I feel like telling them to go to a few discos and pubs and they'll meet a nice girl. But I wouldn't advise them to go on the internet. People spin an image of themselves over the web and when you meet them you're disappointed. And it strikes me as a very cold and inhuman way to go looking for love. When you're dealing with emotions, there has to be a bit of magic.'

While the fee for women is lifelong membership of his matchmaking agency, he charges men the same for just a year. 'We don't get enough women. And anyway women have an awful habit of changing their minds. You never know when they're going to leave the husband or the boyfriend and look for someone new.'

Willie says times have changed since his father used to introduce maidens to wealthy farmers. 'At the time, it was called the Lisdoonvarna Bachelor Festival. Some of the men who come here every year have been coming for fifty-odd years. They say to me Lisdoonvarna is not the same. But that's because they don't have as many women after them. These would have been the Casanovas of their time. Some of these men are lively enough – I've seen men in their seventies who do all the dances until the small hours. And any fella under sixty-five is spoilt rotten with all the lovely girls coming in.' And, while his female clients got picky during the Celtic Tiger years, once the recession hit, he was soon swamped with pleas from desperate housewives-to-be. 'Now the Irish women are after security. They don't mind if the man hasn't a tooth in his head or a bit of hair. They don't even care if he hasn't had a wash for a good while – as long as he has a bit of cash under the mattress and a few cows. The farmers are a safe bet. The bankers and solicitors are not considered a good match any more – sure some of them haven't the arse in their trousers. So Lisdoonvarna is back to being what it was when it began nearly two hundred years ago – a festival where a farmer goes to find a wife.'

He makes it sound like a cattle mart – and agrees that it is similar. 'For some of them, it is like buying a cow. And it's the same for the women.' Indeed he has nothing against the kind of woman who was looking for a cash-cow to keep her in clover.

In 2008, Willie got his first gay client. 'But I had to turn him down. I told him I've never matched gays before, so I wouldn't be any good at it.' So I was puzzled when he offered to fix me up with a ride – on Pamela Anderson! It turned out she was one of the horses at his riding centre. I settled for a bareback romp on Colin Farrell and Brad Pitt. While blue-eyed Brad was a perfect gent, Colin was a bit frisky, as you'd expect. But Brad was a gelding and Colin was a fine filly. . . .

The most romantic moment for me came at 3 AM in front of the chip-van on the main street, when a nice old couple told me it was the fortieth anniversary of their first date – at Lisdoonvarna. 'Wille Daly matched us. It's our little secret,' the woman said as they went off to have a bop in the Hydra.

The hotel, which doubled up as the festival headquarters, was booked out, but I got plenty of offers of a room for the night. However, like a seasoned Lisdoonvarner, I went home alone.

Mrs Whippy

Neighbours know her as a quiet mum-of-one. And most of her visitors were just looking for a massage to ease their aching backs. But others hoped to go away with a few new pains, and scratches, and red bums, and aching private parts. . . . Because this was Mistress Amethyst – one of Ireland's top bondage mistresses. And the three-bedroom semi in a quiet cul-de-sac in Clonee, on the border between counties Meath and Dublin, was her dungeon. Her sex slaves came to be tortured with whips and chains – and to wear women's underwear. And there was no shortage of men willing to pay €250 a pop for the kinky sessions which took place in the spare bedroom.

'I see myself as a healer, whether I'm curing pain – or inflicting it. It's all about touch,' she told me when I brought a male friend to her house of horrors. We were posing as a couple looking for a bit of slap-and-tickle to spice-up our sex lives. My male friend, a businessman and amateur photographer from Mayo, was not a journalist by profession but he was up for the craic.

We had booked just a half-hour (for €150). But the dominatrix held us 'prisoner' for more than two hours as she taught me how to dominate my man. As beginners, we were what S&M enthusiasts call 'vanilla'. But in one afternoon she turned me into Mrs Whippy.

For an awkward moment, I wondered if we had come to the wrong house. Casually dressed with no make-up, the pretty girl who answered the door didn't look like a sadist who could reduce grown men to quivering wrecks. 'I don't answer the door dressed as a dominatrix. It could be the gas man or Jehovah's Witnesses,' she explained.

Inside, the house was as pristine as a showhouse. 'It's not very dungeonesque – the dungeon is a cliché,' she said, pointing out that her clients got turned on by the idea that something kinky was happening in an 'ordinary setting'. On the landing, I spotted meat-hooks and chains hanging from the bedroom doors. And we were to find out later just what they were for.

We had booked on the web using fake names – like most of her clients – but she still made us call from Clonee village to get directions to her house. 'I never tell people until the last minute because I like to play games with them. And I need to talk to them on the phone to make sure they're not weirdos.'

At an arranged time, we had called the dominatrix from my car, in a pub car-park. *Sunday World* snapper Liam O'Connor followed us in a jeep; his job was to discreetly photograph Mistress Amethyst for the obligatory pixellated image (we were not going to totally 'out' her – we save that for criminals, and beating people up with their consent was not yet a crime).

Liam also doubled up as security; if we were not out in half an hour, he was to call the Gardaí. We were not sure who Mistress Amethyst really was, or whether or not she had heavies in the house; this, after all, was a woman whose website listed 'financial domination' as a service.

She had told us to call her Lucy when we arrived, but admitted that that might not be her real name, adding: 'When I meet clients on the street, we ignore each other.' She said her sixteen-year-old son, who lived with her on and off, had no idea what his mum got up to. 'He wouldn't mind but his father would – and his friends' parents, and the teachers at his school!'

The separated mum, who was thirty-nine but looked younger without make-up, said she found it hard to hang on to a man – but not because she had beaten them up. 'They get jealous of my clients.' She said her only true friends were other dommes, including Mistress Maeve, who regularly held 'bondage boot camps' in her country house near Athlone. Lucy had helped her out on a particularly demanding day. 'We had four male slaves. They went away very sore!'

Mistress Amethyst had been initiated five years before, by a couple she had met by chance. She was a regular at fetish parties such as Club Hysteria and Nimhneach, which were both held every month in Dublin nightclubs.

My own initiation started in her horror chamber upstairs, which had just a single bed and stool – it doubled up as her massage clinic. She sent 'Dave' to undress in the bathroom and took me into the master bedroom. Kinky latex and PVC costumes were strewn across the bed and in the wardrobe. 'Some of my clients are cross-dressers,' she said. 'Size fourteen-to-sixteen fits most guys. I make them wear big bras and knickers.' But she didn't hand out Spanx! 'The frillier and pinker the more humiliating! Sometimes I make them wear those disposable panties which are used in tanning salons – they look pathetic!'

I watched as she transformed herself into Mistress Amethyst. In black leggings, a mesh vest over a purple Wonderbra and a black corset-belt, she looked more sex-kitten than dominatrix – until she put on thigh-high biker boots and a black wig, cut in a severe bob. It made her look like an X-rated version of Katie Holmes. I just had to obey when she ordered me to strip to my undies –a red lacy bra and g-string. I had deliberately chosen a flimsy set so she'd see there was no hidden camera in it, just in case she got suspicious. Of course, the camera was in the bum-bag I had been carrying, its tiny pinhole lens poking out of the zipper. I put the bum-bag on the end of the bed, angled to capture all the action.

She made me put on a top hat, explaining: 'Height helps when you're a domme'. Then she gave me a pair of her thigh-boots and fishnet hold-ups, and a black top hat with a tulle veil at the back. A quick dab of her strong red 'slut lipstick', as she called it, and we were ready to kick arse – literally.

She knocked on the door. 'Are you ready, slave? Come forward and let us look at you. Turn, slave, and let us examine this worthless male!' She commanded my man to bend over the bed while she spanked him with a child's riding crop – it was purple and looked like something you'd use to get a ride out of My Little Pony.

'Are you a good slave?' she whispered in his ear. 'What kind of slave are you?'

'A bad slave,' he said with a cocky grin.

'A useless slave!' she hissed and spanked him on the bum.

Next she trussed him up with a white cotton rope, expertly tying sailors' knots all along his back, chest – and under his testicles. Bringing the rope back around his hips, she gave it a gentle tug. Not quite a wedgie, it was just enough to give him a fake hard-on – luckily he was wearing extra thick boxers. Not that he could scream, as she then gagged him with PVC tape. 'It only sticks to itself, not to his skin, so it's ideal for hairy men – and it will come off quickly in an emergency. Safety comes first,' the mistress explained. For someone whose business was torture, I thought she was very caring. She stopped short of forcing a ball-gag into his mouth. 'It's not something I'd do to a beginner. It can be terrifying'.

But she put a balaclava over his head – back to front. I was worried – until I heard Dave sniggering. Next she used velvet handcuffs and a dog-lead across his chest to strap him down to the bed. 'Sometimes I just leave a man tied up and blindfolded while I go downstairs to make tea for myself or phone a friend for a chat,' she said. 'But I never leave them too long – slaves must not be neglected.'

I told her not to hold back on the sexy stuff; I was paying for it after all. She obliged by kneeling on his face and whispering in his ear: 'You're worthless!'

She told me she would often taunt her regulars by comparing them to her other slaves. 'It makes them want to please me – men are competitive creatures.'

While Dave was helpless, Mistress Amethyst caressed him, inviting me to join in. We scratched him with our nails, gently so as not to draw blood, and teased him by lying on him in the sixty-nine position. Then she made me sit on his face. In just my g-string, I felt a bit shy, so I hovered the way you do on the loo. Mistress Amethyst said some clients had asked her to pee on them but she had refused. 'I have my boundaries,' she explained. Who would have guessed? I thought as she scraped Dave's torso with a device like a small pizza-cutter. It left little red marks but it could have been much worse – we had asked her not to break his skin. 'I never listen to them when they scream. Words like 'No' and 'Stop' mean nothing to me,' she explained as Dave winced. 'But we agree a word beforehand to end the session.'

But this time I was calling the shots. I asked her to lay off the nipple-clamps – but she gave me a few tips in case we wanted to try it at home. 'When you take off nipple-clamps, you have to keep tweaking the nipples until the pain goes down. If you just take them off, blood will rush to the nipples and it will be excruciating. I inflict pain but not injury. Sex-slaves are toys – and broken toys are useless.'

Spreadeagled across the landing, Dave was helpless as she yelled obscenities into his ear. Moments later, we were all having tea. It was very civilised – until she told us she sometimes got clients to make her tea as part of their 'punishment'. They could even dress up as Mrs. Doyle if that turned them on, go on, go on....

Her own safety was also important, she said, adding that she sometimes had friends hiding in another room of the house – I felt she dropped that in because she was just a little bit scared of us; for a rookie S & M couple, we were probably a bit too eager. She added: 'I've never had a bad client. Estate agents take more risks.'

She was also a stickler for hygiene, and showed us a gigantic black strap-on dildo which she was sterilising in Milton fluid. 'I'd still put a condom on it before I use it on a client,' she said. It was used for anal and oral sex – but she didn't do intercourse. 'Some dommes do but for most of us it's just about domination, nothing intimate.'

Most of her torture tools were ordinary household items – she said fetish shops were a whip-off. 'Clothes pegs make great nipple-clamps,' she said, adding that she often bought gagging tape in hardware shops.

From then on, I would never think of the aptly named Woodies Hardware as a mere DIY shop. Nor would I associate pet shops with cuddly animals, after Mistress Amethyst revealed she regularly visited them to stock up on dog collars and leads – and petting was the last thing on her mind!

A few months after I exposed Mistress Amethyst in the *Sunday World*, I found out just why she was unbeaten in the world of S & M – I was inundated with requests from horny men begging for a beating! But the cruel mistress left hundreds of punters frustrated as she gave up the wicked game. Her website, which had been full of raunchy pics of the dominatrix at work, was closed down and replaced by a notice: 'What you are looking for no longer exists'. Her friends posted messages on bondage website ClubHysteriaIreland.com to say that she had given up because the *Sunday World* exposé made it impossible for her to continue. But, judging by the sheer volume of requests we got for her services, Mrs Whippy could have been rolling in dough. With fees starting at €250 for an hour of one-to-one torture, she could have ridden out the recession in style.

Most of the men asking to be put in touch with Mistress Amethyst were middle-aged or older. One fifty-something man wrote of his desperation. 'I need her services. Please help me. This is a genuine case.' He added that he had also been turned-on by the rest of my XXX-rated Red Hot Republic series which included undercover exposés of swingers' parties, dogging sessions and high-class escorts. Another described in intimate detail what he wanted to have done to him (by me or Mrs Whippy; he wasn't fussy) and his thoughts on the pictures alongside the story. It was unprintable in a family newspaper. A Dundalk pensioner claimed to be a virgin who desperately wanted his first sexual experience to be S&M. 'I never had sex. I don't mind. I am careful to keep away from infections, so I am not weird,' he said, adding: 'It would be quite easy to dominate a man of my age.'

Some of the men who contacted me looking for a beating said they had also stripped off for visiting New York artist Spencer Tunick the previous summer – and had found that just as much of a turn-on.

S&M in the City

It was Saturday night in a Dublin city centre club and an old man was getting beaten up. Everyone rushed over – and just watched. A few feet away, a beautiful young girl was being tortured and caressed by a couple who were clearly playing up the fact that they were the spitting image of Rosemary West and Ian Brady in his Moors Murders days. The girl was handcuffed to a scaffold and her small breasts had come out of her strapless leather dress. The man cruelly twisted the nipples, an intense expression on his face, while his accomplice inserted a riding crop into the girl's vagina. The kinky couple paused to snog, then took turns at kissing their victim. No one called the police, despite the fact that there was a Garda station just across the road. In fact, some of the stern-faced spectators were wearing what look like fake police uniforms. A woman and two men stomped around dressed as Nazis, complete with jackboots. Everyone else was bursting out of PVC – leggings, corsets, vests. Some peeled off layers of rubber to reveal yet another racy outfit underneath – two girls were wearing just nipple-covers on top. And one bloke wore angel wings with his gladiator outfit.

Not that I could point the finger. I was (barely) wearing a PVC dress with matching boots, stockings and suspenders and my g-string was showing above the cut-outs in my dress; it was meant to. My date was pimpcd up in black leatherette trousers, sleeveless PVC vest and a studded dog-collar, all of which he had bought in sex-shops – at my command. I was leading him around on a chain, which I had bought in a pet shop. I had had to tell the lady I wanted it for a Rottweiler – she had been trying to convince me to buy a prettier leash. It had been very easy to find the clothes, if a bit pricey – it took money to look that cheap – but it had been hard to convince my man to dress up like a missing member of the Village People. 'Can't we just wear ordinary clothes?' he pleaded. 'The dress code is strict!' I snapped, putting on my best dominatrix voice as we set off for the Club Hysteria event at Dublin's Cavern Nightclub. It was the second bondage and sado-masochism session to be held at the club, near Dublin's main bus station, Busárus. And it beat the bejaysus out of a night in the pub.

It's no mean feat to be cruel to a bunch of sadists, but I think I managed it by ruining their cool atmosphere with my naff Bondage Barbie look. My pink furry handcuffs earned me some frosty looks from the proper dominatrices.

At least I was carrying a real leather riding-crop. Maybe that's why some men begged me to give them a lash. I thought they were joking and got one of them to strip down to his shorts and bend over a table. When I realised he really wanted me to beat him, I refused – which made me the cruellest mistress there. I felt a pang of guilt as I wondered if a few playful licks of my whip would have saved the old man the brutal flogging he was getting from one of the club's resident mistresses.

Still, he was clearly loving it, his eyes shut in ecstasy – and his bare bum red-raw. He had come on the bus from Leitrim just for that. He told me it was his favourite hobby since he had retired from a manual job a few years ago.

The domme stopped to hook him up to the scaffolding – with nipple-clamps. The metal teeth didn't quite break his skin but it was clear they hurt. He winced as she grabbed the leather thong that covered his manhood and yanked him back – giving him a massive wedgie! All to the tune of Marilyn Manson's 'Tainted Love'.

I glared back at one of the other men who had wanted me to beat them, a middle-aged schoolteacher type with glasses. He would not have looked out of place at a residents' association meeting – but there he was, queuing up for his flogging and eyeballing me. I knew what he was thinking and it wasn't nice.

It was all rather different from what we had expected: a fancy-dress party with a raunchy adult theme, maybe a bit of flirting, couples snogging on the dancefloor and risqué jokes. But the tables and scaffolds with leather handcuffs attached were not just decorations or part of the live stage-show. And while there were several live acts, the real performers were the clubbers themselves, who were aged from early twenties to mid-sixties. Bums of all shapes and sizes were hanging out as they lined up for their fifteen minutes of infamy in front of the other revellers. As Marilyn Manson sings 'Mutilation is the best kind of flattery'.

After his torture session, the old man from Leitrim told me: 'I'm very disappointed in you. I wanted you to be my mistress. You look brilliant. Why are you dressed like that if you won't take part? I can get you lessons from one of the dommes.' I found myself apologising for not wanting to beat him up. He seemed too nice – until he revealed his fantasy. 'What I really want is for someone to piss on me, kick me around, humiliate me and cover me in clingfilm,' he explained. 'Will you do it?' He added that his wife often poured hot candle-wax on his private parts. 'It hurts like hell – I love it! She's into S & M but she didn't come with me tonight.' He was hurt – and not in a pleasant way – when I asked if he ever thought about going to a prostitute. 'I wouldn't go near prostitutes!' he said.

And why would anyone, I thought, when they could pay the €20 cover charge to indulge in a bit of slap and tickle with strangers.

There were just about 50 people in the club. But what they lacked in numbers they made up for in passion. These were hardcore bondage fans who told me they had been to similar events in London. We seemed to be the only couple who had not tried it before – and we weren't going to that night either.

Don't get me wrong. I liked some of the costumes, and could even imagine a bit of playful mock-violence with the right sort of man. It was the pain bit that bothered me. And what struck me most – pardon the pun – was how seriously everyone was taking themselves. Quite literally – there was lots of fumbling with crotches. And manic eye-contact, in the hope of getting hit on – or just hit! Most of the people had come alone – and left alone. The flogging was the most intimate it got. 'It's like a school disco,' my companion noticed. 'Only there are more loners.'

There was even someone in a schoolmistress costume – a voluptuous twenty-two-year-old computer programmer who was done up like Hattie Jacques in the *Carry On* films. In her Mrs Thatcher-style blouse with a striped tie and long, voluminous skirt, she was the kinkiest person there. Her grey-dyed hair stayed in its prim bun even as she danced wildly, kicking out her legs.

There was also a naughty nurse. And one of the live acts involved a syringe, which was far scarier than the whips. I felt I had stepped into a comedy horror film – *The Rocky Horror Picture Show* without the script.

The girl in the Nazi uniform told me she had bought the jacket in London's Camden Market. It was ridiculously tight and looked like one of the costumes from the movie *The Producers*. I half-expected her to start goose-stepping across the floor while singing 'Springtime for Hitler'. She said she had got interested in bondage a few years previously when she worked as a hostess in a London S & M club. Another 'Nazi' had a fake SS officer's suit – in skin-tight black PVC. He could barely walk; it was either the costume or a sore bum.

Even the goodie bags were bad. They contained invitations to various kinky events in the UK, including a 'Bondage Boot Camp'. Mine also contained a plastic ring with jagged edges and what looked like a whistle attached. A week later, I was still asking friends and frantically searching the web to find out what it was. . . . This, above all, made me realise that I had led a sheltered life until then.

A year later, the bottom fell out of Dublin's bondage scene and the club no longer met in its city centre venue opposite Store Street Garda Station. Pictures were removed from the club's website – though yours truly was still able to enjoy a lively online scrap with the members on their online forum. But the site was later shut down.

And it was hard for a novice masochist to get a proper caning anywhere in Ireland, as Club Hysteria had gone underground, holding private parties or mingling with the slap and tickle crowd at Club Nimhneach, which attracted a more genteel crowd who were simply looking for a themed night out.

Swinging in the Country

It looked like a typical family home in rural Ireland. The small, two-story detached house down a country lane had been recently built. And the couple who lived in it, next door to his mother, seemed normal. The good-looking man and woman, he in his early forties, she in her thirties, had been married nearly five years. Both had full-time jobs. He played golf and was into other sports. And they were a dab hand at juggling their complicated social calendar, given the amount of traffic coming through the door. Their house-parties were legendary, not just locally but throughout Ireland and even in the UK. These very hospitable hosts were in fact renowned for giving guests the ultimate *céad míle fáilte*. Because 'John and Shaz', as they were known to their guests, were swingers.

The parties, which only took place when John's recently widowed mother was away, were marathon orgies starting early in the evening and going on until well after the crack of dawn. The couple had posted a tempting ad, complete with lots of raunchy pics of themselves and their friends in action, on two websites, the UK-based Fabswingers, which they joined over a year ago, and Swing4Ireland, using the name

'Swing2Wex'. Both described themselves as bisexual and said: 'The sight of looking at each other shagging someone else blows both of us away.' They said they were looking for 'straight and group sex, three-somes, anal sex, masturbation, orgies, gang-bangs, outdoor sex, S&M, making videos, role-play and exhibitionism.' And they came highly recommended by other punters on Fabswingers, where they were also members of two groups – Wexford Area Swingers and Black Cock Lovers. A Dublin couple described them as 'the most down-to-earth people you could meet . . . so fun-loving and sexy. Their parties are great and they make everyone feel so at ease. If you ever can get to meet them, it will be worth it.'

To get an invitation, all I had to do was send a description of myself and my boyfriend, and a pic showing our faces – a security measure to prevent my employers, the *Sunday World*, infiltrating their party, as they explained in an email. If they had only known . . . A badly lit pic swung it for us. They replied almost immediately: 'We would love to have you down. We are always looking for new couples to come to our parties and widen our circle of friends that have the same sexual interests . . . The gang going are your normal, everyday, run-of-the-mill people, just they like having sex as a way of enjoying life and mixing with new people. None of us are weird in any way, we just love the cut and thrust of swinging and know the difference between having sex with other people and making love to our own partner. The night will not be anything out of the normal as far as sex is concerned, except bisexuality is probably a little bit more open in swing parties for both male and female . . . We will have finger-food for people to nibble on, all you need to bring is what drink you want and condoms. Only rules we have is no drugs and if people want a smoke, it is utility room or outside . . .

We are in a nice country area and want to keep it that way.' They asked us to be there by 9 PM, adding: 'What time people stop shagging at is up to themselves.'

The guests began arriving just after eight. The couple – a curvy brunette and dark, athletic-looking man – greeted them at the front door, which led straight into the pine-floored living room. By midnight, there were twenty people in the house, John told me when I phoned him, using a fake ID.

I had intended to go along with my boyfriend – just to see if it was really happening – but he had changed his mind at the last minute. 'I don't want to be in the same room as that filth,' he said, adding that swinging breaks up relationships. And he was right – it broke us up for twelve hours, even though I had no intention of taking part in the actual orgy. I had been to a few swingers' parties in the course of my work but had always, in the best tradition of tabloid journalists, 'made my excuses and left'. I always brought along a male friend or colleague for protection – which was cold comfort for my man.

On this occasion, he need not have worried; my windscreen wipers broke when I was within yards of the swingers' house. As I waited in the nearby village for the auto-rescue guy to arrive, a local man asked me if I was 'looking for the party', then invited me to 'a party in a house down the road. If your boyfriend turns up he can come too. Never mind him if he doesn't – we'll keep you company'. Two other men with him laughed. Maybe they guessed I was there for the swingers' party – after all I was a hundred miles from home, alone, on a Saturday night.

Swinger John insisted it was not too late to come when I phoned around midnight from a nearby hotel, where I was stranded thanks to the rain and my broken wiper. He shouted above his guests' moans and shrieks: 'There's one single girl here now and one single lad who's never done it before! I mean he's never done swinging – he's not bad at the oul sex! The party will go on as long as the shagging lasts!' he laughed, adding that it was their biggest party yet.

The parties, which had been going on every few weeks for about a year, usually attracted twelve people – six couples, according to a local man who disapproved.

Next morning John said the last of the swingers had left around 8 AM after a very busy night. It was clear that John and Shaz were "all shagged out", as he put it. He answered the door in a grubby grey bathrobe. With his dark eyes, underscored by dark circles from a sleepless night, messy black hair and matching trendy goatee, he was a ringer for Javier Bardem, the male star who gets Scarlett Johanssen and Penelope Cruz into a threesome in steamy movie *Vicky Cristina Barcelona*. He confirmed that, yes, this was the house where the swingers' party had taken place. His wife had gone back to bed – to sleep this time. There would be more parties, of course, and we were still invited, but they hadn't set a date yet. 'We hold them whenever we have the bother on us,' he explained. Then he shooed out their black cat, who had been forced to stay out all night while the swinging took place. As the cat gave me a knowing look, I was suddenly glad to be going back to my straitlaced boyfriend.

A few months later, I met John by chance, at a sporting event. He recognised me first. We had a laugh about it and I realised that, for them, swinging really was just an enjoyable pastime.

The Eco-Dildo

Hard times were a comin' in 2009 – but an Irish couple found a hot way to beat the recession blues. There was just one passion-killer – the banks would not say yes-yes-yes.

Jobless Chris and Janice O'Connor thought bank managers would be up for it when they invented a nifty sex-toy that was also friendly to the environment. The self-powered Earth Angel was the world's very first eco-safe vibrator. It was guaranteed to raise global temperatures in the nicest possible way. The plastic willy, which vibrated without the need for batteries, had just beaten off stiff competition from other sex toys to get a nomination for an award at the Erotic Trade-Only Awards in Birmingham, UK. And within weeks of making the final list for the Best Initiative gong, they sold one thousand of the gadgets, at €69 a pop, proving it was not a flop. Chris's parents pumped €20,000 into the business, and their main customers were sex-shops, though they also sold some online. But while Ireland's then Environment Minister John Gormley was banging on about the Green Economy, our banks were not yet ready for the Blue Economy. Bank of Ireland showed it no longer lived up to its old advertising slogan, 'The bank that likes to say yes!', when their branch manager refused to top-up their start-up loan to produce more of the sex-toys. AIB and Ulster Bank also said no.

'The woman in Ulster Bank actually said: "We wouldn't like to be associated with something like that. It's immoral". We thought, what a bleedin' banker!' Chris fumed. Janice added: 'If it hadn't been for my parents giving us a loan, we'd never have managed to get it up and running.' Far from being shocked, both their families were very supportive. 'My ma was a hundred percent behind me when I told her,' Chris said. Even their two-year-old son, Caden, thought the toy was 'great – though he doesn't know what it is!' Chris laughed.

The gadget looked innocent enough on their mantelpiece; it could easily have passed for a candlestick. They invited me to test-drive it, so I did – literally, in the exhaust of Chris's car. It lent a whole new meaning to 'Pimp my ride'.

Chris described it as 'the perfect toy for singles, couples and even orgies. You can even have phone sex with it – just hook it up with a Nokia phone charger for an extra buzz.' It was made from 100 percent recycled plastic – though the O'Connors hastened to add that it was not second-hand.

Former sheet-metal worker Chris, who had lost his job following a back-injury, hit on the idea while he was 'messing around in the bedroom' three years previously. 'I've always been handy with my hands and I used to make equipment for a band I was in, Spiral Tribe. But when I made this, I knew it was something big. It was very exciting.'

The couple immediately got a worldwide patent and found a UK company, Motion Touch, who arranged to have the prototype made in Japan. Janice and Chris hoped to eventually have them made in Ireland. They also planned to use the technology, which they had patented worldwide, to make self-powering electric toothbrushes – and generators which would provide free electricity for homes and businesses. Janice, who was also out of work, was able to use her talents as a former presenter on raunchy Sky TV phone-in channel Babe Station and her experience as a credit controller to look after the business end.

Yet they were now living on a social welfare Back-to-Work Allowance, while they plunged their profits into the business and, in keeping with their eco-warrior principles, donated to Greenpeace. They hoped to eventually be just as self-sufficient as the dildo itself. 'We're sure it will make us a fortune – because sex sells,' Chris pointed out.

And even though prim banking types were not interested in helping them raise some extra cash, orders were flying in from shops in the US, UK, Australia and Continental Europe, as well as private customers. The vibrators were on sale online at a very enticing price of €69.99. Meanwhile, they made a deal with Dutch erotic wholesaler Escala BV to supply them to sex-shops around the world – including Dublin's Miss Fantasia.

The dildos could also be fitted with 'sleeves' with various finishes, including suede, rubber with knobs on it – and even spikes! And the pair were already hard at work on some follow-ups, including a waterproof version and a 'Dark Angel', which was the same as the Earth Angel, only black – making it the perfect toy for multi-cultural Ireland.

A year later, they were forced to stop trading. 'We offered to send the bank €29,000 worth of vibrators to clear this debt but they don't seem to be interested,' Janice said. 'We are screwed!'

CHAPTER TEN:
Scary Eire

Older folk get nostalgic when they recall nights sitting around the fireside listening to tales about banshees and evil little people. But the Irish fascination for the supernatural hasn't gone away.

We still love a good scare.

Séance in Clonony Castle

I had come across the Ghost Eire team the previous year, 2010, when they invited me to a séance in a castle in County Offaly. When they told me they were pagans who also practised witchcraft and shamanism, and could even cast spells, I was off to meet them before they could say 'Boo'.

Anto Kerrigan and his mate Paul Davis had piqued my interest because they did not fit the conventional image of people who communicate with ghosts. While they could expect plenty of close encounters with creatures of the night as they worked on the door of a Killarney nightclub, the trouble-making spirits were more likely to come in a bottle.

Dublin-born dad-of-one Anto had grown up in Crewe, in Cheshire. Tall and thin, with his multicoloured Mohican and Goth-rocker clothes, he didn't look like your typical bouncer either. Neither did Paul, a quiet and polite Welshman who had moved from his native Barry, near Penarth, to Dublin and later Killarney, and had inherited his fascination with the supernatural from his Welsh mum, Glenda Hubbard, who had come along to take part in the séance. The granny-of-twenty-six and great-grandmother-of-eleven said she had been psychic since the age of seven when she predicted her nephew's death. 'I wish I didn't have the gift. I don't charge for readings because that would be wrong.' The rest of the group was made up of psychic Eric Hood, Anto's pretty blonde girlfriend Jen Cremins, and medium Xak Aroo, an elfin girl from Leicester living in County Cork, who introduced herself to me with the words: 'Us little 'uns are closer to the faeries'.

Together, they scoured the country in search of spooks. Early in 2010, they announced that they had photographed 'mysterious orbs at Wicklow Gaol' and reported that a doll they had left in the former prison began rocking of its own accord. They were soon swamped with requests from terrified householders and claimed to have found evidence of paranormal activity in twenty-nine locations during the first half of 2010, ranging from pubs to farmhouses.

Clonony Castle, near Ferbane, County Offaly was particularly spooktacular. Owner Rebecca Armstrong called them in after she 'felt a presence' in the ruined Norman tower on her land, which she had bought a few years previously. Rebecca said she didn't want the ghosts booted out of the castle, but said guests who rented it for parties had been spooked.

She said it was not her first brush with the supernatural. She had been tempted to call in an exorcist after a terrifying experience some years back in her previous home – Cangot Castle, just down the road. 'My granddaughter [now grown up] came to stay with me – and a spirit possessed her twice. She woke up in the middle of the night and growled at me in a horrible voice: "Get out". It never happened again and I didn't tell anyone. I was afraid her mother would say "You're not staying with your granny again".

'You'd think I'd have had enough of haunted castles,' she laughed, adding: 'I'm trying to sell this place. I hope the ghost doesn't object!'

Built in the sixteenth century by the MacCoughlan clan, Clonony Castle was later ceded to Henry VIII, who in turn gave it to Anne Boleyn's father Thomas, Earl of Ormond. The tragic queen's sisters Mary and Elizabeth Boleyn are believed to be buried in a nearby tomb under a hawthorn tree, after they were exhumed from their previous resting place. Judging by the ruins, it was once a majestic building with a great hall. But all that remains intact is the fifty-foot-high square tower, one room above the other, joined by a winding stone staircase, with some of the steps missing.

Even on a humid summer night, there was a chill about the building, which stood in its own swirling mists. It was located by the side of a winding country lane between the little village of Ferbane and the medieval Christian monastic settlement of Clonmacnoise. To reach its doorway, I had to climb over sharp rocks which protruded from the grassy hill.

Rebecca had masked the damp air with the scent of joss sticks, and decorated the rooms with goatskin rugs and replicas of medieval tapestries. It was perfect for an intimate séance – or so I thought, until the eerie atmosphere was interrupted by the loud crackling of what sounded like a radio in between stations. Anto was broadcasting 'white noise' and 'brown noise' into the air. He explained that some of the decibels were inaudible to the human ear. They were all too audible to me – and I was sure the racket was scaring off the ghosts.

Meanwhile Eric was pointing what looked like a Geiger counter at the walls.

Armed with an array of gadgets, including an electromagnetic field gauge, night-vision video camera, motion-detector and thermal barometer, as well as a Ouija board, rock of amethyst and a wooden mannequin, these people were determined to raise the dead – and if there were any ghosts having a nap, they were in for a rude awakening!

We began our session when it was still bright, around nine, standing in a circle, holding hands. Anto said a prayer to 'Mother and Father God of all creation' and we each introduced ourselves to the spirit world. It felt spooky enough to be on first-name terms with ghosts. Then Xak, Glenda and Eric sat around a table with a wooden heart and placed their hands on it. Xak began: 'I'm Xak. I'm with a group of people here. We mean you no harm. We're here out of love and curiosity. You can use our energy to communicate.' She told the spirit to answer 'yes' by moving towards the questioner. We took turns to sit at the table, using a range of objects – the wooden heart, a tumbler and the wooden mannequin, which they placed in a frame painted in different 'mood' colours so the spirits could show how they were feeling.

For about half an hour it was like fishing – we were waiting for the spirits to bite. The suspense was even better than in the movie *The Others*, starring Nicole Kidman. But as a fan of classic horror movies, I wanted a poltergeist.

Then Xak said her right leg felt cold. 'I'm feeling a female presence,' she said. Meanwhile Glenda said a little boy called Edward was in the room. 'He's about seven or eight – do you like me, Edward? I know it's me you want to talk to.' She added: 'I know you want your mammy – would you not like to see her again? Come on, sweetheart.' Suddenly she gasped: 'My finger! I can't keep it still – he's trying to torture me.' She said the mischievous little ghost was playing with her.

Anto pointed the electromagnetic field gauge at the table. 'Come towards the black box,' he commanded. But the ghost wasn't playing ball. Glenda tried again. 'Edward, did you have a nasty uncle?' Anto asked: 'Edward, is your mother also your sister? Were you destined to become Prince of Wales?' Glenda said Edward's uncle had smothered him. 'Poor little lad. I don't know why he's attaching himself to me'. She turned to me. 'He likes you too.'

Xak cut in: 'Thomas keeps coming in.' Anto called out: 'Step forward, Thomas. We mean you no harm. Come towards us.'

The spirits seemed to be ignoring us again. Anto broke into Irish: '*Conas atá tú?*' (How are you?). Then Xak tried Spanish. But it was No Way José from the ghosts.

Next Anto chanted a rhyme: 'Hear these words, hear these sighs. Come to us from the Other Side.'

Suddenly the wooden heart moved around the table and spelt out a name: 'Rowan'. Xak asked: 'Is there a dog present called Rowan?' The spirit indicated no – but later Rebecca told us she had seen what looked like a wolf loping out of the castle at that moment! 'It went off into the hills'.

At one point, the wooden heart was flying around the table. The cynic in me was sure that, even though they believed it was moving of its own accord, the three of them were unintentionally moving it themselves. But clearly there was nothing fake about their reaction to whatever was in the room. Zak winced: 'My left hand is pulsing like fuck!' Glenda got out of breath and had to take several breaks outside. 'My knees are freezing. I'm shaking!' she said as she sat in her fold-up wheelchair. Later she broke down crying as she told her ghost, little Edward, to 'go towards the white light'. She told me he had 'dark curly hair' and was wearing 'ball-shaped bottoms – it looked like a skirt'. Meanwhile Eric was in a trance as he drew a beautiful young woman – who, he later said, had been in the room.

Next, Anto, Eric and Xak tried baiting the spirits – with a dead fledgling in a plastic box. Baiting a ghost seemed a bit dodgy, but they insisted it was perfectly all right because the bird had been found by chance by the roadside. 'We were meant to find it when we did,' Xak said. Anto described it as a 'trigger object' and said the idea was to prompt some action from the Other Side. But the spirits gave them the bird – by refusing to react. Glenda, Paul and yours truly chickened out of using a dead creature. Paul pointed out: 'When you get into that stuff, you're dealing with the satanic.' Glenda shuddered. 'I don't like this at all. When you start bringing dead creatures into it, you're inviting darkness.' She sat outside the castle and would not come back in until Xak and Eric had taken the bird upstairs, where they put it on a table and said Shamanic prayers over it – all to no avail.

We also gave the Ouija board a *non-nein*. But we didn't need it – by midnight, there were apparently ten ghosts in the castle.

Just after midnight, as we sat in the upstairs room, Xak yelled: 'Come on. I don't scare easily! Show us something.' Suddenly the table rocked violently and hit Xak in the stomach. She was obviously in pain but she was smiling. She said it was a member of the MacCoughlan family who had built it in 1500.

By the end of the night, everyone except yours truly reported tingling, numbness in their hands or feet. Even hard-nosed photographer Ciaran McGowan said he felt cold. Yet when I checked the windows of my car, they were not fogged over. So the chill the others felt could only have come from the Other Side. Meanwhile I was wandering around in bare feet, a light cardigan covering my summer dress, enjoying the balmy air. Clearly I wasn't psychic. Or maybe it was true what parents told over-imaginative children: there really was No Such Thing.

The Poltergoat

It was a horny old problem – with a supernatural twist. When a poltergeist gets your goat, who're you gonna call? Goatbusters! Especially when you've been spooked by a 'poltergoat'!

A blind goatherd on Cape Clear Island, off Baltimore, County Cork, had been puzzled for years over a series of strange events involving his animals. Three kid-goats apparently leapt over two six-foot walls to move from one pen to another in the middle of the night – on six occasions! The ghostly goings-on, which happened over a five-year period in the early-to-mid-1990s, had never been explained.

For Ed Harper, the fact that he was blind only added to the sense of being hoodwinked. But he was prepared to issue a warm Irish welcome to his mysterious visitors – if only they would make themselves known! He said he'd be glad of the company in the remote farmhouse he shared with his fisherman son Duncan. 'I don't know if ghosts exist, but I'm not going to tell them to clear off. The only visitors I get are agricultural students who come to me for short periods to learn traditional goat-herding.'

The Manchester-born dad of two came across as a rational type. He

had been a schoolteacher in England's West Midlands before he moved
to Cape Clear Island with his wife in 1979 to raise their two sons in a
'wholesome ambience', as he put it. He was also active in his community, often travelling to the mainland to take part in marches and demos
on behalf of disabled people, fishermen and rural communities in general.

Yet he had trouble convincing his neighbours and family that the
goat shed really was haunted. His wife, who moved to the mainland
after their marriage broke up but remained a friend, kept an open
mind, he said, adding: 'She doesn't remember the strange incidents at
all.'

But Ed insisted he was not kidding. And he had ruled out a
prankster among his neighbours. With a population of just 140 at the
time, which had dwindled to 125 by 2011, the islanders couldn't afford
to make enemies – or keep secrets. 'Who would do something like that
for three nights in a row, then wait three years to do it again? And no
one approached me looking for a reaction, the way they might if they
had played a prank on me.'

As he recounted his eerie experiences to me, his voice shook just a
little. Ed said nothing could explain the strange goings-on. 'One morning in November, I went to check on my goats and found three of the
kids were moved into the third pen – which was used for sick animals.
They couldn't have moved themselves because the walls are six foot
high and it's on the other side of a passage.' The next morning, the
young goats were yet again found in the wrong pen, so he spent two-
and-a-half hours there that night. 'Nothing happened so I went back to
my house and told my wife the goats were all right. The following
morning the goats were moved again! It happened three nights in a

row – then it stopped, until, three years later, it all began again. Three nights in a row, just like last time – and at the same time of year. It started or ended on November 13th – I can't remember which, but I thought that might be significant.'

And a prank would not explain what came next. 'A few years later, when I thought it had all stopped for good, I had what may have been a supernatural experience – or maybe it was some freak meteorological phenomenon. One night when I was bringing the goats in as usual, they wouldn't come. I walked down and grabbed two of them and tried to get them to lead the others. They were terrified. There was a passage they had to walk through, between the old pig house and the goat house, so I walked through to see what was disturbing them – and I found it was very cold. Even though the air everywhere else was mild, it was freezing in that place. It could be down to the weather – or it could be something in the air that was terrifying my goats. It's as if they sensed something there.'

An old postman, whose great-uncle used to live in the house, once told Ed it might be the ghost of a dead man whose grieving mother had brought him back from the dead – with her prayers. Ed's voice quivered as he recalled the conversation: 'I'll never forget what Jimmy the postman told me before he passed away. He said there were two stories that might explain the haunting. One story went: Before Jimmy's great-uncle lived there, there was a big family. The mother was about to be left on her own because she was a widow and all her sons were dying. There was just one son left, so she said to him: "When you get to Heaven, come back to me and tell me what it's like on the other side." He died soon after that, and within a short while he appeared at the door while she was praying. He said: "Mother, I won't come in because you're praying." In the other story, he came into the house. Then he said: "Please don't ever ask anyone to do this again, because it's very, very hard to get out of Heaven – and even harder to get back."

'Jimmy said: "Well, that's what it'll be. He's just keeping an eye on the goats for his mother because he's trapped here – he can't get back into Heaven." Jimmy didn't know the name of the family or how long ago it was. People lose all sense of time on this island.'

Jimmy's story notwithstanding, Ed also feared he may have upset 'faeries' – by putting an iron roof on the goat house. 'It used to have a soft roof which was more suitable for animals, but there was an Irish language school behind it and the students used to throw stones onto the roof, and this would frighten the goats. So I put a corrugated iron roof on it – but, according to folklore, faeries don't like iron.'

He added: 'Of course, it could have been another spook. People have been living on Cape Clear Island for four-and-a-half thousand years – that's a lot of dead people. And we've got a church on the island which is built on the spot where the first Mass was said for the first time in Ireland. It was built in the tenth century, but the place it was built is an early Christian site.

'There's always been something strange about Cape Clear anyway. Anyone who has visited it or lived on it will tell you it has an atmosphere of its own that's independent of its people. It's as if it is an entity in itself, like a person. I don't know if ghosts exist, but there's some presence here that we're not clever enough to understand.'

Ed's goat house was in fact the original old farmhouse. 'It's so old, it was there before there were deeds,' Ed said. 'When I came here, the house was just walls, there was no roof, and it was full of nettles and brambles. I built concrete walls to divide it into three pens – two for normal use and one for sick goats. One pen is where the hearthstone and open chimney were in the old house.'

In 2011, Ed called in paranormal investigators Ghost Eire – a team of psychics, shamans and electronics boffins who travel around Ireland carrying out experiments which usually involve a séance and tests using light-and-sound gauges. The group, based in West Cork and Kerry, are Ireland's very own *Scooby Doo* team – minus the dog. While they have day-jobs (the two founders came up with the idea when they were working as nightclub bouncers in Killarney) they hope to someday turn professional. Ed got in touch with them after a chance meeting in a friend's house with psychic Xak Aroo who works with the group.

The Ghost Eire crew spent a week trying to communicate with Ed's 'poltergoat'. They spent the first night in the goat house using infra-red detectors, complex sound equipment – and a Ouija board. Sound technician (and nightclub bouncer) Anthony 'Anto' Kerrigan later admitted even he was 'a bit freaked out. This was seriously scary. It's a very eerie place to be at night. It reminded us of that horror film *The Fog*. Most of the team were picking up dizziness, [they were] tired, disorientated – similar to the emotion of being drowned.'

The ghostbusters and Ed Harper himself reckoned that might have something to do with the fact that the Cape Clear was once a notorious shipwreck zone. Ed's house, located about three hundred feet above sea-level, would once have had a commanding view of the ships being wrecked on the rocks below. And even on a still night, the waters around the island are treacherous, Ed said. 'The lighthouse was always shrouded in fog. It was built too high up – the ships couldn't see its beacon. That's why they later built the Fastnet lighthouse.'

Indeed, shortly before the Ghost Eire team arrived to carry out their experiments, there had nearly been another wreck when a yacht taking part in the Fastnet Race capsized. Luckily all twenty-one sailors were saved, but Anto pointed out: 'Thousands of sailors must have lost their lives here. That's a lot of ghosts floating around!'

The ghostbusters felt queasy when they used light and sound sensors in the Napoleonic Tower near the lighthouse. 'Something was making us seasick. We just don't know what – yet,' Anthony said.

They went away without any clear answers, but said they would return periodically to check on some 'ghost gauges' they had left on the island to see if they could get a reaction from the spook. 'We left a goat-skull in powder in the goat shed with magnets hanging on a string,' he added: 'Any disturbance on the magnetic field would trigger movement of the magnets. We also put a temperature gauge there.

'We'll have to look back on that static camera in the goat shed to see if there's any weirdness.'

Ed remains baffled – though he has solved one mystery himself. 'The paranormal investigators told me they felt a strong female presence in the place. But that doesn't surprise me because I have twelve female goats in the place.'

Stubborn Spooks

It was a ghostly dilemma – stubborn spooks! A young couple in Cork had hoped an expert would rid their Council house of some pesky poltergeists. But a week after Paul O'Halloran, a Celtic shaman, performed a 'cleansing' ritual, Laura Burke and her fiancé Richie Hewitt said the house was still most haunted.

Six-months-pregnant Laura (twenty-one), Richie (twenty-four) and their five-year-old son Kyle had endured six months of hell before they went public about it in 2010. Spooks had lifted little Kyle off his bed and flung him across the room, they said. The tot also told his mum 'the eyes' were looking in his window at him. Other scary incidents included shaking chairs, a levitating table, glasses flying out of the kitchen cupboard, lights coming on suddenly, taps running at night, and Laura's keys mysteriously ending up in the bath.

The terrified tenants were so spooked that they moved out and vowed never to return to their home. 'We just wouldn't feel happy there. Our nerves are in bits,' Laura said as she announced their decision to leave. She added that Kyle had to have the light on all night, while she and Richie were having nightmares. 'We wake up sweating every night,' she said. 'We're living in my mum's house. It's very cramped but we'd rather be anywhere than in that house.'

The family were hoping Cork City Council would give them another home and denied allegations by neighbours that they had made up the ghost story so they would get a transfer. 'We were delighted when we moved in. There were hundreds of people in for this house. Kyle's school is just around the corner and it's near the shops, buses – it was our dream house. But we had to leave it,' Laura insisted.

Cork City Council housing official Kieran O'Donovan refused to give them a new house. 'We were made aware of the situation and because of the extraordinary circumstances, we are treating the case sympathetically. But the volume of alleged evidence is not enough to warrant a transfer. And we don't take alleged paranormal activity into account when deciding on such cases.' The council official said he wouldn't be calling in the ghostbusters either.

But the Gardaí had to be called in to control traffic as hundreds of people from all parts of the country descended on the estate to see the 'haunted house'. The house was boarded up and, soon after, was vandalised.

Laura said living there had been 'like hell', from the day they moved in to the night they ran out, screaming. 'First there were little things – I left my keys on the mantelpiece and they ended up in the bath. Lights were coming on and I knew I'd turned them off myself. The taps would suddenly start running and the sink in the kitchen overflowed one day when we were watching TV.

'Then, one day, a glass flew off the kitchen worktop and hit Richie in the head. Another time, the kitchen cupboard opened and all the glasses flew out as if someone was inside the cupboard throwing them out at us.

'Kyle was standing in the corner of his bedroom one night and he saw eyes staring in the window at him. Another time he was thrown out of his bed and flung across the room. He's only five. He was terrified – he still is. He's always talking about "the eyes". I'd never put him through that again.'

Friends of the couple and Richie's mother, Imelda, had a spooky experience in the house too, Laura added. 'Imelda was sitting on a chair praying and the chair started shaking violently. Something just didn't want her to pray in the house.'

Laura said the previous owner, Adrian Peyton, who had sold the house to Cork City Council eighteen months before the family moved in, had his first ever spooky experience when he visited the Burkes. 'He was sitting with Richie in the kitchen and suddenly the table jumped up in the air and came down with a bang.' Adrian later spoke to reporters about his scary experience.

Laura believed 'kids playing with a Ouija board might have brought the spirits into the house. It was vacant for a year and a half before we moved in, and the neighbours told us teenagers used it for drinking parties. They lit fires and burnt the floors and doors. They must have held a séance there with a Ouija board.'

The couple had got two local priests to bless the house and one said Mass there, but the attacks continued. 'Then we got a Baptist minister called Ciaran who has a PhD in Demonology. But it was as if the spirits wanted to fight back – they got worse,' Laura said.

Shaman Paul O'Halloran was the fourth professional to have a pop at evicting the unwelcome house-guest from Number 18 Hollywood Estate, Knocknaheaney, on Cork's northside. DJ Neil Prendeville of Cork's 96 FM called the Galway-based mystic after TV3's Paul Byrne interviewed the couple on the evening news. O'Halloran waived his usual fee of €350.

I interviewed him for the *Sunday World* shortly after he had performed a ceremony to rid the house of ghosts, and he told me: 'I set up a shamanic altar in the house and read some prayers from the *Celtic Book of Dying*. I released the energy and healed the spirits. I asked them to move on to the next life.' O'Halloran, who doubled up as a rugby masseur and used to be in the Army, told me he had sent 'hundreds' of ghosts packing over the past twenty years, adding that he had dealt with 'a lot worse' than the ghosts in Laura and Richie's house.

'The worst ever was a house in Lucan [west Dublin]. It used to be an institution where children were abused. There were the ghosts of priests and nuns there who had all done wrong. And the ghost of a little boy.' And a house in the countryside near Malahide, north Dublin, scared the bejaysus out of him – but he still managed to chase away the spooks, he said. 'There were what I can only describe as 'Draculas' going down the stairs – lots and lots of them. It was terrifying.'

The shaman said Laura and Richie were lucky to have such gentle ghosts, though he added that it would take 'six weeks or so for all the spirits to leave. They are not bad spirits – just young people who are trapped between this life and the next. I asked them to move on and I believe they will.' Paul added that the spirits had been acting up 'because they wanted attention. There was no malice in it.' And he maintained: 'They are not evil spirits. Just souls who were trapped between this life and the next.'

After we ran the story, Paul claimed I had been unfair to him. He thought the *Sunday World* was 'shaman' him when I told him the couple were still afraid to move back into their house.

Dublin's Scare City

When things go bump in the night, most people call Ghost-busters. But some terrified householders prefer to call . . . the *Sunday World*. Shortly after we ran the story about the spooky experiences of Laura Burke, Richie Hewitt and their son Kyle in Cork, a Dublin woman contacted us to say she had had a similar experience.

Martha Cousins said she too had left her house four years previously, after a poltergeist moved in. Her claims were backed up by FM104 presenter Jeremy Dixon who had spent a night in the haunted house – 4 Allenton Green – and recorded the experience for the *Adrian Kennedy Phone Show*. Jeremy told me he was still haunted by his terrifying experience. The normally shock-proof radio jock admitted he had fled after an invisible man sat down beside him on the bed. 'It was the main bedroom. This shape of a man sat down on the bed beside me.' Jeremy said the man's bum 'left an impression on the bed.'

Earlier he had 'felt a presence' in the upstairs back bedroom. 'There was just this chill that you didn't find in any other room. There was no draught, the heater was on. It was the kind of chill that you know someone is in the room with you.'

Jeremy was worried that he might be a magnet for spooks. 'I normally sense these things. We've done some haunted places on the show and it's happened to me a few times.' He had received rope-burns around his neck while reporting on haunted Wicklow Gaol.

Martha said she had put up with the ghosts for ten years before she called in Jeremy. 'I was in the house twelve years and the ghosts started acting up two years after I moved in. Things used to fly around the room. When my husband died [in a car crash] it got worse. It was as if these spirits knew I was alone with the kids and wanted to frighten me. I even got bitten by the spirits – on the top inside of my leg.

'I believe it was because they thought I could see their portal into the other world. I am a clairvoyant but I only found that out later – I was told by a medium who came to clear my house. She couldn't get rid of the spirits – no one could.

'They are still in the house. It is haunted, evil – it is one of the most haunted houses in Ireland and it will never be free,' Martha said.

The house was boarded up after Martha left with her three children. 'I don't go near it – I live in another part of Tallaght. The place where that house is built is haunted. Even if they knock down the house, the land will still be haunted,' she said, adding that the neighbours were apparently unaffected. 'They never heard anything all the time I was having these experiences.'

Martha offered moral support to the Cork couple. 'I want to talk to them and tell them not to give in. The Council will try to get them to move back in but they should hold out for another house. No one should have to live in a haunted house.'

Most of the people who claim to be able to communicate with the spirit world regard themselves simply as messengers. So it was unusual to meet two ghostbusters who were ready to do some actual ghost . . . busting! Dubliners Dez McQuaid (aka Dez Mahon) and Larry O'Brien were a two-man swat team for pesky poltergeists. They boasted a one-hundred-per-cent success rate in getting rid of ghosts.

So I should not have been in the least bit scared when, in 2006, Dez, a professional actor who had appeared on popular Irish soap *Fair City* as a creepy stalker, and Larry, who had been a medium for more than 20 years, invited me along to an 'exorcism'. Still, I felt a chill as we arrived at the house in Finglas, a suburb on Dublin's northside. Maybe it was because this was an ordinary semi-detached house; you don't expect to find ghosts in modern homes. Perhaps it was because it was coming up to Halloween. Or it could have been because Dez, Larry and the woman who answered the door seemed to genuinely believe there was something spooky going on.

The woman, who wanted only to be known by her first name, Irene, said the poltergeist had been driving her 'mental' for two months – turning the heating and lights on and off, running the taps and shower, and breaking the pipe at the back of the wall behind the shower. She said the plumber was amazed to find it had been broken in four places – 'a clean break each time, with no sign of rust or rotting. It's definitely done to annoy me and frighten me.'

Irene's scariest moment came the evening before Larry and Dez arrived to expel the spirit. 'For four hours, non-stop, the kettle was going on and off. I sat with the light on, trying to ignore it, trying to watch the telly, but I was terrified. And I heard footsteps upstairs in the front bedroom – I was afraid to go to bed. It was as if this ghost knew I was getting the lads in to get rid of her.'

Irene had agreed to let me write about it and even have the interior of the house photographed, so the *Irish Mirror* sent top photographer Arthur Carron along with me. Arthur, who was more used to photographing models for the social diaries and fashion pages, was macho about it and kept cracking jokes – until Irene said she believed the ghost was a teenage girl, a friend of her daughter, who had committed suicide in the neighbourhood a few years previously. 'Before my daughter went away to university, she used to sleep in the front room and the CD player kept going on in the middle of the night. I'm sure it's this friend of hers who used to come round to the house a lot. I feel sorry for her, but I want her spirit out of my house.'

Armed with just a candle, Larry and Dez walked silently around the house, stopping in the middle of every room to 'listen for spiritual presences'. Dez explained: 'We can always sense the presence of people who have passed on. They make themselves known to us. Poltergeists want someone to listen to them. That's why they make such a din.'

After ten minutes, Larry confirmed that there was indeed the ghost of a teenaged girl in the house – but she was not the only one. 'There's an older ghost, a man – he's protecting you,' he said. Irene smiled: 'That's my father. He's always here.' Larry said: 'No harm will come to you with him here. We're not going to send him away.'

But it was time to despatch the young female spook to the Other Side. We went up to the bedroom where Irene had heard ghostly footsteps. On entering the room, Dez and Larry stopped suddenly and said in unison: 'Rachel.' Dez turned to Irene: 'The ghost's name is Rachel. She's not your daughter's friend.'

As he said it, in a deadpan voice, I felt a chill. Dez said Rachel had died forty years previously, aged seventeen. Larry cut in: 'She killed herself and the baby she was carrying inside here. She was four months pregnant.'

As Larry stared towards a corner of the room, we all went silent. After several minutes, he turned to me: 'She said she was pregnant by a priest. She told me her family name and the priest's name, but I don't want you to put them in the paper because their relatives are alive. I believe the priest was moved around to different parishes. He's passed on now.'

Irene sighed. 'The poor girl – but I wish she'd leave me alone.' Dez put a hand on her shoulder: 'She's not malevolent. She's just mischievous. But it's better for you that she moves on.'

He and Larry then stood at the end of the bed, listening to the ghost – whose voice only they could hear. Dez said: 'She's a real tough little Dub. She said to me just now: "I'm not leavin." She said she had been wandering around Finglas for twenty years until she found this house. She's actually been here twenty years, but it's only in the last two months that she's made her presence known. She wants you to leave the house so she can have it all to herself. She said this house is "just grand" for her.'

Larry laughed: 'She's an attention-seeker – all poltergeists are.' He was holding a candle in his hand and suddenly its flame went out. But Dez said: 'She's not gone yet.'

Before they sent her spirit away, Larry and Dez said the ghost had a message for the *Irish Mirror* team, which she was about to reveal through Larry. He gazed at Arthur first, telling the photographer that he was going to have a certain minor health problem. Arthur's blasé attitude vanished instantly – the colour drained from his face, as he revealed that he had had an operation for a certain problem some years back.

I stifled a fit of the giggles as Dez lit the candle again, and he and Larry sat on the bed, staring into space for about a minute. Then, just at the moment when Dez and Larry said together 'She's gone,' I felt a surge in my heart – I was overcome with some emotion I couldn't understand. It was as if someone had given me a hug deep inside. I felt silly as I told Dez. He said I had formed some bond with the ghost just as she left. 'She likes you. She feels that you understand her.' I put it down to having heard such a moving story, in such an intense atmosphere. Poor little Rachel, I thought, suddenly close to tears.

Dez said he and Larry had 'called on the spirit guides to come and take her to where she belongs. Relatives of Rachel came for her. She's OK now.' Irene sighed, her tension evaporating visibly.

The ghostbusters said they were relieved, for Irene's sake, that Rachel had been a 'harmless' poltergeist. Dez said: 'Sometimes we can reassure people that the ghost that's haunting their house is not evil. But sometimes we have to tell them that, yeah, this one is a real bogey. We don't spook them – but we have to tell them the truth.'

Four weeks later, in November 2006, I was to come across one of 'the evil ones'. A terrified couple had contacted me after reading the story about the poltergeist in Finglas. They said a poltergeist occupying their house had been terrorising the whole street for seven years.

Now it was the spook's turn to be scared, Dez and Larry said, as they swung into action, armed yet again with just a candle.

It was another semi-detached house, this time in Tallaght, and it looked innocuous, but the couple were visibly upset as they told me that they had sent their four children to stay with relatives while the exorcism was taking place. The woman wanted to be known simply as Maria (not her real name) to protect the children's identities.

She said her son had awoken to find his toy car whizzing around the bedroom – with no batteries. The five-year-old and his ten-year-old brother would no longer sleep in their room after they started to get headaches and nightmares. Whilst dreaming, the older boy had drawn a man – his hand apparently guided by an unseen presence.

Maria said she had had to sleep downstairs because there were 'cold spots' in the master bedroom. She said she often heard footsteps at night, and on other occasions she thought she was going deaf – and felt pressure on her chest. Could it be a panic attack? I asked. She said that couldn't be the case, because she wasn't suffering from any stress other than that caused by the poltergeist.

Larry suddenly interrupted us and said in a monotone: 'This spirit is the most evil we have ever come across.' Dez shuddered: 'He has definitely murdered and raped – and sacrificed animals. It's disgusting – I want to retch!'

As I followed Dez from the hall into the sitting room, my skirt snagged on a nail that was sticking out of a table. Dez took this as a sign that the ghost had noticed me. 'He hates you. He hates everyone, but he especially hates women. I wouldn't like to tell you want he's saying about you.' I pressed him to tell all, but he said: 'Just disgusting things, foul language, he's calling you a whore, that sort of thing,' Larry added: 'He's saying horrible things to you.'

I mentally gave the ghost the two fingers as the ghostbusters invited him to blow out a candle. With no hint of a breeze, the flame suddenly went out. 'This has never happened before,' Larry said, then gazed towards the ceiling. Dez said: 'He's still here'. He said the ghost was telling them he had been a bailiff, born in the 1800s, who had died of a heart-attack on the land where Maria's house was built.

In chorus, Dez and Larry asked the spirit guides to take him away, but the ghost was refusing to budge, Dez said. 'He has a message for us – about an injury. Someone in the room has an injured leg.' Maria said she had a pin in her knee. Why the ghost wanted to tell us about it, we never did find out, but soon after that – an hour after we had entered the house – Dez and Larry pronounced him gone.

However, that night Dez called me to say his left leg was mysteriously covered in fingernail scratches. He was sure it was the bailiff's ghost – but, to me, it sounded more like the handsome actor had been attacked by an all-too-real woman.

A Swift Return from the Other Side

In life, he taunted pompous politicians – but, in death, Jonathan Swift seemed to have gone all soft. When the Dean of St Patrick's Cathedral, Victor Griffin, told me in 1990 that the deanery next door was haunted, I expected to hear tales of a particularly mischievous poltergeist.

But the great satirist apparently preferred to delegate his duties as a ghost to a servant. 'If there's a presence here, it's probably a footman of Swift's – an old retainer who's happy to see the house used,' he said.

He revealed that his wheelchair-bound wife had often felt 'a benevolent presence' near the portrait, which hung in the dining room. 'She feels someone leaning over her – as if to wish her well. My wife is often alone here, but she's never felt lonely.'

He added: 'Swift put a curse on anyone who would dare remove that portrait. Even when it has to be restored, the people from the National Gallery restore it in the deanery. We decorate the wall around it, but no one knows what's behind the painting.'

Spook Head

With Halloween just around the corner it was only natural to confess to a little fear – of the dark. So I thought I was just being sensible when I headed off to find myself the biggest ever flashlight – a lighthouse! *The Lonely Planet Guide 2011* had just declared Hook Head lighthouse the 'World's Number One Flashiest Lighthouse', and I was sure it would do the trick-or-treat.

The goosebumps began even before I reached the end of the peninsula. The narrow, winding road to the lighthouse took me past Loftus Hall, a gothic mansion where Lucifer himself is said to have turned up! What the Devil was Old Nick doing in one of Ireland's most scenic tourist spots, you might wonder on a sunny day. But on a stormy day, it's easy to see why he would have chosen that spot to make an appearance. According to local folklore, a well-dressed gentleman came to the door on a stormy night, claiming his horse had bolted. He was invited to join a game of cards – but when one of the ladies bent down to pick up a card from the floor, she spotted his cloven hoof! Some reports say he shot up through the ceiling in a cloud of smoke. Others claim he ran through the wall – leaving his imprint.

Locals believed that the Evil One had chosen the house because the owner, Henry Loftus, was known for his debauchery – and the fact that he was willing to send sailors to their death if the British Crown did not renew his lease on the lighthouse on his terms. Loftus turned off the light until he got his way, a decision that is said to have caused several shipwrecks.

Loftus Hall was later razed to the ground, and the rebuilt house was turned into a convent. The nuns got a local priest to bless it, before selling it to the Devereaux family, who ran it as a hotel in the 1980s. It has changed hands several times since then, and is currently owned by a local property developer, who plans to restore it to its former splendour.

The spooky tale is being made into a movie – but not even a Hollywood horror flick could hold a candle to the lighthouse itself, I realised. I arrived around midday, and the sun was shining until I approached the Hook. With the mist swirling around the tower, sea-spray lashing its base and waves clawing the rocks, the lighthouse was shrouded in its very own winter's night.

Paranormal investigation team Ghost Eire said they had contacted four spirits while they were carrying out scientific and psychic experiments in the lighthouse earlier that year. Ghosthunter Anto Kerrigan said the spooky stuff began even before they reached the lighthouse. 'We actually broke down outside Loftus Hall. The shock absorber went in the car when we were turning a corner – the metal spring snapped off. But we went on to the lighthouse to carry out our experiments. The name Frank came up on the Talking Board. He was a sailor drowned at sea from around 1536.'

Scarier still was when two spirits actually called out their names on a radio known as Frank's Box or a Ghost Box. The device is believed to communicate with the other side through 'white noise' frequencies. Meanwhile a table tilted of its own accord. And psychic Xak Aroo said she 'picked up on children, blood and gunpowder' in the lighthouse's Liberty Room. 'We found out afterwards from that there was a child blown up from a gunpowder explosion,' Anto said. He added: 'I could hear gentle whispering from the spiral staircase [but] I didn't feel at unease – I only felt we were being watched and reviewed.'

So did I when I visited the lighthouse with local photographer Mary Browne – but, luckily, the life-sized ghoul was just a member of the staff, dressed up as a monk for a Halloween prank on the visitors. He was lurking in the shadows as I climbed the 115 stone steps of the narrow, steep spiral staircase, along with lighthouse keeper Liam Colfer. Ghosts are supposed to vanish once they're spotted – but not this one! He followed us into the circular rooms, jumped out at us from alcoves and ambushed us on the balcony that runs around the lighthouse just under the light.

But, while the staff in the visitor centre next door admitted that this ghost was fake, they said the place was genuinely haunted. Ann Waters, Cathy Dowling and Mary Dunne revealed that a psychic 'clearer' had to be called in during 2010 after tourists reported suffering from sudden headaches in the visitor centre, where the lighthouse keepers had lived until 1996. 'The psychic clearer took out a pendulum and asked Ann to stand in the middle of the floor. She got a headache and the pendulum went wild!' Mary said. Ann added: 'We've had no complaints since. Whatever he did, it must have worked!'

Things have been going bump around here for centuries. The 800-year-old tower is the oldest working lighthouse in Europe and the sea-bed is believed to be littered with shipwrecks – many lured to their death by wreckers, who took advantage of Henry Loftus's protest. The lighthouse has been automatic since 1996 and its haunting foghorn was heard for the last time in 2011, but generations of lighthouse keepers had lived in the cottage next door and at one point it was manned by a hermitage of monks.

In austere times, even ghosts must earn their keep, so in October 2011 the staff decided to turn the spooks into a tourist attraction, giving guided tours and teaching children how to make Halloween masks, pumpkin lanterns, spell-catchers and magic wands. They even spooked up the snack menu in the café, which is in the old lighthouse-keeper's cottage; instead of the usual scones and tea, they served up pumpkin soup, 'burnt critters from the grave' and 'blood and guts red fruit pavlova'. And they plan to do it every Halloween, Ann said, adding: 'If the real ghosts turn up, they're very welcome to join in.'